PTCB
STUDY GUIDE
2024-2025

THE ALL-IN-ONE TOOL YOU NEED
TO FACE THE EXAM FEARLESSLY

270 Test Questions
Answer Explanations
Just the Key Information
to Pass, No Fluff Included!

- ## 3 FULL-LENGTH PRACTICE TESTS

- ## COMPREHENSIVE TOP DRUGS LIST

- ## PLAIN LANGUAGE FOR EFFORTLESS UNDERSTANDING

 HIGH SCORE
PUBLISHING

Bonus Flashcards

Dear student, thank you for the trust you are giving us by choosing our "PTCB Study Guide 2024". Go to page 68 to receive your printable bonus Flashcards now.

TABLE OF CONTENTS

SECTION 1: Medications

This section covers the classification of drugs, indications and contraindications, drug interactions, route of drug administrations, allergies, Narrow therapeutic index and drug compounding and storage.

Drug Names and Classification

Pharmacology encompasses the study of the effects and actions of drugs or medications on living organisms, including their interactions with human physiological systems. It can be broadly categorized into two branches: pharmacodynamics and pharmacokinetics.

Pharmacodynamics

Pharmacodynamics is the field dedicated to understanding how drugs exert their effects. One of the primary ways drugs achieve this is by interacting with specific receptors found in cell membranes or intracellular fluid.

Agonist and antagonist:

- The degree of receptor activation and the resulting biological response is directly influenced by the concentration of the activating drug, known as the 'agonist.' The potency of a drug, acting as an 'agonist', is determined by its concentration, which in turn affects the degree of receptor activation and the resulting biological response. As the dose of the drug increases, so does its effect, up to a point where the maximum response is achieved. Beyond this point,
- further increases in dose will not produce a greater effect. This relationship is quantified using a dose-response curve, which delineates the escalation of the drug's effect with increasing doses, illustrating the saturation of receptors as the drug concentration rises. This curve is vital for understanding the drug's efficacy and establishing the optimal therapeutic range.

Various factors, including patient-specific elements such as age and underlying medical conditions, can influence the interplay between drugs and receptors.

- Additionally, other drugs competing for binding at the same receptor, known as receptor *'antagonists,'* can also impact the pharmacodynamic relationship.

Different drugs acting on the same receptor or tissue can exhibit varying levels of efficacy, determining the magnitude of their biological responses and potency, which denotes the required drug dosage for a response. Drug receptors can be categorized based on their specific response to various drugs, enabling a more comprehensive understanding of their mechanisms.

Pharmacokinetics

The principle of pharmacokinetics, influenced by the philosophy of Paracelsus, states that "only the dose makes a thing not a poison." In essence, the dose determines whether a substance acts as a drug or a poison.

At therapeutic doses, a chemical substance is considered a drug, whereas, at higher or non-therapeutic doses, it becomes toxic.

Pharmacokinetics is a scientific field that examines drug absorption, distribution, metabolism, and excretion **(ADME)** within the body. It delves into how the body processes and interacts with drugs, including the study of associated toxicity **(ADMET).**

All four processes (ADME) require in-depth investigation to fully understand the pharmacokinetics of a drug. These processes involve the movement of drugs across cellular membranes within the body. *Nonpolar, lipid-soluble (lipophilic) drugs* can directly dissolve into the lipid bilayer of membranes, allowing them to cross easily. On the other hand, polar drugs face challenges in crossing membranes.

Let us look more closely at the four processes:

- *Absorption*, the first process, refers to the drug's movement from the site of administration into the bloodstream. Drugs can cross membranes through passive absorption, facilitated diffusion, or carrier-mediated diffusion.
  - Factors such as molecule size, lipophilicity, and pH environment influence the rate of absorption.
  - For instance, acidic drugs are better absorbed in the stomach's acidic pH, while basic drugs are more efficiently absorbed in the alkaline pH of the intestine.
- *Distribution*, the next process, involves the movement of drug molecules throughout the body to reach their target sites.
  - Tissue perfusion rates (blood flow to tissues) play a crucial role in determining drug distribution. Highly perfused tissues receive a greater proportion of the drug.
- *Metabolism*, or biotransformation, is the process by which the body transforms drugs into water-soluble metabolites for easy excretion through the kidneys. This process is essential because drugs and chemicals are considered foreign substances (xenobiotics) in the body. **Metabolism converts lipophilic drugs into hydrophilic forms, promoting their elimination**. In some cases, the metabolites may even be more active than the original drug. Enzymes act as biological catalysts in the metabolism process. Some enzymes are highly specific, targeting specific compounds, while others, like pepsin, have broader enzymatic activity.
  - **Phase I metabolism** chemically transforms drugs through oxidation, reduction, and hydrolysis.
  - **Phase II metabolism** involves conjugating the drug or its metabolites with polar groups, such as sulfates and glucuronides, to facilitate excretion.
- *Excretion* is the final process of eliminating drugs from the body. Some drugs exit the body unaltered, while others are transformed into hydrophilic metabolites and excreted via urine or bile. Natural routes of drug elimination include tears, sweat, breath, and saliva. Patients with kidney or liver impairment may have elevated drug levels in their system due to decreased metabolism, necessitating careful monitoring of drug dosage to avoid toxicity.

Applications of Pharmacokinetics extend to various areas of biomedical sciences:

- **Pharmacological Testing:** Here, pharmacokinetic principles are vital for establishing the relationship between drug concentrations and their pharmacological effects. This is key in determining the optimal therapeutic dose that maximizes efficacy while minimizing side effects, as well as in choosing the most effective route of administration.
- **Toxicological Testing:** Pharmacokinetics plays an important role in evaluating the distribution of drugs within tissues and their potential toxicity, providing insights crucial for safety assessments.

- **Drug Development:** In the realm of drug development, pharmacokinetics is essential for understanding the absorption, distribution, metabolism, and excretion (ADME) of new pharmaceuticals, guiding dosage and delivery system design.
- **Clinical Pharmacology:** Pharmacokinetics informs clinical pharmacology by helping to predict drug interactions, effects in different patient populations, and adjustments needed for specific patient conditions, such as renal or hepatic impairment.
- **Personalized Medicine:** It also contributes significantly to personalized medicine, allowing for tailored drug regimens based on individual pharmacokinetic responses, thus improving treatment outcomes and reducing adverse effects.".

Drug Metabolism

Drug metabolism plays a crucial role in the body's defense against toxic reactions caused by lipid-soluble substances, which tend to accumulate and pose a risk. To counteract this, the body possesses a powerful metabolic system that transforms these lipophilic, water-insoluble, and nonpolar drugs into ionized and hydrophilic water-soluble metabolites. This transformation facilitates easy excretion from the body and is often referred to as a detoxification process.

The liver's smooth endoplasmic reticulum serves as the primary site for drug metabolism due to its abundance of various enzymes. This process, known *as hepatic metabolism*, takes place predominantly in the liver.

However, other organs such as the lungs, kidneys, placenta, epithelial cells of the gastrointestinal tract, adrenal glands, and skin also participate in biotransformation.

Drug metabolism involves intricate chemical processes wherein biological enzymes play a vital role in converting one chemical species to another, influencing their activity. These enzymes can be classified into two types: microsomal enzymes, such as *cytochrome P450 (CYP) enzymes*, associated with a specific fraction of the liver, and *non-microsomal enzymes* found in the cytoplasm and other tissues apart from the liver.

- *Phase I reactions*, considered detoxification reactions, predominantly involve microsomal enzymes like CYP450. These reactions encompass various transformations, including oxidation, reduction, hydrolysis, cyclization, and de-cyclization.
    - **Oxidation** is a common type of reaction that enhances drug solubility by introducing polar functional groups like -OH. Reduction reactions involve the addition of hydrogen or removal of oxygen, resulting in the formation of amino and hydroxyl groups.
    - **Hydrolysis** reactions lead to significant changes in the substrate, often observed in the metabolism of ester and amide prodrugs.
        - *Prodrugs* are a class of compounds designed to be administered in an inactive or less active form, which undergo biotransformation within the body, often through enzymatic processes like hydrolysis. This metabolic conversion results in the release of the active pharmacological agent, thereby enhancing drug efficacy, improving bioavailability, or reducing undesirable side effects compared to the administration of the active drug alone.
- *Phase II reactions*, known as **conjugation** reactions, occur subsequent to Phase I and mainly involve the products obtained from Phase I reactions. Conjugation entails the addition of polar moieties like glucuronic acid, glutathione, sulfate, and glycine to Phase I metabolites or directly to the active drug molecule.

o Transferase enzymes, including uridine diphosphate (UDP)-glucuronosyltransferases, sulfonyl transferase, and glutathione transferases, catalyze these reactions. The resulting conjugated metabolites have increased molecular structure, size, weight, and polarity.

Drug metabolism holds significant importance as it leads to the pharmacological inactivation of drugs, rendering metabolites with reduced or no pharmacological activity. Conversely, it can also result in toxicological activation, producing metabolites that exhibit high tissue reactivity and potential harm. Additionally, drug metabolism can facilitate the pharmacological activation of prodrugs, converting them into highly active forms to enhance their therapeutic effects.

Drug Elimination

Elimination of drugs and their metabolites from the body occurs through a vital process known as excretion. This process involves the transfer of substances from the internal environment of the body to the external environment. Effective excretion of the unchanged drug is crucial for terminating its pharmacological effects. Among the various organs involved in drug excretion, the kidneys play a primary role.

Non-renal excretion through organs such as the

- Lungs
- Intestines
- Biliary system
- Salivary glands

Drugs and metabolites can be excreted through several pathways, including:

- Urine
- Feces
- Exhaled air
- Saliva
- Sweat
- Milk

Urine: Polar, non-volatile, and relatively small-sized drugs or metabolites (less than 500 Daltons) that undergo slow metabolism are typically excreted in the urine. The kidneys primarily handle drugs' excretion and metabolites to varying extents.

- For instance, Gentamicin is exclusively eliminated through renal excretion.

Feces: The unabsorbed fraction of drugs found in feces is derived from bile. The liver plays a role in transporting organic acids, organic bases, lipophilic drugs, and steroids into bile through specific active transport mechanisms. Relatively larger molecules (with a molecular weight greater than 300 Da) are eliminated through bile.

- Examples of drugs that exhibit higher concentrations in bile include erythromycin, ampicillin, rifampin, tetracycline, oral contraceptives, and phenolphthalein. Some drugs, such as anthracene purgatives and heavy metals, may also be excreted directly in the colon.

Exhaled Air: Gases and volatile liquids, including general anesthetics, paraldehyde, and alcohol, are eliminated through the lungs. The transfer of these substances occurs in the alveoli and depends on their partial pressure in the blood.

- Additionally, the lungs serve as a filtering mechanism, eliminating any particulate matter that may have been injected intravenously.

Saliva and Sweat: Certain drugs can be excreted in sweat and saliva. Saliva and sweat can contain significant amounts of substances such as lithium, rifampicin, potassium iodide, and heavy metals.

- In the case of saliva, most of it, along with any drug present, is swallowed and follows a similar pathway to orally administered drugs.

Milk: During lactation, some drugs may be excreted in breast milk. While this excretion may not pose significant concerns for the mother, the nursing infant unintentionally receives the drug. Drugs mainly enter breast milk via the process of passive diffusion.

- Lipid-soluble drugs with lower protein binding are more readily excreted in milk. The administration of tetracyclines to lactating mothers can have adverse effects on the nursing infant, such as tooth discoloration.

Generic and Brand Names

Each medication possesses a designated *generic name*, which serves as its approved name. Medications with similar therapeutic actions often share similar-sounding generic names, creating groups of related medicines. For instance, phenoxymethylpenicillin, ampicillin, amoxicillin, and flucloxacillin belong to a single group of antibiotics.

The *brand name* is the selection of a name made by the manufacturing company. It is possible for multiple companies to produce the same generic medicine, each with its own unique brand name.

The choice of brand name is often influenced by factors such as memorability for advertising purposes or the desire for a name that is easier to pronounce or spell compared to a generic name. For instance, **"paracetamol"** is a generic name, while various companies produce it under brand names such as Panadol®, Calpol®, and others.

OTC (Over-the-Counter) Medications

Over-the-counter (OTC) medications, also known *as non-prescription medicines*, provide a convenient solution for addressing various health concerns without the need for a prescription. These readily available products are safe and effective when used as directed, making them a *popular choice for individuals seeking relief from common symptoms*. These include drugs such as pain relievers and cough suppressants.

- In the United States, the market offers more than **80 classes of OTC medications**, catering to a multitude of health needs.
- Renowned examples include **well-known pain relievers** like:
    o Acetaminophen (Tylenol)
    o Ibuprofen (Advil, Motrin)
    o Cough suppressants such as dextromethorphan (Robitussin)
    o Antihistamines like loratadine (Claritin 24H)

- These products can be easily found on shelves in pharmacies, grocery stores, and even gas stations, ensuring accessibility for consumers.

The oversight and evaluation of OTC medications in the United States fall under the purview of the **US Food and Drug Administration (FDA).**

- The FDA's Division of Drug Information (CDER), the Office of Drug Evaluation, and the Non-prescription Drug Advisory Committee play crucial roles in reviewing OTC ingredients and labels.
- To streamline the process, an *OTC drug monograph* is established for each class of product. This monograph outlines acceptable ingredients, doses, formulations, and labeling guidelines.
    - OTC products that adhere to an existing monograph can be marketed without further FDA review.
    - However, products that deviate from the established monographs must undergo approval through the FDA's New Drug Approval System, ensuring the safety and efficacy of non-monographed OTC medications.

While OTC medications offer convenience and accessibility, remember that they can still carry certain risks. While a prescription isn't necessary, there can be side effects, interactions with other drugs, or harm due to excessive dosages. For safe consumption, it's important for users to thoroughly review the "Drug Facts" label on all over-the-counter (OTC) items. This label provides crucial information on proper usage, dosing instructions, and potential warnings.

- It is advisable to consult with the healthcare provider, pharmacist, or doctor if a consumer has any queries or concerns regarding the use of OTC medications.
- Additionally, **pregnant women** should not be prescribed an OTC without consulting with a healthcare provider. This includes any medication, vitamin, or herbal supplement, even if it falls under the OTC category.

Supplement Drugs

Vitamins are essential nutrients that our bodies need to function properly. They are also given as drug supplements. They can be divided into two categories based on their solubility in water or fat:

- **Water-Soluble Vitamins**: These include B vitamins (such as thiamine, riboflavin, niacin, and folic acid) and vitamin C. Vitamins that are water-soluble dissolve in water and aren't retained in the body, necessitating daily replenishment. These vitamins are crucial for energy production, nerve function, and sustaining a strong immune system.
- **Fat-Soluble Vitamins**: This group consists of vitamins A, D, E, and K. They accumulate in the body's fat tissues and liver and play a role in a range of functions including vision, maintaining bone health, providing antioxidant protection, and aiding in blood clotting.

Fat-Soluble Vitamins:

Vitamin A (Retinol/Retinal):

- Function: Supports vision, skeletal growth, and regulation of mucous membranes.
- Sources: Carrots, spinach, sweet potatoes, and liver.
- Indications: Vision problems, growth disorders, skin conditions.
- Contraindications: Pregnancy (high doses), liver disease, hypervitaminosis A.

Vitamin D (Calciferol):

- Function: Aids in bone and teeth formation and helps with the absorption of calcium and phosphorus.
- Sources: Sunlight, fortified dairy products, and fatty fish.
- Indications: Vitamin D deficiency, rickets, osteoporosis.
- Contraindications: Hypercalcemia, sarcoidosis, certain cancers.

Vitamin E (Tocopherols):

- Function: Acts as an antioxidant, protecting cells from damage.
- Sources: Nuts, seeds, vegetable oils, and leafy greens.
- Indications: Vitamin E deficiency, antioxidant support, skin health.
- Contraindications: Bleeding disorders, high doses without medical supervision.

Vitamin K (Phytomenadione):

- Function: Essential for blood clotting (coagulation).
- Sources: Leafy greens, broccoli, and vegetable oils.
- Indications: Vitamin K deficiency, bleeding disorders, osteoporosis.
- Contraindications: Anticoagulant therapy and certain medications (e.g., warfarin).

Water-Soluble Vitamins:

Vitamin C (Ascorbic Acid):

- Function: Aids in the healing of wounds, the functioning of the immune system, and the synthesis of collagen.
- Sources: Citrus fruits, peppers, berries, and leafy greens.
- Indications: Vitamin C deficiency, immune support, skin health.
- Contraindications: Iron overload conditions, kidney disorders (high doses).

Vitamin B1 (Thiamine):

- Function: Important for normal appetite and nervous system function.
- Sources: Whole grains, beans, nuts, and pork.
- Indications: Thiamine deficiency, nerve disorders, alcoholism.
- Contraindications: Allergy or hypersensitivity to thiamine.

Vitamin B2 (Riboflavin):

- Function: Essential for vision and maintaining healthy skin.
- Sources: Dairy products, mushrooms, leafy greens, and lean meats.
- Indications: Riboflavin deficiency, skin disorders, migraines.
- Contraindications: Allergy or hypersensitivity to riboflavin.

Vitamin B3 (Niacin):

- Function: Supports digestion, appetite, and healthy skin.
- Sources: Meat, fish, whole grains, and legumes.
- Indications: Niacin deficiency, high cholesterol, pellagra.
- Contraindications: Liver disease, active peptic ulcers.

Vitamin B5 (Pantothenic Acid):

- Function: Involved in hormone formation and nutrient metabolism.
- Sources: Meat, avocados, broccoli, and whole grains.
- Indications: Pantothenic acid deficiency, skin conditions, adrenal support.
- Contraindications: None known.

Vitamin B6 (Pyridoxine):

- Function: Important for red blood cell formation, insulin production, and hemoglobin synthesis.
- Sources: Poultry, fish, bananas, and potatoes.
- Indications: Pyridoxine deficiency, anemia, PMS symptoms.
- Contraindications: High doses without medical supervision.

Vitamin B7 (Biotin):

- Function: Supports protein and carbohydrate metabolism.
- Sources: Eggs, nuts, seeds, and sweet potatoes.
- Indications: Biotin deficiency, hair and nail health, glucose metabolism.
- Contraindications: None known.

Vitamin B9 (Folic Acid):

- Function: Essential for red blood cell formation and prevention of neural tube defects during pregnancy.
- Sources: Leafy greens, legumes, fortified grains, and citrus fruits.
- Indications: Folic acid deficiency, pregnancy support, heart health.
- Contraindications: Recent chemotherapy, untreated vitamin B12 deficiency.

Vitamin B12 (Cobalamins):

- Function: Necessary for red blood cell production, energy metabolism, and provides nutrients for collagen synthesis.
- Sources: Meat, fish, dairy products, and fortified cereals.
- Indications: Vitamin B12 deficiency, anemia, nerve disorders.
- Contraindications: Allergy or hypersensitivity to cobalamin, certain medications (e.g., metformin).

Therapeutic Equivalence and Dosage

Therapeutic Equivalence can be defined as the combination of Bioequivalence and Pharmaceutical Equivalence.

Therapeutic Equivalence = Bioequivalence + Pharmaceutical Equivalence

In order for drugs to be considered therapeutic equivalents and suitable for substitution, they must fulfill certain requirements, including being both pharmaceutical equivalents and bioequivalent. For drug products to be classified as therapeutic equivalents, they need to be pharmaceutical equivalents and expected to produce the same clinical effect and safety profile when administered to patients under specified conditions mentioned in the labeling. The FDA establishes criteria for products to be classified as therapeutically equivalent, which include:

- Approval is safe and effective.
- Being pharmaceutical equivalents, which means drug ingredients, are presented in the same dosage form, follow the same route of administration, and comply with established standards related to strength, quality, purity, and identity.
- Being bioequivalent implies either the absence of known or potential bioequivalence issues and adherence to an acceptable in vitro standard, or, in cases where such issues exist, showing compliance with an appropriate bioequivalence standard.
- Having adequate labelling.
- Manufactured in compliance with Current Good Manufacturing Practice regulations.

Pharmaceutical Equivalents are drug products that meet the following three criteria:

- They contain the same active ingredient.
- They are of the same dosage form and route of administration.
- They are identical in strength or concentration.

Pharmaceutically equivalent drug products may have variations in characteristics such as shape, release mechanism, labeling (to some extent), scoring, and excipients (including colors, flavors, and preservatives).

Drug Dosage Forms

Calculating drug dosage forms is a crucial aspect of pharmacology that involves determining the appropriate drug dosage in various units. Conversion factors are employed to convert measurements between different units, such as pounds to kilograms or liters to milliliters. This method allows us to work with diverse units of measurement, simplifying the calculations.

There are four methods commonly used for drug dosage calculations: the Ratio (Rainbow) Method, Proportion Method, Formula Method, and Dimensional Analysis:

1. **Ratio (Rainbow) Method**: This method, widely employed for drug dosage calculations, relies on ratios and involves only multiplication and division.

Step 1: Establish ratios.

Step 2: Multiply the means and extremes.

Step 3: Solve for "x" algebraically.

2. **Proportion Method**: Like the Ratio (Rainbow) Method, the Proportion Method utilizes cross-multiplication.

Step 1: Set up proportions.

Step 2: Cross multiply.

Step 3: Solve for "x" algebraically.

3. **Formula Method**: The Formula Method employs an equation to calculate an unknown quantity (x), like the ratio/proportion method.

Conversion factors are utilized in drug calculations.

D/H × Q = Dose

Dose ordered (D) / supply on hand (H) × Quantity (Q) = answer

4. **Dimensional Analysis**: This method follows the formula

Dose ordered (D) × Quantity (Q) / supply on hand (H) = dose.

Dimensional Analysis is employed when calculating the number of medications or drugs needed for a patient, given that the medication's strength is already known.

Additionally, drug dosage strategies involve considering the **volume of distribution (V_d)** and are categorized into loading dose and maintenance dose. A loading dose, administered initially, aims to quickly achieve the steady-state, while a maintenance dose is given subsequently to maintain a lower plasma concentration of the drug. This strategy is implemented for patients experiencing severe pain or emergencies requiring rapid relief.

Half-Life

Half-life is the time required for the drug concentration in the body or plasma to decrease by half. It is **denoted as t½.** The half-life refers to the period needed for the concentration of a medication in the body or plasma to reduce by fifty percent. It is represented as t½. The plasma half-life refers to the duration it takes for the concentration of the medication in plasma to diminish by half of its initial amount. Understanding half-life is essential as it determines the duration of action, time to reach a steady state, and dosing frequency.

The estimation of time for drug elimination is critical for determining the total drug elimination duration. *The elimination half-life (t1/2)* is the time taken for the drug amount and plasma concentration to decline by 50% from the initial value. It depends on parameters such as *clearance (CL)* and apparent *volume of distribution (V_d)*.

$$t_{1/2} = 0.693\ V_d/Cl$$

Note: The half-life is directly proportional to V_d and inversely proportional to CL, meaning an increase in V_d prolongs the half-life, while a decrease in clearance shortens it.

Approximately five half-lives are required for a drug to be eliminated by about 97%. Thus, it is commonly stated that a drug has no pharmacological action after four half-lives since approximately 97% of it is eliminated from the body. The **elimination rate constant (KE)** describes the rate at which a drug is

removed or excreted from the body. It is represented as a fraction of the substance eliminated per unit of time. KE is the sum of rate constants for various elimination processes, including urinary excretion, metabolism, biliary excretion, and pulmonary excretion.

Drug Classifications

Drugs Related to The Nervous System

1. Central Nervous System (CNS) Depressants:
   - **Benzodiazepines**: These drugs enhance the effects of gamma-aminobutyric acid (GABA) in the brain, leading to sedation, anxiety relief, and hypnotic effects. They are indicated for anxiety disorders, insomnia, and seizure disorders. Contraindications include a history of substance abuse and respiratory depression.
     - Examples include diazepam, lorazepam, alprazolam, and clonazepam.

Note: Benzodiazepines end with the suffix "pam" or "lam".

   - **Barbiturates**: Acting on GABA receptors, barbiturates depress the CNS. They are prescribed as sedatives, hypnotics, and anticonvulsants. Barbiturates are contraindicated in individuals with porphyria, respiratory conditions, and a history of drug dependence.
     - Examples include Phenobarbital, and amobarbital (amytal).

Note: Barbiturates end with the suffix "barbital".

   - **Other Sedative-Hypnotics**: These drugs promote relaxation and induce sleep by depressing CNS activity. They are indicated for short-term treatment of insomnia and anxiety. Contraindications include respiratory insufficiency and sleep apnea.
     - Examples include zolpidem and eszopiclone
   - **Alcohol**: As a CNS depressant, alcohol produces sedative and anxiolytic effects. It is commonly consumed recreationally but should be avoided during pregnancy, liver disease, and when operating machinery or driving.
2. CNS Stimulants:
   - **Amphetamines**: These drugs increase the release and inhibit the neurotransmitter reuptake, leading to increased alertness and focus. They are indicated for attention-deficit hyperactivity disorder (ADHD) and narcolepsy. Contraindications include cardiovascular disease, anxiety disorders, and hyperthyroidism.
     - Examples include amphetamine and dextroamphetamine.
   - **Methylphenidate**: These drugs act by enhancing the release of norepinephrine and dopamine. These are prescribed for ADHD and narcolepsy. Contraindications include glaucoma, agitation, and severe anxiety.
     - Examples include Ritalin and Concerta.
3. Antidepressants:
   - **Selective Serotonin Reuptake Inhibitors (SSRIs):** These drugs increase the level of levels by inhibiting their reuptake. They are indicated for depression, anxiety disorders, and obsessive-compulsive disorder. Contraindications of SSRIs are the concurrent use of monoamine oxidase inhibitors (MAOIs) and untreated narrow-angle glaucoma.
     - Examples include Fluoxetine, Sertraline and Escitalopram
   - **Tricyclic Antidepressants (TCAs):** Blocking the reuptake of serotonin and norepinephrine, TCAs are prescribed for depression and chronic pain. Contraindications include recent myocardial infarction and glaucoma.
     - Examples include Amitriptyline, Nortriptyline, Imipramine and Desipramine.
   - **Monoamine Oxidase Inhibitors (MAOIs):** These drugs inhibit the enzyme monoamine oxidase, thereby increasing the availability of neurotransmitters. They are indicated for

depression and certain anxiety disorders. Contraindications include concurrent use of SSRIs, TCAs, and foods high in tyramine.
   o Examples include Phenelzine, Tranylcypromine and Isocarboxazid.
4. Antipsychotics:
   • **Typical Antipsychotics**: Blocking dopamine receptors, typical antipsychotics are used for treating schizophrenia and other psychotic disorders. They should be avoided in individuals with Parkinson's disease, blood dyscrasias, and liver disease.
   • **Atypical Antipsychotics**: Acting on various neurotransmitter systems, including dopamine and serotonin receptors, atypical antipsychotics are prescribed for schizophrenia and bipolar disorder. Contraindications include QT prolongation, dementia-related psychosis, and uncontrolled diabetes.
5. Anxiolytics:

Anxiolytics are used to reduce anxiety and promote relaxation in the treatment of generalized anxiety disorder and other anxiety-related conditions.

   • **Buspirone** is A non-benzodiazepine anxiolytic drug acting on serotonin receptors. Buspirone is prescribed for generalized anxiety disorder. Contraindications include concurrent use of MAOIs, liver impairment, and hypersensitivity.
6. Antiepileptic Drugs (AEDs):
   • **Sodium Channel Blockers**: These drugs inhibit abnormal neuronal firing by blocking voltage-gated sodium channels. They are prescribed for epilepsy and seizure disorders. Contraindications include heart block, liver impairment, and pregnancy.
      o Examples include Phenytoin, Carbamazepine, Lamotrigine and Oxcarbazepine.
   • **GABAergic Drugs**: Increasing the inhibitory effects of GABA, these drugs reduce neuronal excitability. They are indicated for epilepsy, neuropathic pain, and mood disorders and are also known as GABA enhancers. Contraindications include hepatic encephalopathy and porphyria.
      o Examples include Valproic acid, Gabapentin and Pregabalin.
7. Analgesics:
   • **Nonsteroidal Anti-Inflammatory Drugs (NSAIDs)**: These drugs reduce pain, inflammation, and fever by inhibiting the enzyme cyclooxygenase (COX). They are indicated for mild to moderate pain and inflammatory conditions. Contraindications include peptic ulcers, renal impairment, and bleeding disorders.
      o Examples include Ibuprofen, Naproxen and Diclofenac.
Note: Commonly used NSAIDs have the suffix "profen", "proxen", or "fenac"

   • **Opioids**: Acting on opioid receptors, opioids provide moderate to severe pain relief. They are prescribed for acute and chronic pain management. Contraindications include respiratory depression, bowel obstruction, and substance abuse disorders.
      o Examples include Morphine, Oxycodone, Hydrocodone and Codeine.
8. Local Anesthetics: Local anesthetics cause reversible numbing or loss of sensation and pain in the specific area. These drugs block sodium channels, leading to local anesthesia by preventing nerve impulse generation and conduction. They are used for various surgical and dental procedures.
      o Contraindications include known hypersensitivity and infection at the injection site.
      o Common examples are Lidocaine, Bupivacaine, Procaine and Mepivacaine.

Cardiovascular System Drugs

1. **Antihypertensive Drugs:** Antihypertensive drugs are medications used to manage high blood pressure. They are classified based on their mechanisms of action.
   * **ACE Inhibitors**: ACE inhibitors are commonly used in the treatment of hypertension, heart failure, and diabetic nephropathy. Their mechanism of action involves the inhibition of the ACE enzyme, which leads to a decrease in the production of a hormone known as angiotensin II.
     o This hormone causes blood vessels to narrow, leading to increased blood pressure. ACE inhibitors help lower blood pressure and reduce strain on the heart. They are indicated for patients with high blood pressure, heart failure, and certain kidney conditions.
     o However, individuals with a history of angioedema or those who are pregnant should avoid using ACE inhibitors.
     o Examples include Lisinopril, Enalapril, and Ramipril
   * **Angiotensin II Receptor Antagonists/Blockers**: Angiotensin II receptor antagonists/blockers also play a significant role in managing hypertension, heart failure, and diabetic nephropathy. They act by blocking the effects of angiotensin II at specific receptors, resulting in blood vessel relaxation and lowered blood pressure.
     o These are indicated for patients with high blood pressure, heart failure, and certain kidney conditions. However, individuals with a history of angioedema or those who are pregnant should avoid using these drugs.
     o Examples include Losartan, Valsartan, Irbesartan
   * **Beta-Blockers**: Beta-blockers are versatile drugs used for various cardiovascular conditions. They are prescribed for hypertension, angina (chest pain), arrhythmias (irregular heart rhythms), and heart failure. Beta-blockers block the effects of adrenaline on beta receptors in the heart, which leads to a decreased heart rate and relaxed blood vessels.
     o By reducing the heart's workload, they help lower blood pressure.
     o Examples include Atenolol, Metoprolol, and Propranolol

Point to remember: Beta-blockers are contraindicated in individuals with severe bradycardia (slow heart rate), heart block, and asthma

Note: Beta-blockers have the suffix "olol".

   * **Calcium Channel Blockers**: Calcium channel blockers are used for the management of hypertension, angina, and arrhythmias. They work by blocking calcium channels in blood vessel walls and the heart, leading to the relaxation of blood vessels and reduced cardiac contractility. This leads to a reduction in blood pressure and an enhancement in blood flow.
     o Examples include Nifedipine, Amlodipine, Diltiazem, and Verapamil

Note: They should be avoided in individuals with heart block, severe hypotension (low blood pressure), and acute myocardial infarction.

   * **Diuretics**: Diuretics increase urine production, helping to lower blood pressure and reduce fluid retention. They are used for the treatment of hypertension, edema (fluid accumulation), and heart failure. Diuretics increase the excretion of sodium and water from the body, resulting in decreased fluid volume and reduced blood pressure.
     o They are indicated for patients with high blood pressure, fluid retention, and heart failure. However, diuretics should be used with caution in individuals with anuria (lack of urine production) and those at risk of electrolyte imbalances.
     o Examples include Hydrochlorothiazide, Furosemide, and Spironolactone.

Note: Diuretics are described in detail in the renal drugs section.

2. **Antiarrhythmic Drugs:** Antiarrhythmic drugs are used to manage irregular heart rhythms and restore normal cardiac function. They can be classified based on their mechanisms of action.
   - **Sodium Channel Blockers**: Class I antiarrhythmics are effective in managing both ventricular and atrial arrhythmias. They work by blocking sodium channels in cardiac cells, which helps stabilize the heart's electrical activity.
     - Individuals with certain heart block conditions and severe heart failure should avoid using Class I antiarrhythmics.
     - Examples include Procainamide, Lidocaine, and Flecainide
   - **Beta-Blockers:** Class II antiarrhythmics help manage hypertension and suppress supraventricular and ventricular arrhythmias. They work by reducing the heart's response to adrenaline, leading to a decreased heart rate and improved rhythm.
     - Severe bradycardia and heart block are contraindications for using Class II antiarrhythmics.
     - Examples include Propranolol, Metoprolol, and Esmolol
   - **Potassium Channel Blockers**: Class III antiarrhythmics are prescribed for the treatment of various arrhythmias. They work by prolonging the action potential duration in cardiac cells, helping to regulate the heart's electrical activity and stabilize heart rhythms.
     - Certain types of heart block and severe bradycardia are contraindications for Class III antiarrhythmics.
     - Examples include Amiodarone, Sotalol, and Dofetilide
   - **Calcium Channel Blockers:** Class IV antiarrhythmics, which are also calcium channel blockers, are effective in managing supraventricular arrhythmias. They work by blocking calcium channels in the heart, decreasing heart rate and reducing irregular heart rhythms.
     - They should be avoided in individuals with heart block and severe hypotension.
     - Examples include Diltiazem and Verapamil
3. **Lipid-Lowering Agents:** Lipid-lowering agents or drugs are also known as hypolipidemic agents. These drugs reduce elevated levels of lipids in the blood. They are usually prescribed for the management of high cholesterol and triglyceride blood levels, which are risk factors for cardiovascular diseases.
   - **Statins**: Statins are the most commonly used lipid-lowering drugs which act by inhibiting an enzyme involved in cholesterol synthesis. This helps in reducing the production of cholesterol in the liver. These drugs also increase the ability of the liver to remove cholesterol from the bloodstream.
     - Examples include atorvastatin, simvastatin, and rosuvastatin.

Note: Statins have the suffix "statin".

   - **Bile Acid Sequestrants**: These drugs reduce blood cholesterol levels by removing bile acids.
     - Examples include Cholestyramine, Colesevelam, and Colestipol.
   - **Fibrates**: Fibrates reduce the production of triglycerides in the body, thus, reducing their levels in the blood. They also promote the removal of LDL (Low-density lipoprotein) molecules.
     - Examples include Clofibrate, Fenofibrate and Gemfibrozil
4. **Anticoagulant and Antiplatelet Drugs:**
   - **Anticoagulants**: Anticoagulants are medications used to prevent and treat blood clots. They are prescribed for individuals with thromboembolic disorders (conditions where blood clots form and travel through the bloodstream) and atrial fibrillation (an irregular heart rhythm).

Anticoagulants work by interfering with the blood clotting process, thus reducing the risk of clot formation.

- o Examples include Warfarin, Heparin, and Rivaroxaban

Note: Anticoagulants should be avoided in individuals with active bleeding, certain bleeding disorders, and those who have recently undergone surgery.

- **Antiplatelet Drugs:** Antiplatelet drugs are used to prevent blood clot formation by preventing aggregation of platelets. They are commonly prescribed for individuals with coronary artery disease and for stroke prevention. Antiplatelet medications work by inhibiting the activation of platelets, which are essential for blood clotting.
  - o They should be avoided in individuals with active bleeding, a history of bleeding disorders, and those who have recently undergone surgery.
  - o Examples include Aspirin, Clopidogrel, Prasugrel

Digestive System Drugs

1. **Antacids**: Antacids are used to relieve symptoms of acid reflux and indigestion by neutralizing stomach acid. Indications: They are indicated for individuals with occasional mild acid reflux and indigestion. Antacids should be used with caution in individuals with kidney problems or those on a sodium-restricted diet.
   - o Examples include magnesium hydroxide, calcium carbonate, and aluminum hydroxide.
2. **Proton Pump Inhibitors (PPIs):** PPIs are used to reduce stomach acid production, providing long-lasting relief from conditions like gastroesophageal reflux disease (GERD), ulcers, and gastritis. They are indicated for individuals with frequent or severe acid reflux, GERD, ulcers, and certain stomach conditions. PPIs should be used with caution in individuals with problems in the liver.
   - o Examples include Omeprazole, Esomeprazole, and Lansoprazole.

Note: PPIs have the suffix "prazole".

3. **H2 Blockers**: H2 blockers reduce acid production in the stomach. They are prescribed in the management of acid reflux, GERD, ulcers, and gastritis. They are indicated for individuals with moderate to severe acid reflux, GERD, ulcers, and certain stomach conditions. H2 blockers should be used with caution in individuals with kidney or liver problems or those taking certain medications.
   - o Examples include Ranitidine, Famotidine, and Cimetidine.

Note: H2 blockers have the suffix "tidine".

4. **Prokinetics**: Prokinetics improve gastrointestinal motility and are used to treat conditions like gastroparesis (delayed stomach emptying) and gastroesophageal reflux. They are indicated for individuals with gastroparesis, acid reflux, and other motility disorders. Prokinetics should be used with caution in individuals with certain heart conditions or those taking certain medications.
   - o Examples include Metoclopramide and Domperidone.
5. **Laxatives**: Laxatives are used to relieve constipation and promote bowel movements. They are indicated for individuals with occasional constipation or when a softer stool is needed (e.g., after surgery or childbirth). Laxatives should be used with caution in individuals with certain bowel conditions or those experiencing severe abdominal pain.
   - o Examples: Psyllium, Bisacodyl, and Polyethylene glycol.
6. **Antiemetics**: Antiemetics are used to prevent or treat nausea and vomiting in conditions such as chemotherapy, motion sickness, and post-operative recovery. They are indicated for individuals

experiencing nausea and vomiting due to various causes. Antiemetics should be used with caution in individuals with certain heart conditions or those taking certain medications.
  o Examples: Ondansetron, Meclizine, and Promethazine.

Renal System Drugs

1. **Diuretics**: Diuretics are the drugs that increase urine production and promote the elimination of excess water and electrolytes from the body. They are used to treat hypertension, edema (fluid retention), and certain kidney disorders. Diuretics can be further classified into different types based on their site of action and mechanism of action:
   - **Thiazide Diuretics:** Thiazide diuretics, such as hydrochlorothiazide, chlorthalidone, and indapamide, work by inhibiting the reabsorption of sodium and chloride from the distal convoluted tubules of the kidneys. This results in higher excretion of both water and electrolytes.
   - **Loop Diuretics**: Loop diuretics, such as furosemide, bumetanide, and torsemide, act on the ascending limb of the loop of Henle in the kidneys. They inhibit the reabsorption of sodium, potassium, and chloride, resulting in a powerful diuretic effect.

Note: Loop diuretics have the suffix "ide".

   - **Potassium-Sparing Diuretics**: Potassium-sparing diuretics, such as spironolactone and amiloride, work by inhibiting the reabsorption of sodium and reducing the excretion of potassium in the distal tubules. They are often used in combination with other diuretics to maintain potassium levels.
   - **Carbonic Anhydrase Inhibitors**: Carbonic anhydrase inhibitors (CAIs) inhibit the enzyme carbonic anhydrase, which is responsible for the reabsorption of bicarbonate ions in the proximal tubules (PCT) of the nephron. This increases urine output by limiting the reabsorption of salt, bicarbonate, and water.
     o Examples include acetazolamide and methazolamide.

Note: Carbonic anhydrase inhibitors have the suffix "amide".

   - **Osmotic Diuretics**: Osmotic diuretics are diuretics that increase urine production by creating an osmotic pressure to prevent the reabsorption of water.
     o Examples include Mannitol.
2. **Angiotensin-Converting Enzyme (ACE) Inhibitors**: ACE inhibitors are medications that block the enzyme ACE, which is responsible for converting angiotensin I to angiotensin II. By inhibiting this enzyme, ACE inhibitors decrease the production of angiotensin II, a potent vasoconstrictor. This leads to vasodilation, reduced blood pressure, and decreased sodium and water retention.
   - ACE inhibitors are used to commonly to treat hypertension, heart failure, and certain kidney conditions.
   - Examples include Lisinopril, Enalapril, and Ramipril.
3. **Angiotensin II Receptor Blockers (ARBs):** ARBs work by blocking the receptors for angiotensin II in blood vessels and other tissues. By doing so, they prevent angiotensin II from exerting its vasoconstrictive effects, leading to vasodilation, decreased blood pressure, and reduced sodium and water retention. ARBs are used to treat hypertension, heart failure, and certain kidney conditions.
   - Examples include Losartan, Valsartan, and Irbesartan.
4. **Calcium Channel Blockers**: Calcium channel blockers inhibit the influx of calcium into smooth muscle cells, including those in blood vessels. By doing so, they promote vasodilation, reduce peripheral resistance, and decrease blood pressure. These drugs are used to treat hypertension, angina (chest pain), and certain arrhythmias.

- Different types of calcium channel blockers, including dihydropyridines and non-dihydropyridines, have varying selectivity and effects on cardiac and vascular tissues.
- Examples include Amlodipine, Diltiazem, and Verapamil.

5. **Antidiuretic Hormone (ADH) Antagonists**: ADH antagonists, also known as vasopressin receptor antagonists, block the action of antidiuretic hormone (ADH) or vasopressin. ADH normally acts on the kidneys to increase water reabsorption and concentrate urine. By blocking ADH, these drugs increase water excretion and are used in the treatment of hyponatremia (low sodium levels) and fluid retention.
   - They are used in the treatment of hyponatremia, heart failure and polycystic kidney disease.
   - Examples include Conivaptan and Tolvaptan.

Note: ADH antagonists have the suffix "vaptan".

6. **Renin Inhibitors**: Renin inhibitors interfere with the renin-angiotensin-aldosterone system, which plays a crucial role in blood pressure regulation. These medications inhibit the enzyme renin, which initiates the production of angiotensin I. By blocking renin, these drugs decrease the production of angiotensin II, leading to vasodilation and reduced blood pressure. Renin-inhibitors are used in the treatment of hypertension.
   - Examples include Aliskiren.

Respiratory System Drugs

1. Bronchodilators
   - **Beta-2 Adrenoreceptor Agonists**: These drugs stimulate beta2-adrenergic receptors located in the smooth muscle of the airway leading to relaxation and bronchodilation.
     o These drugs are used to treat asthma and COPD.
     o Examples include albuterol and salmeterol.

Note: Beta-2 adrenoreceptor agonist drugs have the suffix "terol"

   - **Anticholinergic**: These drugs are a type of bronchodilator that block the acetylcholine neurotransmitter.
     o These drugs are used in the treatment of asthma and COPD.
     o Examples include ipratropium bromide and tiotropium.
   - **Methylxanthines**: These drugs act as bronchodilators and also have anti-inflammatory properties. They act by causing inhibition of the enzyme phosphodiesterase, which increases the level of cyclic adenosine monophosphate (cAMP) in the airway smooth muscles.
     o These drugs are used in the management of asthma and COPD.
     o Examples include theophylline.
2. Leukotriene Modifiers: Leukotriene modifiers are used for the management of asthma and may also be used as an alternative or along with corticosteroids.
     o These drugs act by inhibiting the action of leukotrienes, which are inflammatory mediators involved in bronchoconstriction and inflammation of the airways.
     o Examples include Montelukast and Zafirlukast.

Note: Leukotriene modifiers have the suffix "lukast"

3. Expectorants: Expectorants loosen the mucus in the respiratory tract to make coughing up the mucus easier thus, help in clearing the airways. They are used in the treatment of productive cough associated with respiratory infections.
     o Examples include Guaifenesin

4. Antitussives: Antitussives are used to relieve coughing. These drugs act by reducing the sensitivity of the cough reflex, providing temporary relief from non-productive or dry cough.
   o Examples include Dextromethorphan and Codeine.

Endocrine System Drugs

1. Hormone Replacement Therapy (HRT): Hormone replacement therapy involves the administration of hormones to replace or supplement deficient endogenous hormones. HRT is commonly used in conditions such as menopause, hypothyroidism, and adrenal insufficiency. The specific hormones used in HRT can vary depending on the condition being treated.
   - **Estrogen and Progestin:** Estrogen and progestin are used in menopausal hormone therapy to relieve menopausal symptoms and prevent osteoporosis. Common examples include conjugated estrogens, estradiol, and medroxyprogesterone acetate.
   - **Thyroid Hormones**: Synthetic thyroid hormones, such as levothyroxine sodium, are used in the treatment of hypothyroidism to replace or supplement thyroid hormone levels.
   - **Corticosteroids**: Corticosteroids, such as hydrocortisone and prednisone, are used in the treatment of adrenal insufficiency to replace or supplement cortisol and other adrenal hormones.
2. Thyroid Drugs: Thyroid drugs specifically target the thyroid gland and are used to regulate thyroid hormone levels in conditions such as hypothyroidism and hyperthyroidism.
   - **Thyroid Hormone Replacement**: Synthetic thyroid hormones, such as levothyroxine sodium, are used in the treatment of hypothyroidism to supplement or replace thyroid hormone levels.
   - **Antithyroid Drugs**: Antithyroid drugs, like methimazole and propylthiouracil, are used in the treatment of hyperthyroidism to inhibit the production of thyroid hormones.
3. Glucocorticoids: Glucocorticoids are a type of corticosteroid hormone that have anti-inflammatory and immunosuppressive effects. They are used in the treatment of various endocrine and non-endocrine conditions.
   - These drugs act by binding to glucocorticoid receptors present in various cells of the body and affect gene expression.
   - Synthetic glucocorticoids, such as prednisone and dexamethasone, are used in the treatment of conditions such as adrenal insufficiency, autoimmune disorders, and allergic reactions. Prednisone helps to reduce inflammation and suppress the immune system response. Dexamethasone also has benefits in managing severe respiratory symptoms in certain viral infections.
4. Antidiabetic Drugs: Antidiabetic drugs are used in the management of diabetes mellitus to regulate blood glucose levels.
   - **Insulin**: Insulin regulates glucose metabolism. It binds to the insulin receptors usually located on the surface of adipose cells, liver cells and muscle cells. This enhances glucose uptake reducing the blood glucose level.
     o It is used in the treatment of type 1 diabetes and sometimes in type 2 diabetes when oral antidiabetic medications are insufficient.

Point to remember: Insulin therapy requires proper dosing and close monitoring of blood glucose levels to minimize the risk of hypoglycemia.

   - **Oral Antidiabetic Drugs**: There are several classes of oral antidiabetic drugs, including:
     - Biguanides: Metformin is a commonly used biguanide that reduces glucose production in the liver and improves insulin sensitivity in type II diabetes.
     - Sulfonylureas: Sulfonylureas, such as glipizide and glyburide, stimulate insulin secretion from the pancreas.

- Thiazolidinediones: Thiazolidinediones, such as pioglitazone and rosiglitazone, improve insulin sensitivity in peripheral tissues.
- Dipeptidyl Peptidase-4 (DPP-4) Inhibitors: DPP-4 inhibitors, like sitagliptin and saxagliptin, elevate the levels of incretin hormones, promoting the release of insulin and decreasing glucagon secretion.
- Sodium-Glucose Cotransporter 2 (SGLT2) Inhibitors: SGLT2 inhibitors, such as empagliflozin and dapagliflozin, reduce glucose reabsorption in the kidneys, leading to increased glucose excretion.

5. Adrenal Hormone Drugs: Adrenal hormone drugs target the adrenal glands and are used to regulate the production and release of adrenal hormones.
   - **Mineralocorticoids**: Mineralocorticoids, such as fludrocortisone, mimic the actions of aldosterone and are used in the treatment of conditions such as adrenal insufficiency and salt-losing disorders.
     o Mineralocorticoids should be used with caution in individuals with hypertension or congestive heart failure because they can cause exacerbation of these conditions. They are contraindicated in patients with primary hyperaldosteronism (excessive production of aldosterone) and those with known hypersensitivity to the medication.
   - **Glucocorticoids**: Glucocorticoids, such as hydrocortisone and prednisone, have anti-inflammatory and immunosuppressive effects and are used in the treatment of adrenal insufficiency, autoimmune disorders and allergic reactions.
     o Glucocorticoids should be used with caution in patients with systemic fungal infections as they can worsen the infection.

Antimicrobial Drugs

1. **Antibiotics**:
   - **Penicillin**: Penicillin is the first ever discovered antibiotic that is commonly used to treat streptococcal infections such as tonsillitis, pharyngitis, endocarditis and urinary tract infections. It is also used in the treatment of meningitis.
     o This type of antibiotic prevents the formation of cell walls during bacterial reproductive division. This results in bacterial cells swelling up and eventually bursting and dying. It is contraindicated in people who are allergic to penicillin.
     o Examples include penicillin G, penicillin V, amoxicillin, and ampicillin.
   - **Cephalosporins**: Cephalosporins act similar to penicillin and are classified further into different generations. These are contraindicated in patients with hypersensitivity due to the antibiotic.
     o They prevent the formation of peptidoglycans in the bacterial cell wall thus, are bactericidal.
       ▪ First generation: cefazolin and cephalexin
       ▪ Second generation: cefuroxime and cefoxitin
       ▪ Third generation: ceftriaxone and ceftazidime
       ▪ Fourth generation: cefepime
       ▪ Fifth generation: ceftaroline and ceftobiprole

Point to remember: In neonates ≤ 28 days, it is important to avoid the coadministration of Ceftriaxone IV with IV solutions that contain calcium, including continuous calcium-containing infusions like parenteral nutrition. This caution is necessary to prevent the risk of precipitation of ceftriaxone-calcium salt.

Note: Cephalosporins have the prefix "ceph" or cef".

- **Macrolides**: Macrolide antibiotics are used to treat respiratory tract infections, such as community-acquired pneumonia, as well as skin and soft tissue infections caused by susceptible bacteria.
  - They act by preventing protein synthesis in the bacterial cells by binding to the 50s subunit of the ribosome.
  - Macrolides should be used with caution in individuals with known liver impairment, as they can potentially worsen liver function. They may also interact with certain medications, so careful consideration is necessary when prescribing them alongside other drugs.
  - Examples include azithromycin and clarithromycin.
- **Fluoroquinolones**: Fluoroquinolones are broad-spectrum antibiotics used to treat various bacterial infections, including urinary tract infections, respiratory tract infections, skin and soft tissue infections, and certain sexually transmitted infections.
  - These antibiotics act by inhibiting DNA replication in the bacteria. These should be used with caution in individuals with a history of tendon disorders, as they can increase the risk of tendon rupture.

Point to remember: Fluoroquinolones are generally not recommended for children and pregnant women due to potential adverse effects on bone and cartilage development.

  - Examples include ciprofloxacin and levofloxacin.

Note: Fluoroquinolones have the suffix "floxacin".

- **Tetracyclines**: Tetracycline antibiotics are used to treat respiratory tract infections, acne, urinary tract infections, and certain sexually transmitted infections. They are also used for the treatment of Lyme disease, cholera, and certain types of pneumonia.
  - Tetracyclines prevent protein synthesis in bacteria by binding to the 30s ribosomes.

Point to remember: Tetracyclines should be avoided in pregnant women, children under the age of eight, and individuals with severe liver or kidney disease. They can interfere with bone growth and tooth development in children, and they may also cause photosensitivity reactions in some individuals.

  - Examples include doxycycline and minocycline.

Note: Tetracyclines have the suffix "cycline"

2. **Antiviral Drugs**:
   - **Nucleoside/Nucleotide Analogues**: Nucleoside/nucleotide analogues are used to treat viral infections such as herpes simplex virus (HSV), varicella-zoster virus (VZV), hepatitis B virus (HBV), and human immunodeficiency virus (HIV).
     - These work by incorporating into the viral DNA or RNA, disrupting viral replication. They act as chain terminators and prevent the synthesis of new viral DNA or RNA strands.

Point to remember: These drugs should be used with caution in individuals with impaired kidney function, as dose adjustments may be necessary.

     - Some nucleoside/nucleotide analogues may also have interactions with other medications, so careful monitoring is required.
     - Examples include acyclovir and lamivudine.

- **Protease Inhibitors**: Protease inhibitors are primarily used in the treatment of HIV infection. They are combined with other antiretroviral drugs to suppress viral replication and slow down the progression of the disease.
    - These drugs prevent the maturation of new viral particles and reduce viral replication by inhibiting the activity of the viral protease enzyme.
    - Protease inhibitors may have interactions with other medications and can cause side effects such as gastrointestinal disturbances and metabolic abnormalities.

Point to remember: They should be used with caution in individuals with liver disease or impaired liver function.

- Examples include ritonavir and lopinavir.

Note: Most antiviral drugs have the suffix "vir"

- **Neuraminidase Inhibitors**: Neuraminidase inhibitors are used for the treatment and prevention of influenza A and B viral infections.
    - These prevent the action of neuraminidase, which prevents the release of new viral particles from infected cells to limit the spread of the virus in the respiratory tract.
    - These drugs should be used with caution in individuals with underlying respiratory conditions, as they may cause bronchospasm or exacerbate respiratory symptoms. They should also be used with caution in individuals with known allergies to the drug.
    - Examples include oseltamivir and zanamivir.

3. **Antifungal Drugs**:
- **Azoles**: Azole antifungals are used to treat a wide range of fungal infections, including vaginal yeast infections, oral thrush, systemic fungal infections, and certain types of skin infections.
    - Azoles inhibit the synthesis of ergosterol, a key component of the fungal cell membrane resulting in the inhibition of fungal growth and replication.
    - Azoles should be used with caution in individuals with liver dysfunction, as they can affect liver enzymes and potentially lead to liver toxicity. They may also have interactions with other medications, so careful consideration is necessary when prescribing them alongside other drugs.
    - Examples include fluconazole and itraconazole.

Note: Azoles have the suffix "azole:

- **Polyenes**: Polyene antifungals are primarily used for the treatment of systemic fungal infections, including severe cases of candidiasis and invasive fungal infections.
    - Polyenes bind to ergosterol which is a component of the fungal cell membrane. This results in the formation of spores that disrupt the fungal cell membrane's integrity.
    - Polyene antifungals should be used with caution in individuals with impaired kidney function, as they can cause kidney toxicity. They may also have interactions with other medications, and certain formulations may have specific contraindications, so close monitoring is necessary.

Point to remember: Adequate hydration and monitoring of renal function are important during treatment using polyenes.

- Examples include amphotericin B and nystatin.

- **Echinocandins**: Echinocandin antifungals are used to treat invasive fungal infections, particularly those caused by Candida species. Echinocandins should be used with caution in individuals with known allergies to the drug.
    - These drugs inhibit the synthesis of β-(1,3)-D-glucan, which is a component of the fungal cell wall
    - They may also have interactions with other medications, so careful consideration is necessary when prescribing them alongside other drugs.
    - Examples include caspofungin and micafungin.
4. **Antiparasitic Drugs**:
    - **Antimalarials**: Antimalarial drugs are primarily used for the prevention and treatment of malaria, a parasitic infection transmitted by mosquitoes. Some antimalarial drugs, such as chloroquine, should be used with caution in individuals with pre-existing cardiac conditions, as they can cause cardiac toxicity.
        - They inhibit the growth and replication of the malarial parasites by acting on different stages of their life cycle. Some antimalarials, such as amodiaquine and chloroquine, inhibit the detoxification of heme which accumulates and is toxic to the parasite.
        - They may also have interactions with other medications, so careful consideration is necessary when prescribing them alongside other drugs.
        - Examples include amodiaquine, chloroquine, hydroxychloroquine, and artemisinin derivative.
    - **Anthelmintics or Antinematodal Agents**: Anthelmintic drugs are used to treat helminthic infections, such as intestinal worms (e.g., roundworms, hookworms). Anthelmintics should be used with caution in individuals with liver dysfunction or impaired liver function, as they can affect liver enzymes.
        - These drugs disrupt the microtubule formation leading to inhibition of glucose uptake, ultimately leading to the death of helminths.
        - They may also have interactions with other medications, so careful consideration is necessary when prescribing them alongside other drugs.
        - Examples include albendazole and mebendazole.

Note: Anthelminthics have the prefix "dazole", which should not be confused with "azoles" for some antifungal drugs.

- **Other Drugs**: Other drugs, also known collectively as Antiprotozoal drugs, are used to treat various protozoan infections, including amoebiasis, giardiasis, trichomoniasis, and certain types of malaria. Antiprotozoals should be used with caution in individuals with liver dysfunction or impaired liver function, as they can affect liver enzymes.
    - They may also have interactions with other medications, so careful consideration is necessary when prescribing them alongside other drugs.
    - Examples include metronidazole and quinine.

Reproductive System Drugs

1. **Contraceptives**: Contraceptives play a crucial role in preventing pregnancy.
    - Combination Oral Contraceptives (COCs): These contain a combination of estrogen and progestin hormones.
        - Common examples include ethinyl estradiol/levonorgestrel (Alesse), and norgestimate/ethinyl estradiol (Ortho Tri-Cyclen).

- Progestin-Only Contraceptives: These contraceptives contain only progestin and are also known as mini-pills.
  - Examples include norethindrone (Micronor), levonorgestrel (Plan B), and etonogestrel implant (Nexplanon).

2. **Prostaglandin Analogs**: These medications mimic the effects of naturally occurring prostaglandins and are used for labor induction, cervical ripening and managing postpartum hemorrhage. Examples include misoprostol and Dinoprostone

3. **Phosphodiesterase Type 5 (PDE5) Inhibitors**: These are used to treat erectile dysfunction.
   - Sildenafil (Viagra): Sildenafil is a widely used medication for erectile dysfunction. By increasing blood flow to the penis, it helps in achieving and maintaining an erection.
   - Tadalafil (Cialis): Due to its extended duration of action, tadalafil provides a broader window of opportunity for sexual activity when compared to sildenafil.
   - Vardenafil (Levitra): Vardenafil promotes increased blood supply to the penis working similarly to sildenafil and tadalafil.

4. **Alpha-Blockers**: Alpha-blockers are drugs that have the ability to relax the smooth muscles of the prostate and bladder neck, which leads to improved urine flow and a reduction in urinary symptoms.
   - Alpha-blockers are primarily used to relieve symptoms such as urinary frequency, urgency, weak urine flow, and incomplete bladder emptying. They are often the first-line treatment for Benign Prostatic Hyperplasia.
   - Examples: Tamsulosin (Flomax), Alfuzosin (Uroxatral), Silodosin (Rapaflo)

5. **5-Alpha Reductase Inhibitors**: 5-alpha reductase inhibitors block the enzyme 5-alpha reductase and convert testosterone to dihydrotestosterone (DHT). By inhibiting DHT production, these medications help reduce prostate size over time.
   - These are effective in shrinking the prostate gland in Benign Prostatic Hyperplasia, relieving urinary symptoms, and preventing disease progression.
   - Examples: Finasteride (Proscar), Dutasteride (Avodart)

Most Common Drugs List

Now that you know the classification of drugs of various systems, here is the list of the 240 most common drugs whit generic names and brand names, along with their classes, that you should know for your PTCB exam.

Generic Name	Brand Name	Drug Class
Acetaminophen	Tylenol	Analgesic
Acetylsalicylic acid	Aspirin	Antiplatelet
Acyclovir	Zovirax	Antiviral
Albuterol	Proventil, Ventolin	Beta-2 Agonist
Alendronate	Fosamax	Bisphosphonate
Allopurinol	Zyloprim	Xanthine Oxidase Inhibitor
Alprazolam	Xanax	Benzodiazepine
Amitriptyline	Elavil, Vanatrip	Tricyclic Antidepressant
Amlodipine	Norvasc	Calcium Channel Blocker
Amoxicillin	Amoxil, Trimox	Penicillin Antibiotic

Amoxicillin + Clavulanic acid	Augmentin	Penicillin antibiotic and Beta-lactamase inhibitor
Ampicillin	Principen	Penicillin Antibiotic
Aripiprazole	Abilify	Atypical Antipsychotic
Aspirin	Bayer, Ecotrin	Nonsteroidal Anti-inflammatory
Atenolol	Tenormin	Beta Blocker
Atomoxetine	Strattera	Selective Norepinephrine Reuptake Inhibitor
Atorvastatin	Lipitor	HMG-CoA Reductase Inhibitor (Statin)
Azathioprine	Imuran	Immunomodulator
Azithromycin	Zithromax	Macrolide Antibiotic
Baclofen	Lioresal	Muscle Relaxant
Bevacizumab	Avastin	Vascular Endothelial Growth Factor Inhibitor
Bisacodyl	Dulcolax	Laxative
Bisoprolol	Zebeta	Beta Blocker
Brimonidine	Alphagan	Alpha-2 Agonist
Budesonide	Rhinocort, Pulmicort	Corticosteroid
Buprenorphine	Subutex, Suboxone	Opioid Analgesic
Calcium carbonate	Tums	Antacid
Carbamazepine	Tegretol	Anticonvulsant
Carvedilol	Coreg	Beta Blocker
Cefdinir	Omnicef	Cephalosporin Antibiotic
Ceftriaxone	Rocephin	Cephalosporin Antibiotic
Cefuroxime	Ceftin	Cephalosporin Antibiotic
Celecoxib	Celebrex	Nonsteroidal Anti-inflammatory
Cephalexin	Keflex	Cephalosporin Antibiotic
Cetirizine	Zyrtec	Antihistamine
Chlorpheniramine	Chlor-Trimeton	First Generation Antihistamine
Chlorpheniramine + Hydrocodone	Tussionex, PennKinetic	Narcotic antihistamine
Cimetidine	Tagamet	H2 Receptor Antagonist
Ciprofloxacin	Cipro	Fluoroquinolone
Citalopram Hydrobromide	Celexa	Selective Serotonin Reuptake Inhibitor
Clarithromycin	Biaxin	Macrolide Antibiotic
Clindamycin	Cleocin	Macrolide Antibiotic
Clonazepam	Klonopin	Benzodiazepine

Clopidogrel	Plavix	Antiplatelet
Clotrimazole+ Betamethasone	Lotrisone	Antifungal
Clozapine	Clozaril	Atypical Antipsychotic
Codeine	Tylenol with Codeine	Opioid Analgesic
Colchicine	Colcrys, Mitigare	Antigout
Cyclobenzaprine	Flexeril	Muscle Relaxant
Cyclosporine	Neoral, SandIMMUNE	Calcineurin Inhibitor
Desmopressin	DDAVP	Antidiuretic Hormone
Desmopressin	DDAVP	Antidiuretic Hormone
Dexamethasone	Decadron	Corticosteroid
Dextromethorphan	Robitussin	Antitussive
Diazepam	Valium	Benzodiazepine
Diclofenac	Voltaren, Cataflam	Nonsteroidal Anti-inflammatory
Dicyclomine	Bentyl	Antispasmodic
Digoxin	Lanoxin	Cardiac Glycoside
Diltiazem	Cardizem	Calcium Channel Blocker
Dimenhydrinate	Dramamine	Antiemetic
Diphenhydramine	Benadryl	Antihistamine
Docusate	Colace	Laxative
Donepezil	Aricept	Cholinesterase Inhibitor
Doxazosin	Cardura	Alpha-1 Blocker
Doxycycline	Vibramycin, Adoxa	Tetracycline Antibiotic
Doxylamine	Unisom	Antihistamine
Duloxetine	Cymbalta	Serotonin-Norepinephrine Reuptake Inhibitor
Enalapril	Vasotec, Epaned	ACE Inhibitor
Epoetin alfa	Epogen, Procrit	Erythropoiesis-Stimulating Agent
Escitalopram	Lexapro	Selective Serotonin Reuptake Inhibitor
Esomeprazole	Nexium	Proton Pump Inhibitor
Estradiol	Estrace	Estrogen
Eszopiclone	Lunesta	Sedative-Hypnotic
Ethinyl estradiol/Levonorgestrel	Alesse, Aviane, Seasonique	Contraceptive
Ezetimibe	Zetia	Cholesterol Absorption Inhibitor
Famotidine	Pepcid	H2 Receptor Antagonist
Famotidine/calcium carbonate/magnesium hydroxide	Pepcid Complete	Antacid

Ferrous sulfate	Feosol	Iron Supplement
Fexofenadine	Allegra	Antihistamine
Filgrastim	Neupogen	Granulocyte Colony-Stimulating Factor
Finasteride	Proscar	5-alpha Reductase Inhibitor
Fluconazole	Diflucan	Antifungal
Fluoxetine	Prozac, Sarafem	Selective Serotonin Reuptake Inhibitor
Fluticasone	Flonase, Flovent	Corticosteroid
Fluvoxamine	Luvox	Selective Serotonin Reuptake Inhibitor
Formoterol	Foradil, Perforomist	Beta-2 Agonist
Furosemide	Lasix	Loop Diuretic
Gabapentin	Neurontin	Anticonvulsant
Gentamicin	Garamycin	Aminoglycoside Antibiotic
Glargine	Lantus	Long-acting Insulin
Glimepiride	Amaryl	Antidiabetic
Glipizide	Glucotrol	Antidiabetic
Glyburide	Diabeta, Glynase Pres Tab, Micronase	Antidiabetic
Guaifenesin	Mucinex	Expectorant
Heparin	Heparin sodium	Anticoagulant
Hydralazine	Apresoline	Vasodilator
Hydrochlorothiazide	Microzide, HydroDiuril	Thiazide Diuretic
Hydrocodone + Acetaminophen	Vicodin, Norco	Opioid Analgesic
Hydrocortisone	Cortef, Ala-Cort	Corticosteroid
Hydroxychloroquine	Plaquenil	Antimalarial
Ibandronate	Boniva	Bisphosphonate
Ibuprofen	Advil, Motrin	Nonsteroidal Anti-inflammatory
Indomethacin	Indocin	Nonsteroidal Anti-inflammatory
Infliximab	Remicade	Monoclonal antibody
Insulin	Humulin, Novolin	Antidiabetic
Insulin Aspart	NovoLog	Antidiabetic
Ipratropium	Atrovent	Anticholinergic
Isosorbide mononitrate	Imdur	Nitrate
Ketoconazole	Nizoral Topical	Antifungal
Ketorolac	Toradol	Nonsteroidal Anti-inflammatory
Lactulose	Duphalac, Constulose	Osmotic Laxative

Lamotrigine	Lamictal	Anticonvulsant
Lansoprazole	Prevacid	Proton Pump Inhibitor
Latanoprost	Xalatan	Prostaglandin Analog
Levodopa	Inbrija, Dopar, Larodopa	Antiparkinsonian medicine
Levodopa+ Carbidopa+ Entacapone	Stalevo 50	Antiparkinsonian medicine
Levofloxacin	Levaquin	Fluoroquinolone
Levonorgestrel	Plan B, Mirena	Contraceptive
Levothyroxine	Synthroid	Thyroid Hormone Replacement
Lidocaine	Lidoderm	Local anesthetic
Linezolid	Zyvox	Oxazolidinone Antibiotic
Lisinopril	Zestril, Prinivil, Qbrelis	ACE Inhibitor
Lispro	HumaLOG	Insulin Analogue
Lithium	Lithobid	Mood Stabilizer
Loratadine	Claritin	Antihistamine
Lorazepam	Ativan	Benzodiazepine
Losartan	Cozaar	Angiotensin II Receptor Blocker
Lovastatin	Mevacor, Altoprev	HMG-CoA Reductase Inhibitor (Statin)
Lubiprostone	Amitiza	Chloride Channel Activator
Meclizine	Bonine	Antihistamine
Meloxicam	Mobic	Nonsteroidal Anti-inflammatory
Memantine	Namenda	NMDA Receptor Antagonist
Metformin	Glucophage	Antidiabetic (Oral)
Methadone	Dolophine	Opioid Analgesic
Methimazole	Tapazole	Antithyroid
Methocarbamol	Robaxin, Carbacot	Muscle Relaxant
Methotrexate	Trexall, Otrexup	Antimetabolite
Methylergonovine	Methergine	Uterine Stimulant
Methylergonovine	Methergine	Uterine Stimulant
Methylphenidate	Ritalin, Concerta	Stimulant
Methylprednisolone	Medrol	Corticosteroid
Metoclopramide	Reglan	Antiemetic
Metoprolol	Lopressor	Beta Blocker
Metronidazole	Flagyl	Antimicrobial
Minocycline	Minocin	Tetracycline Antibiotic
Mirabegron	Myrbetriq	Beta-3 Agonist
Mirtazapine	Remeron	Alpha-2 Antagonist
Montelukast	Singulair	Leukotriene Receptor Antagonist

Morphine	MS Contin	Opioid Analgesic
Moxifloxacin	Avelox	Fluoroquinolone
Mupirocin	Bactroban	Antibacterial (Dermatological)
Naloxone	Narcan	Opioid Receptor Antagonist
Naloxone	Narcan	Opioid Receptor Antagonist
Naltrexone	Revia	Opioid Receptor Antagonist
Naltrexone	Revia	Opioid Receptor Antagonist
Naproxen	Aleve, Naprosyn	Nonsteroidal Anti-inflammatory
Nifedipine	Procardia	Calcium Channel Blocker
Nitrofurantoin	Macrobid, Macrodantin	Urinary Tract Antibiotic
Nitroglycerin	Nitrostat	Nitrate
Nortriptyline	Pamelor	Tricyclic Antidepressant
NPH Insulin	Humulin N, Novolin N	Intermediate-acting Insulin
Olanzapine	Zyprexa	Atypical Antipsychotic
Omeprazole	Prilosec	Proton Pump Inhibitor
Omeprazole/sodium bicarbonate	Zegerid	Proton Pump Inhibitor
Ondansetron	Zofran	Antiemetic
Oseltamivir	Tamiflu	Antiviral
Oxybutynin	Ditropan	Anticholinergic
Oxycodone	OxyContin	Opioid Analgesic
Oxytocin	Pitocin	Uterine Stimulant
Oxytocin	Pitocin	Uterine Stimulant
Pancrelipase	Creon, Pancreaze	Pancreatic Enzyme
Pantoprazole	Protonix	Proton Pump Inhibitor
Paroxetine	Paxil	Selective Serotonin Reuptake Inhibitor
Pegfilgrastim	Neulasta	Granulocyte Colony-Stimulating Factor
Pemetrexed	Alimta	Anticancer drug
Perindopril	Aceon	ACE Inhibitor
Phenobarbital	Luminal	Barbiturate
Phenylephrine	Sudafed PE	Decongestant
Phenytoin	Dilantin	Anticonvulsant
Piroxicam	Feldene	Nonsteroidal Anti-inflammatory
Polyethylene Glycol	Miralax	Laxative
Polyvitamin with iron	Ferrous Fumarate	Multivitamin with Iron
Prednisolone	Prelone, Flo-Pred	Corticosteroid
Prednisone	Deltasone	Corticosteroid

Pregabalin	Lyrica	Anticonvulsant
Probenecid	Benemid	Uricosuric Agent
Progesterone	Prometrium	Progestin
Promethazine	Phenergan	Antiemetic
Pseudoephedrine	Sudafed	Decongestant
Psyllium	Metamucil	Laxative
Quetiapine	Seroquel	Atypical Antipsychotic
Ramipril	Altace	ACE Inhibitor
Ranitidine	Zantac	H2 Receptor Antagonist
Regular Insulin	Humulin R, Novolin R	Short-acting Insulin
Risperidone	Risperdal	Atypical Antipsychotic
Rituximab	Rituxan	CD20-Directed Cytolytic Antibody
Rizatriptan	Maxalt	Triptan
Ropinirole	Requip	Dopamine agonist (Antiparkinsonian drug)
Rosuvastatin	Crestor	HMG-CoA Reductase Inhibitor (Statin)
Salmeterol	Serevent	Beta-2 Agonist
Salmeterol + Fluticasone	Advair	Bronchodilator
Senna	Senna Lax, Senokot, Ex-Lax, MiraLAX	Stimulant Laxative
Sertraline	Zoloft	Selective Serotonin Reuptake Inhibitor
Sildenafil	Viagra	Phosphodiesterase Inhibitor
Simethicone	Gas-X	Antiflatulent
Simvastatin	Zocor	HMG-CoA Reductase Inhibitor (Statin)
Sirolimus	Rapamune	mTOR Inhibitor
Sitagliptin	Januvia	Antidiabetic
Solifenacin	Vesicare	Anticholinergic
Spironolactone	Aldactone	Potassium-Sparing Diuretic
Sulfamethoxazole/Trimethoprim	Bactrim, Septra	Sulfonamide Antibiotic
Sumatriptan	Imitrex	Triptan
Tacrolimus	Prograf	Calcineurin Inhibitor
Tadalafil	Cialis	Phosphodiesterase Inhibitor
Tamsulosin	Flomax	Alpha-1 Blocker
Temazepam	Restoril	Benzodiazepine
Terazosin	Hytrin	Alpha-1 Blocker

Testosterone	AndroGel	Androgen
Timolol	Timoptic	Beta Blocker
Tiotropium	Spiriva	Anticholinergic
Tizanidine Hydrochloride	Zanaflex	Muscle Relaxant
Tobramycin	Tobrex	Aminoglycoside Antibiotic
Tramadol	Ultram	Opioid Analgesic
Tranexamic acid	Lysteda	Hemostatic Agent
Tranexamic acid	Lysteda	Hemostatic Agent
Trastuzumab	Herceptin	HER2 Inhibitor
Trazodone	Desyrel	Serotonin Antagonist and Reuptake Inhibitor
Triamterene	Dyrenium	Potassium-Sparing Diuretic
Ustekinumab	Stelara	Monoclonal antibody
Valacyclovir	Valtrex	Antiviral
Valproic acid/Valproate sodium	Depakote	Anticonvulsant
Valsartan	Diovan	Angiotensin II Receptor Blocker
Vancomycin	Vancocin	Glycopeptide Antibiotic
Vardenafil	Levitra	Phosphodiesterase Inhibitor
Venlafaxine	Effexor	Serotonin-Norepinephrine Reuptake Inhibitor
Verapamil	Calan	Calcium Channel Blocker
Warfarin	Coumadin	Anticoagulant
Zafirlukast	Accolate	Leukotriene Receptor Antagonist
Zolmitriptan	Triptan	Triptan
Zolpidem	Ambien	Sedative-Hypnotic

Drug Interactions, Indications, Contraindications

Drug Interactions

Drug interactions can occur in different ways and can be classified into pharmacokinetic interactions and pharmacodynamic interactions.

- Pharmacokinetic interactions are seen when a drug impacts how another drug is absorbed, distributed, metabolized, or excreted. These interactions can impact the concentration and response of one or both drugs at the site of action in the body.
  - There are four types of pharmacokinetic interactions: absorption interactions, distribution interactions, metabolism interactions, and excretion interactions.

- Pharmacodynamic interactions, on the other hand, involve alterations in the biological response of one or both drugs without affecting their pharmacokinetics.
  - These interactions can result in additive effects, potentiation (increased response due to synergy), or antagonism (reduction in effects). Antagonism can be chemical, physiological, pharmacological, or due to physicochemical incompatibility between drugs. Additionally, pharmacodynamic interactions may increase adverse effects when the combined action of drugs enhances their side effect profiles or leads to unforeseen toxicities.

Drug-Drug Interactions: Drug-drug interactions are seen when two or more medications interact with each other and affect the pharmacological actions or increase the risk of adverse effects. This type of interactions can occur due to different mechanisms, including changes in the absorption, distribution, metabolism, or excretion of the drug. Drug-drug interactions can lead to altered drug concentrations, diminished therapeutic effects, or increased toxicity.

Examples of drug-drug interactions include:

- Synergism: **When two drugs with similar effects are taken together**, resulting in an additive or enhanced effect. An example of this is seen in the combination of opioids and nonsteroidal anti-inflammatory drugs (NSAIDs) for better pain control.
- Antagonism: **When one drug interferes with the actions of another drug**, reducing its effectiveness. For example, diuretic medications (thiazides) may have reduced diuretic activity when taken along with NSAIDs.
- Potentiation: **When one drug increases the effects of another drug** beyond what would be expected. An example is the combination of aspirin and warfarin, which can increase the risk of excessive bleeding.

Drug-Food Interactions: Drug-food interactions occur when certain foods or beverages interfere with the absorption, metabolism, or effectiveness of medications. Food can affect the bioavailability and pharmacokinetics of drugs, leading to changes in their therapeutic effects or safety profiles. These interactions can occur due to interactions with enzymes, alteration of gastric pH, or competition for absorption sites.

- Bioavailability: In pharmacology, bioavailability is the measure of the fraction of a drug that reaches the bloodstream and becomes available for action at its intended site. It determines the necessary dosage for achieving desired therapeutic effects. Bioavailability is influenced by the drug's characteristics, how it's administered (e.g., orally, intravenously), and individual patient variables such as metabolism and interactions with other substances.

Examples of drug-food interactions include:

- Decreased Absorption: Some foods can bind to drugs, reducing their absorption. For instance, consuming dairy products with tetracycline antibiotics can form insoluble complexes that hinder drug absorption.
- Altered Metabolism: Certain foods can affect the activity of drug-metabolizing enzymes, potentially leading to changes in drug concentrations.
  - Grapefruit juice, for example, can inhibit the metabolism of some medications, such as statins (lipid-lowering medications), resulting in higher drug levels in the body.
- Impaired Effectiveness: Some foods can interfere with the therapeutic effects of medications. For instance, consuming foods high in vitamin K can have a negative impact on the effectiveness of anticoagulant medications like warfarin.

Point to remember: Regular monitoring of the international normalized ratio (INR) is important if a patient is taking warfarin.

Additionally, specific interactions can lead to increased drug activity, such as insulin or oral diabetic agents with alcohol, which can dangerously enhance the drug's hypoglycemic effect. Conversely, warfarin's anticoagulant action can be decreased when taken with vitamin K-rich foods due to competitive antagonism. Furthermore, certain food-drug combinations can produce toxic responses; for example, combining tyramine-rich foods like aged cheese with monoamine oxidase inhibitors can precipitate a hypertensive crisis, and co-administration of acetaminophen with alcohol can elevate the risk of liver toxicity. These examples illustrate the critical need for careful management of diet when on medication regimens.

Drug-Disease Interactions: When a medication intended to treat one condition adversely affects another existing medical condition or interacts with the disease process itself, this type of drug interaction is called a drug-disease interaction. Certain medications may worsen symptoms, interfere with treatment outcomes, or interact negatively with the physiological processes of a specific disease.

Examples of drug-disease interactions include:

- Asthma and Beta-Blockers: Non-selective beta-blockers such as propranolol or metoprolol, commonly used to treat hypertension and heart conditions, can worsen asthma symptoms by constricting airways. For example, if a patient with asthma takes a beta-blocker, it can potentially trigger bronchospasms and make breathing more difficult.
- Kidney Disease and Nephrotoxic Drugs: Patients with kidney disease may be more susceptible to the toxic effects of certain medications that are cleared by the kidneys. Some nephrotoxic drugs, like ibuprofen (NSAIDs) or antibiotics like Gentamicin, can further compromise kidney function. For instance, a patient with kidney disease who takes NSAIDs regularly for pain relief may experience worsening kidney function and potential kidney damage.
- Depression and Selective Serotonin Reuptake Inhibitors (SSRIs): SSRIs, such as fluoxetine (Prozac) or sertraline (Zoloft), are the drugs that are commonly used in the management of

depression. However, when some SSRIs are taken with other medications that affect serotonin levels, an increase in the risk of serotonin syndrome may occur. For example, taking SSRIs with pain medications like tramadol or migraine drugs like triptans can potentially lead to serotonin syndrome. Serotonin syndrome is a potentially life-threatening syndrome that has symptoms such as increased agitation, confusion, rapid heart rate, dilated pupils, muscular stiffness, and tremors. Patients with depression need to be cautious when taking other medications that can interact with SSRIs and increase serotonin levels.

Drug interactions can occur at different stages, such as during drug absorption, distribution, metabolism, and excretion. Here are some examples of drug interactions at each stage:

During drug absorption:

- Certain substances like calcium, iron, or antacids can form insoluble complexes with drugs, impairing their absorption.
- Antibiotics can reduce the metabolism of drugs like digoxin, leading to increased concentrations and potential toxicity.
- Some drugs, when taken together, can delay the absorption of others, potentially causing adverse effects.

During drug distribution:

- Drug interactions can occur when one drug displaces another from protein-binding sites, altering their free concentrations in the body.

During drug metabolism:

- Drug interactions can involve the induction or inhibition of drug-metabolizing enzymes, such as cytochrome P450 enzymes. Inhibition can increase the plasma concentration of a drug, leading to toxicity or enhanced side effects.

During drug excretion:

- Alterations in urinary pH, tubular secretion, or glomerular flow can affect the amount of drug excreted in the urine, potentially impacting its efficacy.
- Some drugs can inhibit the tubular secretion of certain drugs, prolonging their presence in the body.

Common Drug Interactions to Know for The PTCB Exam:

- **Statins and Grapefruit Juice**: The consumption of grapefruit juice introduces furanocoumarins into the body, which interact with enzymes involved in the metabolism of statins. This interaction heightens the likelihood of experiencing side effects like muscle pain and aches when using statins such as atorvastatin, simvastatin, or lovastatin.
- **Antiplatelet Drugs, NSAIDs, and Anticoagulant Drugs**: When taken individually, antiplatelet drugs (e.g., clopidogrel), NSAIDs (e.g., aspirin, ibuprofen), and anticoagulant drugs (e.g., warfarin, heparin) increase the risk of bleeding. When combined, the risk of bleeding becomes even more pronounced. Additionally, the concomitant use of other medications like SSRIs further amplifies the risk of bleeding.
- **Multivalent Ions and Various Drugs**: Substances containing multivalent ions, such as milk, antacids, calcium, magnesium, and iron, have the potential to interact with several medications. This interaction diminishes the efficacy of drugs like levothyroxine, tetracyclines, fluoroquinolones, and bisphosphonates, thereby impeding their ability to achieve desired therapeutic outcomes.

- **Nitrates and PDE5 Inhibitors**: Combining nitrates and PDE5 inhibitors (e.g., sildenafil, tadalafil) can lead to severe hypotension due to their respective hypotensive effects. Consequently, the simultaneous administration of these drugs poses a substantial risk.

- **ACE Inhibitors and Potassium-Elevating Drugs**: ACE inhibitors (e.g., ramipril, lisinopril) elevate potassium levels, consequently increasing the likelihood of developing hyperkaliemia. Therefore, it is advisable to avoid combining ACE inhibitors with potassium-elevating drugs like trimethoprim or potassium supplements.

- **Ritonavir and Protease Inhibitors**: The inhibition of CYP enzymes by ritonavir alters the metabolism of protease inhibitors. This interaction enables the use of lower doses of protease inhibitors (e.g., lopinavir) to achieve equivalent clinical effects without inducing excessive side effects.

- **Beta-Blockers and Calcium Channel Blockers**: The combination of beta-blockers (e.g., metoprolol) with calcium channel blockers (e.g., verapamil, diltiazem) heightens the risk of heart failure and bradycardia (reduced heart rate).

- **Broad-Spectrum Antibiotics and Warfarin**: Broad-spectrum antibiotics (e.g., penicillin, cephalosporins) eradicate the gut flora responsible for synthesizing vitamin K. This interaction elevates the risk of bleeding when these antibiotics are taken concurrently with warfarin.

- **Digoxin and Loop/Thiazide Diuretics**: Loop diuretics (e.g., furosemide) and thiazide diuretics (e.g., hydrochlorothiazide) increase the probability of digoxin toxicity by inducing low potassium levels.

- **Aminoglycosides and Loop Diuretics**: The administration of aminoglycosides (e.g., Gentamicin, amikacin) in combination with loop diuretics (e.g., furosemide) heightens the risk of experiencing ototoxicity and kidney damage.

Routes of Drug Administration:

The route of administration is the method used for administering a drug into the body. Each route of administration plays a crucial role in achieving optimal bioavailability and determining the drug's action and response within the body.

Enteral Route:

The "enteral route" refers to the administration of medication through the gastrointestinal tract. It is one of the most common methods for drug delivery, primarily because it is convenient, safe, and cost-effective for both outpatient and inpatient care. Medications administered via the enteral route are typically in the form of tablets, capsules, liquids, or suspensions, and are absorbed into the bloodstream through the lining of the stomach or intestines.

The following list elaborates on the various routes of administration that fall within the broad scope of the enteral route:

Oral Route: The oral route involves administering the drug through the mouth to get absorbed into the systemic circulation as it passes through the gastrointestinal tract.

- This route is widely used and convenient for patients, as they can self-administer medications in various forms, such as tablets, capsules, syrups, or suspensions.
- However, the oral route has limitations, including potential low bioavailability, first-pass metabolism in the liver, irritation to the gastric mucosa, and slower onset of action.
  - The "First-Pass Effect" occurs when a significant portion of a drug is metabolized by the liver before it enters systemic circulation. This phenomenon primarily affects orally administered drugs, as they are absorbed from the gastrointestinal tract and transported directly to the liver via the portal vein. In the liver, hepatic enzymes metabolize the drug, potentially reducing its concentration in the bloodstream and affecting its pharmacological effectiveness.

Sublingual Route: The sublingual route involves placing medications under the tongue, where they are absorbed through the buccal mucous membrane and directly enter the systemic circulation, bypassing the first-pass effect.

- This route offers a quick onset of action and the patient can take the drug by themselves.
- It is not suitable for certain drugs and may cause taste and compliance issues.

Buccal Route: The buccal route involves placing the drug formulation between the gums and the inner cheek. The drug gets absorbed from the buccal mucosa rapidly and directly enters the systemic circulation, bypassing the first-pass metabolism.

  - First-Pass Metabolism: This is a specific aspect of the first-pass effect, focusing solely on the metabolic transformation of a drug in the liver during its first pass through the hepatic circulation. It describes the biochemical alterations the drug undergoes, leading to the formation of metabolites (which can be either active or inactive) and can impact the concentration and effectiveness of the drug reaching systemic circulation.

- This route provides both systemic and localized effects, making it suitable for specific conditions such as mouth ulcers.
- Buccal tablets and chewing gum are common dosage forms used in this route.

Rectal Route: The rectal route is an alternative for drugs that can also be administered orally. Medications in the form of suppositories or pessaries are inserted into the rectum, where they are readily absorbed due to the thin rectal wall and rich blood supply.

- This route is useful when oral administration is not feasible, such as in unconscious patients or those with nausea or difficulty swallowing.
- Drug absorption may be incomplete and inconsistent, and patient acceptance can be a challenge.

Vaginal Route: The vaginal route involves administering drugs to women vaginally using solutions, tablets, creams, gels, suppositories, rings, or pessaries.

- This route is commonly used to administer drugs during hormone replacement therapy in women in the menopausal period. It can be administered in unconscious patients or those experiencing nausea or vomiting.
- Irritation and variable absorption are possible drawbacks.

Local Route:

The "local route" involves applying medication directly to a targeted area for immediate effect, minimizing systemic impact. Key forms include creams, ointments, eye drops, ear drops, and inhalers, focusing on treating specific local conditions. The local route offers the advantage of delivering medication efficiently to the affected area, ensuring rapid and focused therapeutic effects.

The following list elaborates on the various routes of administration that fall within the scope of the local route:

Topical Route:

The topical route involves applying drugs directly to the skin or mucous membranes for localized action. Different sites can be targeted, such as the oral cavity, rectum, anal canal, eyes, ears, nose, bronchi, and skin.

- Dosage forms include suspensions, ointments, jellies, drops, and sprays.
- This route is suitable for specific conditions in each site, providing localized effects and reducing systemic side effects.

Otic/Ear Route: The otic or ear route involves administering medication into or through the ear using formulations such as ear drops.

- This route offers a localized effect, targeting specific conditions or infections in the ear.
- Self-administration can be challenging with this route, and patients may find it time-consuming as they need to remain in a tilted position for a few minutes after instilling the ear drops.

Ocular/Eye Route: The ocular or eye route involves administering medication into the eye using formulations such as eye drops or eye ointments.

- This route offers advantages such as reduced systemic side effects and achieving a localized effect within the eye.
- Eye drops may cause temporary blurring of vision after administration, and certain barriers, such as poor manual dexterity or poor vision, can impede proper administration.

Inhalation: Inhalation involves the administration of volatile liquids and gases for systemic effects or the treatment of nasal disorders. This route is usually used for medications like general anesthetics and bronchodilators.

- Inhalation offers several advantages, including a quick onset of action due to the direct delivery of the medication to the respiratory system. The required dosage for inhalation is typically low, minimizing the risk of systemic toxicity.
  - Inhalation allows for better regulation of the number of drugs administered.
  - A potential disadvantage of inhalation is the possibility of local irritation in the nasal cavity or nasopharyngeal tract, which can lead to increased respiratory secretions and bronchospasm.

Parenteral Route

The "parenteral route" is used to administer drugs directly into the systemic circulation without passing through the gastrointestinal tract. It can be classified into two classes: with injections (intravascular, intramuscular, subcutaneous) and without injections (inhalations). The parenteral route offers advantages such as the rapid onset of action, suitability for emergency situations, and precise control over drug plasma concentration. However, it requires aseptic conditions and trained personnel and may cause pain or local tissue injuries.

The following list elaborates on the various routes of administration that fall within the scope of the parenteral route:

Intravenous Route: The intravenous route delivers drugs directly into a vein through injections or infusions.

- This route provides an immediate onset of action, precise control over drug concentration, and suitability for unconscious patients.
- It has risks of certain complications such as infections, allergic reactions, and phlebitis. So, it requires skilled administration.

Intramuscular Route: The intramuscular (I.M.) route involves administering medication directly into specific muscles, such as the gluteus Medius and deltoid. This route offers several advantages, such as the immediate onset of action and allowing for quick therapeutic effects.

- This route enables the use of depot or sustained-release formulations, which are beneficial for treating chronic diseases by providing a controlled and extended release of the drug.
- The intramuscular route bypasses the first-pass metabolism, meaning the medication can directly enter the bloodstream without being extensively metabolized in the liver. Moreover, compared to the intravenous route, the intramuscular route is relatively easier to administer.
- Certain drugs administered intramuscularly may cause pain or discomfort due to their irritating nature.

- The absorption of the drug can alter depending on the specific muscle group used and the blood flow to the muscle.

Subcutaneous Route: The subcutaneous (S.C.) route involves injecting medication into the subcutaneous tissue through direct infusion or injection. This route offers several advantages. Patients can self-administer the medication in certain cases, providing convenience and control over their treatment.

- Additionally, the subcutaneous route is particularly suitable for drugs with a long duration of action, as it helps reduce the overall duration of drug effects.
- The subcutaneous route carries a lower risk of systemic infection compared to other routes of administration.

NOTE: It's important to note that the absorption of the drug can vary based on blood flow to the subcutaneous tissue. Thus, a fine needle should be used for SC injection administration.

Intradermal Route: In the intradermal route of drug administration, medication is injected into the dermis, which is the skin layer found just below the epidermis. This method is commonly utilized for diagnostic purposes, such as performing skin tests for allergies or tuberculosis screening. One significant advantage of the intradermal route is the ability to produce a localized response that is easily visible and measurable.

- Compared to other routes, the dermis has a rich supply of blood vessels, which facilitates faster absorption of the medication. This can be advantageous when a rapid systemic effect is desired.
- Administering medication intradermally requires a precise injection technique to ensure accurate placement in the dermis. Injections into the dermis can be more painful or uncomfortable compared to other routes.

NOTE: Due to the highly vascularized nature of the dermis, there is a potential for rapid absorption of the medication into the bloodstream. This can lead to unintended systemic effects if the medication is intended for local action only.

The explanation below explains the technique of drug administration in intramuscular, subcutaneous, intravenous and intradermal routes of drug administration:

Intramuscular injections are given directly into the muscle tissue at a 90-degree angle to the body. Subcutaneous injections are administered into the tissue layer between the skin and muscle at a 45-degree angle. Intravenous injections are delivered straight into the vein at a shallow angle of around 25 degrees, and intradermal injections are made just under the skin at an angle between 10 to 15 degrees. Each method targets different layers of tissue to optimize the delivery and absorption of medications.

Special Drug Handling

When it comes to drug handling, the safety and integrity of medications is crucial.

1. Temperature-Sensitive Medications: Certain medications require specific temperature controls to maintain their stability and effectiveness. For example, **vaccines, insulin,** and some biological medications need to be stored in a refrigerated environment. Pharmacy technicians should be aware of the proper storage requirements and handling procedures for temperature-sensitive drugs, including monitoring temperature logs and addressing any deviations.

2. Hazardous Medications: Some medications pose a risk to healthcare workers if proper precautions are not taken during handling. Hazardous drugs, such as **chemotherapy agents**, require specialized handling techniques to minimize exposure. Pharmacy technicians should be familiar with the guidelines for handling hazardous drugs, including the use of personal protective equipment (PPE), proper disposal methods, and spill management protocols.

3. Controlled Substances: Controlled substances, such as **opioids and certain sedatives,** have a higher potential for abuse and are subject to strict regulations. Pharmacy technicians must adhere to legal requirements for the storage, documentation, and dispensing of controlled substances. This includes maintaining accurate inventory records, ensuring appropriate security measures, and following procedures for controlled substance reconciliation.

4. Compounded Medications: Compounded medications are customized formulations prepared based on the specific needs of the patients. Pharmacy technicians may assist in the compounding process by measuring ingredients, preparing sterile compounding, or labeling compounded products. They should understand the principles of the aseptic technique, proper compounding calculations, and the importance of maintaining sterility and accuracy during the compounding process.

5. Special Packaging and Labeling: Some medications require special packaging or labeling due to specific patient requirements or regulatory guidelines such as medications that are dispensed in child-resistant packets, blister packs, or unit-dose packaging. Pharmacy technicians should be familiar with different packaging systems, labeling requirements, and how to ensure proper identification and patient safety when dispensing these medications.

Side Effects, Adverse Effects and Allergies

This section provides a comprehensive overview of the various side effects, adverse effects, and allergic reactions associated with medication use. It categorizes and details common and severe effects on different bodily systems, including gastrointestinal, cardiovascular, central nervous, respiratory, musculoskeletal, dermatological, hematological, renal, and endocrine systems. The section also delves into the specifics of drug allergies, outlining common symptoms and identifying medications with higher allergenic potential. It serves as an essential guide for understanding the wide spectrum of drug reactions, crucial for ensuring patient safety in pharmacy practice.

Drug Side Effects and Adverse Effects

1. **Gastrointestinal System**:
   - Common Side Effects: Nausea and vomiting are common gastrointestinal side effects that can occur with medications such as opioids (e.g., morphine) or chemotherapy drugs (e.g., cisplatin). Upset stomach, indigestion, and acid reflux may be experienced with nonsteroidal anti-inflammatory drugs (NSAIDs) like ibuprofen.
     - Medications that affect bowel movements, like opioids, can cause diarrhea or constipation. Note: Opioids are commonly associated with constipation and only rarely with diarrhea.
     - Anticholinergic medications such as certain antihistamines (e.g., diphenhydramine) can result in a dry mouth sensation.
   - Severe Adverse Effects: NSAIDs can cause gastrointestinal bleeding or ulceration, leading to serious complications. For example, long-term use of NSAIDs like ibuprofen can increase the risk of gastric ulcers.
     - Pancreatitis, though rare, can occur as a severe adverse effect of medications like valproic acid.
     - Liver toxicity is a severe adverse effect associated with certain medications such as acetaminophen, some antibiotics (e.g., isoniazid), or antifungals (e.g., fluconazole).
2. **Cardiovascular System**:
   - Common Side Effects: Headache is a common side effect reported with cardiovascular medications like nitroglycerin, used for angina.
     - Dizziness may occur due to changes in blood pressure with medications like antihypertensives.
     - Flushing, a sensation of warmth and redness of the skin, can be seen with certain medications like niacin used to manage cholesterol levels.
   - Severe Adverse Effects: Certain medications, such as some antiarrhythmics like amiodarone, can cause cardiac arrhythmias, including prolonged Q.T. interval, leading to potentially life-threatening irregular heart rhythms.

Note: The QT interval is the period on an electrocardiogram (ECG) that represents the time it takes for the heart's ventricles to contract and then recover, or repolarize.

   - Myocardial infarction (heart attack) can occur as a severe adverse effect of medications like hormonal contraceptives containing estrogen.
   - Congestive heart failure can be a severe adverse effect associated with medications like some antidiabetic drugs (e.g., pioglitazone).

o Hypertension can also be a severe adverse effect of medications like oral contraceptives.

3. **Central Nervous System**:
   - Common Side Effects: Drowsiness and sedation are common side effects of medications like antihistamines (e.g., diphenhydramine), opioids (e.g., codeine), or benzodiazepines (e.g., diazepam).
     - o Headache and dizziness can occur with various medications, including analgesics or antihypertensives.
     - o Some medications can also cause mood changes, including irritability or alterations in emotional well-being. For example, certain antidepressants (e.g., selective serotonin reuptake inhibitors - SSRIs) may cause initial agitation or changes in mood.
   - Severe Adverse Effects: Serotonin syndrome is a potentially life-threatening condition that can occur with the use of certain medications, such as SSRIs (e.g., fluoxetine) or tramadol, resulting in agitation, confusion, rapid heart rate, dilated pupils, tremors, or seizures.
     - o Neuroleptic malignant syndrome, though rare, can occur as a severe adverse effect of antipsychotic medications like haloperidol, characterized by hyperthermia, altered mental status, muscle rigidity, and autonomic dysfunction.
     - o Seizures or extrapyramidal symptoms like tardive dyskinesia (involuntary repetitive movements) can also occur as severe adverse effects of certain medications like antipsychotics.

4. **Respiratory System**:
   - Common Side Effects: Cough and shortness of breath can occur with various medications. For example, angiotensin-converting enzyme (ACE) inhibitors may lead to persistent cough.
     - o Some medications, including opioids and some sedatives, can slow breathing by causing respiratory depression.
   - Severe Adverse Effects: Hypersensitivity pneumonitis is a rare but severe adverse effect of certain medications, such as some antibiotics (e.g., nitrofurantoin) or nonsteroidal anti-inflammatory drugs (NSAIDs), causing inflammation of the lung tissue and leading to symptoms like cough, shortness of breath, and flu-like symptoms.
     - o Bronchospasm, a severe adverse effect, can occur with medications like beta-blockers or certain antibiotics (e.g., penicillins), causing sudden constriction of the airways and difficulty in breathing.
     - o Respiratory distress can also be seen as a severe adverse effect of medications like certain chemotherapy drugs (e.g., bleomycin).

5. **Musculoskeletal System**:
   - Common Side Effects: Muscle weakness and joint pain can occur with certain medications like corticosteroids (e.g., prednisone) or statins (e.g., atorvastatin).
   - Severe Adverse Effects: Rhabdomyolysis, a severe adverse effect, can occur with medications like statins, causing the breakdown of muscle tissue and leading to symptoms such as severe muscle pain, weakness, and dark-colored urine.
     - o Tendon rupture can also be a severe adverse effect associated with certain medications like fluoroquinolone antibiotics (e.g., ciprofloxacin).

6. **Dermatological System**:
   - Common Side Effects: Skin rash and itching can be common side effects of medications, including antibiotics (e.g., penicillin) or anticonvulsants (e.g., lamotrigine). Photosensitivity, an increased sensitivity to sunlight, may occur with certain medications like tetracyclines.

- Severe Adverse Effects: Severe skin reactions such as Toxic Epidermal Necrolysis (TEN) and Stevens-Johnson Syndrome (SJS) can occur as adverse effects of medications, including antiepileptic drugs (e.g., carbamazepine) or sulfonamides. These conditions cause widespread blistering and skin detachment, requiring immediate medical attention.

7. **Hematological System**:
   - Common Side Effects: Easy bruising or bleeding can occur with medications that affect platelet function, such as antiplatelet drugs (e.g., aspirin) or anticoagulants (e.g., warfarin).
   - Severe Adverse Effects: Bone marrow suppression, leading to decreased production of blood cells, can occur as a severe adverse effect of medications like chemotherapy drugs (e.g., methotrexate).
     - Aplastic anemia and agranulocytosis, rare but severe adverse effects, can be associated with certain medications like antithyroid drugs (e.g., propylthiouracil) or clozapine.

8. **Renal System**:
   - Common Side Effects: Increased urination, known as diuresis, can occur with medications like diuretics (e.g., furosemide) or some antihypertensives.
   - Severe Adverse Effects: Kidney damage, acute renal failure, or nephrotoxicity can be severe adverse effects associated with certain medications like nonsteroidal anti-inflammatory drugs (NSAIDs) or certain antibiotics (e.g., vancomycin).

9. **Endocrine System**:
   - Common Side Effects: Weight gain or weight loss can occur with various medications, including antipsychotics (e.g., olanzapine) or certain antidepressants (e.g., fluoxetine).
   - Severe Adverse Effects: Adrenal suppression can be a severe adverse effect of long-term use of corticosteroids, resulting in decreased adrenal gland function.
     - Some medications, such as certain antipsychotics or glucocorticoids, can lead to diabetes mellitus or worsen existing diabetes.
     - Thyroid dysfunction, including hypothyroidism or hyperthyroidism, can be associated with certain medications like amiodarone.

Allergic Reactions

Drug allergies are adverse immune reactions that occur in response to exposure to a specific medication. Unlike side effects, which are common and expected effects of a medication, allergies involve an abnormal response of the immune system. Drug allergies can be mild, severe and even life-threatening.

Common Symptoms: Drug allergy symptoms can manifest in different ways, including:

- Skin Reactions: These may include hives (itchy, raised welts on the skin), rash, itching, and swelling.
- Respiratory Symptoms: These can include wheezing, shortness of breath, coughing, or nasal congestion.
- Gastrointestinal Symptoms: Symptoms related to the gastrointestinal tract may comprise nausea, vomiting, diarrhea, or abdominal pain.
- Anaphylaxis: This is a potentially life-threatening allergic reaction characterized by a rapid onset of symptoms such as difficulty in breathing, low blood pressure (hypotension), rapid heartbeat, swelling in the throat or tongue and dizziness. Anaphylaxis requires immediate medical attention.

Common Allergenic Medications: Some medications that are more likely to cause drug allergies include:

- Antibiotics: Penicillins (such as amoxicillin), cephalosporins, sulfonamides.
- Nonsteroidal Anti-Inflammatory Drugs (NSAIDs): Aspirin, ibuprofen, naproxen.
- Chemotherapy Drugs: Cisplatin (a platinum-based drug), taxanes, monoclonal antibodies.
- Contrast Agents: Used in imaging procedures like C.T. scans or angiograms.

Drug Stability

Drug stability refers to the ability of a pharmaceutical substance to maintain its therapeutic properties over its intended storage period or shelf life. Understanding drug stability is essential to make sure that the drugs are safe to use and are effective. The Food and Drug Administration (FDA) enforces regulations known as Current Good Manufacturing Practices (CGMPs), which require drug manufacturers to conduct stability testing to assess the effectiveness of their products.

Factors Affecting Drug Stability Several factors can influence drug stability, including environmental conditions and the inherent properties of the drug itself. The following are the three general categories of stability loss:

1. **Chemical Stability**: Chemical stability refers to a drug's ability to remain unchanged when exposed to various environmental conditions that could cause degradation. One common type of chemical degradation is hydrolysis, where the drug reacts with water, resulting in its breakdown. Certain functional groups present in pharmaceutical compounds are prone to hydrolysis. Formulating drugs with chemical shields that protect against hydrolysis is a challenge in developing stable medications.
2. **Physical Stability**: Physical stability refers to a drug's ability to maintain its physical properties over time. Crystallization of precipitation of some pharmaceutical compounds out of solution may occur at extreme temperatures. For instance, when certain drugs are mixed with incompatible intravenous solutions, they can precipitate. Additionally, volatile components of drugs may evaporate, leaving behind solid residues. Denaturation, which involves changes in the molecular structure of the active component, can also affect physical stability, especially in complex protein-based drugs.
3. **Microbiological Stability**: Microbiological stability relates to the prevention of microbial contamination during the storage and transportation of drugs. Contamination can occur through exposure to dirty equipment, storage containers, airborne microorganisms, or personnel handling the drugs. Manufacturing, storage, and sale of drugs must adhere to strict aseptic conditions to maintain microbiological stability.

Different drug categories require specific considerations for maintaining stability. Here are a few examples:

1. **Oral Suspensions and Reconstitutables**: Oral suspensions consist of solid particles suspended in a liquid phase. To ensure stability, excessive settling of particles must be prevented.
   - The manufacturers of the drugs often thicken the suspension liquid using certain additives such as *glycerin or polyethylene glycol*.
   - Reconstitutables, which are powdered drugs mixed with a liquid solvent by the patient, include pre-packaged solvents to prevent deactivation and maintain stability.
2. **Insulin**: Insulin storage varies based on the type and presentation (vials, pens, or small syringes). Unopened insulin can remain stable until the expiration date if *refrigerated*, while opened insulin is typically usable for about a month.
   - Extreme temperatures and sunlight exposure should be avoided to maintain insulin stability. Note that these vials should not be shaken before use.
3. **Injectables**: Injectable drug stability depends on the specific drug and its packaging. Some injectables require refrigeration, while others may need special packaging, like foil, to protect against temperature and light sensitivity.
   - Sterilization processes are employed to *prevent microbial contamination*, and durable materials like *polyethylene and polypropylene* are commonly used for packaging.

4. **Vaccinations**: Vaccine stability is crucial to preserve the complex molecules they contain, including live attenuated microorganisms. *Temperature control* has a crucial role in maintaining the stability of a vaccine.

   - For example, mRNA vaccines for COVID-19 require ultra-low temperature storage, while refrigerated vaccines should be kept between 36 and 46 degrees F.

Narrow Therapeutic Index (NTI) Medications

Narrow Therapeutic Index (NTI) medications are drugs that have a small difference between the therapeutic dose (the dose that provides the desired effect) and the toxic dose (the dose that can cause harmful or toxic effects). These medications require careful dosing and monitoring to make sure that they are safe and effective.

NTI medications have a narrow margin of safety, meaning that small changes in dosage or blood concentration can lead to significant differences in therapeutic response or adverse effects.

- Examples: warfarin (an anticoagulant), digoxin (used in heart failure and arrhythmias), levothyroxine (a thyroid hormone replacement), and phenytoin (an antiepileptic drug).
  - These medications require close monitoring of blood levels and dosage adjustments to maintain their therapeutic effects within a safe range.
  - To monitor the effectiveness and safety of warfarin therapy, patients need regular blood tests to measure their *International Normalized Ratio* (INR). INR is a standardized measure of the duration taken for blood to clot. The target INR range for patients on warfarin varies depending on their medical condition but is typically between 2.0 and 3.0.
  - Monitoring the INR helps healthcare providers determine the appropriate dosage adjustments to maintain the therapeutic effects of warfarin within a safe range.

Due to the narrow therapeutic index, the FDA has established strict standards for the bioequivalence of generic versions of NTI medications. Generic versions of these drugs must demonstrate that they are pharmaceutically equivalent and bioequivalent to their brand-name counterparts. This ensures that the generic versions have similar absorption, distribution, metabolism, and elimination properties.

- Pharmacy technicians play a crucial role in counseling patients about the importance of adhering to the prescribed dosage regimen, reporting any adverse effects, and scheduling regular follow-up appointments for monitoring. Due to the narrow margin of safety, errors in prescribing, dispensing, or administration of NTI medications can have serious consequences.
- Pharmacy technicians must be diligent in their roles to prevent medication errors, including double-checking prescriptions, verifying dosage calculations, and ensuring accurate dispensing of these medications.

Drug Compounding and Storage

Drug compounding refers to the process of preparing customized medications for patients with specific needs. It involves combining or altering ingredients to create medications that are not readily available in commercially manufactured forms. Compounding can be performed by pharmacists, pharmacy technicians, or other trained professionals in compliance with state and federal regulations.

During the drug compounding process, various techniques are employed to prepare medications in different forms, such as creams, ointments, capsules, solutions, suspensions, or suppositories. Compounded medications are often tailored to address specific patient requirements, such as adjusting dosages, removing allergens, or providing alternative administration routes.

Sterile Compounding

Sterile compounding refers to the preparation of medications in a sterile environment to reduce the risk of contamination and safe compounding to ensure patient safety. Sterile compounded medications are typically administered through intravenous (IV) injections, intramuscular injections, or directly into the eye or other sterile body sites.

- The process of sterile compounding involves strict adherence to aseptic techniques to prevent the introduction of microorganisms. Compounding personnel must work in a designated cleanroom or sterile compounding area equipped with specialized equipment, including a laminar airflow hood or isolator, to maintain a sterile environment.

Key considerations for sterile compounding include:

1. Personal Protective Equipment (PPE): Compounding personnel must wear appropriate PPE, including sterile gloves, masks, gowns, and head coverings, to minimize the risk of introducing contaminants.
2. Cleanroom Environment: The sterile compounding area should have controlled airflow, HEPA (high-efficiency particulate air) filtration systems, and surfaces that are easy to clean and disinfect. Regular cleaning and disinfection of the cleanroom are essential to maintain sterility.
3. Sterilization Techniques: Sterile Compounding often involves the use of sterilization techniques, such as filtration or autoclaving, to eliminate microorganisms from ingredients, equipment, and containers. Sterilized components, such as syringes, vials, and IV bags, are used to maintain sterility throughout the compounding process.
4. Aseptic Technique: Compounding personnel must follow strict aseptic technique, which includes proper hand hygiene, disinfection of work surfaces, and the use of sterile tools and equipment. Any breach in the aseptic technique can introduce contaminants and compromise the sterility of the final product.

Non-Sterile Compounding

Non-sterile Compounding involves the preparation of customized medications that do not require a sterile environment. These medications are typically administered orally, topically, or through other routes that do not carry a high risk of introducing contaminants.

- Non-sterile Compounding can include activities such as mixing ingredients, altering dosage forms, flavoring medications, or preparing topical creams and ointments.
- However, even though non-sterile compounding does not require a sterile environment, it still requires strict adherence to cleanliness and quality control measures to ensure the safety and effectiveness of the compounded medications.

Key considerations for non-sterile compounding include:

1. Clean Environment: Non-sterile Compounding should be performed in a clean and well-maintained area to minimize the risk of contamination. This involves routine cleaning of work surfaces, utensils, and equipment.
2. Sanitization: Compounding personnel must sanitize equipment, such as mortar and pestle, mixing utensils, and measuring devices, before use. Proper cleaning and sanitization procedures help prevent cross-contamination between different medications.
3. Ingredient Quality and Compatibility: It is essential to use high-quality ingredients and ensure their compatibility to maintain the stability and effectiveness of compounded medications. Compounding personnel should carefully select ingredients and verify the suitability of the ingredients and the medication for use.
4. Accurate Measuring and Compounding Techniques: Precise measurement and compounding techniques are crucial to ensure accurate dosing and consistent quality of compounded medications. Proper training and following standard operating procedures (SOPs) help minimize errors and maintain quality control.
5. Packaging and Labeling: Non-sterile compounded medications should be appropriately packaged and labeled with clear instructions for use, ingredients, and expiration dates. Proper packaging and labeling help ensure the accurate identification, appropriate storage, and patient safety.

Procedures to Compound Non-Sterile Products

Non-sterile compounding plays a significant role in pharmacy practice, involving the preparation of customized medications such as ointments, mixtures, liquids, emulsions, suppositories, and enemas. Pharmacy technicians are responsible for following precise procedures to ensure accuracy, safety, and quality. It is crucial for pharmacy technicians to adhere to relevant compounding guidelines, such as the United States Pharmacopeia (USP) General Chapter 795 (USP795 regulations) for non-sterile compounding. Here are step-by-step procedures for compounding non-sterile medications:

Procedure Overview:

1. Formula Creation: Using the prescription or compounding formula provided, create a formula for the intended product. Perform any necessary calculations to determine the specific amounts of ingredients needed.
2. Preparation: Prior to compounding, wash hands thoroughly and wear all required personal protective equipment (PPE) to maintain a clean and sterile work environment.
3. Equipment Acquisition: Gather the necessary hardware supplies, such as a balance or graduated cylinder, to accurately measure the ingredients.
4. Ingredient Measurement: Weigh or measure out all ingredients using appropriate tools and techniques to ensure precise measurements.
5. Mixing and Blending: Follow the compounding formula instructions to combine the ingredients in the correct ratios and proper order. For ointments, utilize the process of spatulation, which involves

geometric mixing of semi-solids and powders on an oil slab using a spatula. Ensure thorough and uniform mixing.

6. Documentation and Labeling: Record the exact amounts of each ingredient used in the compounding process. Properly label the final product, including the strengths of the ingredients, to ensure accurate identification.

Ointments:

Ointments are topical medications used to treat various dermatologic conditions. They differ from creams, which are water-based preparations. Ointments are oil-based and consist of water in oil. Mixing ointments involves spatulation, where equal parts of each ingredient are geometrically mixed on an oil slab until a uniform mixture is achieved. Ointments are typically stored in jars, as mixing may be necessary before administration.

Mixtures:

Mixtures encompass a range of formulations that consist of multiple active and inactive ingredients. They can involve the combination of solids and liquids, two liquids, or two solids. Geometric mixing is crucial to ensure consistency and uniformity in mixtures. For example, a liquid mixture like magic mouthwash, used to treat mouth pain and mucositis, requires a 1:1:1 ratio of lidocaine 2% viscous, liquid antacid, and diphenhydramine. All ingredients are mixed together to create a uniform solution.

Liquids:

While some medications come commercially in liquid form, others require compounding. Liquids comprise a solute (active drug component) dispersed homogeneously in a solvent (liquid vehicle). During compounding, it is important to dissolve the solute completely in the solvent to achieve the desired concentration. Suspensions, a type of liquid formulation, may require thorough mixing before use to prevent settling.

Emulsions:

Emulsions consist of two immiscible liquids dispersed throughout each other. For instance, an oil-in-water emulsion involves dispersing oil droplets throughout the water. Emulsions are commonly used in topical creams and serve as bases for ointments and lotions.

Suppositories:

Suppositories are solid formulations primarily used rectally and sometimes vaginally. They contain medication suspended in a base, such as cocoa butter. Suppositories can be prepared through hand rolling, fusion molding, or compression molding. Hand rolling involves mixing the suppository base with medication and forming it into a cone-shaped mold.

Enemas:

Enemas are solution formulations administered rectally to treat various conditions, such as constipation or ulcerative colitis. They work locally on the colon lining and are not systemically absorbed.

Physical and Chemical Compounding Incompatibilities

Physical and chemical incompatibilities can occur during non-sterile compounding and reconstitution processes. These incompatibilities can lead to alterations in drug stability, effectiveness, and safety. It is crucial for pharmacy technicians to be aware of these incompatibilities to ensure the appropriate preparation and administration of compounded medications. Here are some examples of physical and chemical incompatibilities that can occur:

1. Precipitation: Precipitation refers to the formation of solid particles when incompatible substances are combined. It can result in the formation of visible particles or a cloudy appearance in the final product. Precipitation can occur due to interactions between two or more drugs, pH changes, or temperature variations.
2. pH Incompatibility: pH plays a critical role in the stability and effectiveness of certain drugs. Incompatibility can arise when acidic and alkaline substances are combined, leading to changes in drug solubility, degradation, or loss of activity. pH adjustments may be required to maintain compatibility during compounding or reconstitution.
3. Chemical Decomposition: Some drugs can undergo chemical decomposition when exposed to certain substances or conditions. For example, oxidation reactions can occur when drugs are exposed to air, light, or certain metals. This can result in a loss of drug potency or the formation of potentially harmful degradation products.
4. Drug-Excipient Incompatibility: Excipients are inactive ingredients used in formulations to enhance the stability, solubility, or other characteristics of the drug. However, certain excipients may interact with the active ingredient, leading to incompatibilities. For example, preservatives, antioxidants, or surfactants used in formulations may cause destabilization or degradation of the active drug.
5. Solubility Issues: Incompatibility can arise from the poor solubility of drugs in the chosen vehicle or diluent. Insoluble drugs may precipitate or form aggregates, rendering the medication ineffective or unsafe. Selecting appropriate solvents and vehicles based on the drug's solubility characteristics is important to ensure compatibility.
6. Container-Drug Incompatibility: Certain drugs may interact with the materials used in containers or administration devices. This can lead to leaching of substances from the container or adsorption of the drug onto the container surface, affecting drug stability or introducing contaminants. Compatibility between the drug and the container material should be considered during compounding and storage.

To mitigate physical and chemical incompatibilities during non-sterile compounding and reconstitution, pharmacy technicians should:

1. Review drug compatibility references and available stability data.
2. Follow manufacturer guidelines and product labeling instructions.
3. Use appropriate solvents, vehicles, and excipients based on drug characteristics.
4. Conduct compatibility testing when necessary, such as visual inspection, pH adjustment, or stability studies.
5. Monitor and control environmental factors, such as temperature, light exposure, and humidity.
6. Ensure proper cleaning and maintenance of equipment and containers to minimize contamination or leaching.
7. Document all compounding processes and ingredients used to facilitate traceability and identification of potential incompatibilities.

SECTION 2: Federal Drug Regulations

Section 2 offers an exploration of Federal Drug Regulations, highlighting how key laws such as the Food Drug and Cosmetic Act and HIPAA influence pharmacy practice. It also sheds light on the pivotal role of pharmacy technicians in record-keeping and the complexities involved in the management of controlled substances. This section serves as a comprehensive guide to the intricate legal framework essential to pharmaceutical care.

Handling and Disposal of Pharmaceutical Substances and Waste

Pharmacy practice is governed by a combination of federal and state laws that aim to ensure the safe and effective delivery of pharmaceutical care.

Federal Laws

1. **Food, Drug, and Cosmetic Act (FD&C Act):** The Food, Drug, and Cosmetic Act is a pivotal federal law that grants the Food and Drug Administration (FDA) authority to oversee the *safety, efficacy, and labeling of drugs*. It sets forth the requirements for drug approval, manufacturing practices, labeling standards, and post-marketing surveillance. Pharmacists are responsible for ensuring that all drugs dispensed comply with FDA regulations and meet quality and safety standards.
2. **Health Insurance Portability and Accountability Act (HIPAA):** HIPAA is a federal law that safeguards the *privacy and security of the protected health information* and medical records of patients. Pharmacists must adhere to strict guidelines to maintain the confidentiality of patient health records, implement appropriate security measures to protect against unauthorized access or disclosure, and ensure the secure transmission of patient data.
3. **Drug Enforcement Administration (DEA) Regulations**: The DEA enforces federal *laws pertaining to controlled substances*. Pharmacists must comply with DEA regulations, which include obtaining and maintaining a DEA registration, proper storage and security of controlled substances, accurate record-keeping, conducting periodic inventories, and reporting suspicious activities or losses of controlled substances.
4. **The Drug Quality and Security Act (DQSA)**: The Drug Quality and Security Act (DQSA) is a federal law that *enhances the safety and security of the pharmaceutical supply chain.*
   - It consists of two main provisions: the Drug Supply Chain Security Act (DSCSA) and the Compounding Quality Act (CQA).
     - The DSCSA establishes tracing, serialization, and verification systems to prevent counterfeit drugs.
     - The CQA regulates compounding practices for patient safety and quality, distinguishing between traditional compounding and manufacturing. It introduces outsourcing facilities subject to FDA oversight.

- The DQSA emphasizes adherence to quality standards, such as current Good Manufacturing Practices (cGMPs), and grants the FDA authority to inspect facilities and enforce compliance.

State Laws

State laws governing pharmacy practice may vary from one jurisdiction to another, but they generally cover similar areas and are designed to complement federal laws. Here are some key aspects typically addressed by state pharmacy laws:

1. **Pharmacist Licensing and Practice**: Each state establishes its own requirements for pharmacist licensure, which encompass educational qualifications, examinations, and ongoing professional development. State laws define the scope of practice, delineating their roles and responsibilities in providing patient care, medication management, and other pharmacy services.
2. **Pharmacy Ownership and Operation**: State laws regulate the ownership of a pharmacy and its operation. These laws encompass licensing requirements, permits, and ownership restrictions.
3. **Prescription Requirements and Drug Dispensing**: State laws define the specific requirements for valid prescriptions, including the types of prescribers who are authorized to issue prescriptions and the necessary information that must be included in the prescription document.
4. **Medication Errors and Reporting**: Many states have laws that mandate the reporting of medication errors, adverse drug events, or dispensing discrepancies to appropriate regulatory authorities. These reporting systems aim to identify and analyze errors, facilitate learning and improvements in pharmacy practice, and ensure patient safety.
5. **Medication Synchronization**: Some states have enacted legislation to facilitate medication synchronization programs. These programs allow pharmacists to align the refill dates of multiple medications for patients, promoting medication adherence and enhancing patient convenience.
6. **Collaborative Practice Agreements**: In certain states, pharmacists are authorized to collaborate with other healthcare providers with the help of collaborative practice agreements. These agreements enable pharmacists to engage in collaborative patient care activities such as medication therapy management, immunizations, and ordering laboratory tests under specific protocols and with the appropriate supervision and oversight.

Pharmacy Technician Code of Ethics

As a pharmacy technician, adhering to a Code of Ethics is essential to maintain the highest standards of professionalism and patient care. These may vary from one state to the other. Pharmacy practice regulations and standards can differ between jurisdictions and organizations. The following are key principles outlined in the Pharmacy Technician Code of Ethics:

1. **Patient Welfare:** The primary focus of a pharmacy technician is the well-being and safety of patients. Technicians must prioritize patient care by ensuring accuracy in medication dispensing, maintaining patient confidentiality, and promoting patient education and counseling.
2. **Integrity**: Pharmacy technicians should conduct themselves with honesty, integrity, and trustworthiness. They should follow all laws and regulations governing pharmacy practice, including proper handling of controlled substances, maintaining accurate records, and avoiding conflicts of interest.
3. **Professional Competence**: Technicians should consistently seek to improve their knowledge and skills by pursuing continuing education and engaging in professional development opportunities.

They should stay up-to-date with advancements in pharmacy practice, technology, and regulations to provide the best possible care to patients.

4. **Collaboration and Respect:** Pharmacy technicians should work collaboratively with pharmacists, other healthcare professionals, and colleagues in a respectful and professional manner. They should foster a positive work environment to promote open communication, effective teamwork and mutual respect.

5. **Ethical Decision Making**: Technicians should approach ethical dilemmas with thoughtful consideration, applying ethical principles and professional judgment to make sound decisions. They should prioritize patient well-being and consult with pharmacists or other healthcare professionals when faced with ethical challenges.

6. **Confidentiality**: Pharmacy technicians must respect patient confidentiality and privacy rights. It is crucial for them to uphold strict confidentiality when dealing with patient information, prescription records, and any other confidential data.

7. **Professional Conduct**: Technicians should consistently demonstrate professionalism in their behavior and conduct. This includes adhering to dress codes, maintaining appropriate personal hygiene, and practicing proper communication skills with patients and colleagues.

8. **Quality Assurance and Safety**: Pharmacy technicians are responsible for ensuring the accuracy and quality of medications and pharmacy operations. They should follow established procedures for medication storage, handling, labeling, and disposal. They should also report any errors, adverse events, or safety concerns to the appropriate individuals or regulatory bodies.

9. **Advocacy**: Pharmacy technicians should advocate for the profession and the well-being of patients. They should support initiatives that promote access to affordable healthcare, patient safety, and the advancement of pharmacy practice.

Role of Pharmacy Technician in Record-Keeping and Documentation

Supporting pharmacists and ensuring the safe and efficient delivery of medications and healthcare services is a crucial responsibility of pharmacy technicians. Their responsibilities may vary depending on the practice setting, but here are some common roles and responsibilities of pharmacy technicians:

1. **Prescription Processing**: Pharmacy technicians assist in the processing of prescriptions by receiving written or electronic prescriptions, verifying patient information, and ensuring the prescription is complete and accurate. They may also perform data entry tasks to input prescription information into the pharmacy computer system.

2. **Medication Dispensing**: Pharmacy technicians are responsible for accurately dispensing medications. They retrieve the prescribed medication from the pharmacy inventory, count or measure the appropriate quantity, and package it according to pharmacy standards. They also label the medication containers with proper instructions and warnings.

3. **Inventory Management**: Pharmacy technicians play a vital role in managing the pharmacy inventory. They receive incoming medication and supply shipments, check them for accuracy, and ensure proper storage. They monitor inventory levels, rotate stock to maintain freshness and assist with placing orders to replenish supplies.

4. **Prescription Filling and Compounding**: Pharmacy technicians assist in the filling of prescriptions by retrieving the necessary medications, measuring or counting the correct amounts, and assembling them into patient-specific packages. In some settings, they may also assist pharmacists in compounding medications by following established formulas and procedures.

5. **Patient Interaction and Customer Service**: Pharmacy technicians often interact directly with patients. They answer phone calls, address inquiries, and provide information regarding prescription

availability, insurance coverage, and medication instructions. They may also assist with over-the-counter product recommendations and provide general healthcare guidance.

6. **Pharmacy Operations Support**: Pharmacy technicians support the overall operations of the pharmacy. They adhere to high standards of cleanliness and organization in their work areas, ensuring that all equipment is thoroughly sanitized and adequately stocked. They follow safety protocols for handling hazardous medications, dispose of expired or unused medications appropriately, and comply with regulatory guidelines.

7. **Technology Utilization**: Using pharmacy computer systems, pharmacy technicians are responsible for prescription processing, patient profile maintenance, and report generation. They ensure accurate prescription data entry, handle insurance claims, and contribute to administrative functions, including billing and record-keeping. They may also operate automated dispensing systems and assist with medication-related technology implementation.

Federal Requirements for Controlled Substance

In the United States, the Drug Enforcement Administration (DEA) enforces the Controlled Substances Act (CSA), a comprehensive federal law that governs the manufacturing, distribution, dispensing, and possession of controlled substances. DEA also oversees controlled substance regulations in the United States. Based on their potential for abuse and accepted medical purposes, substances are categorized into five schedules. Pharmacy technicians must have a thorough understanding of each schedule's requirements and restrictions, as they vary in terms of prescription regulations, storage, and record-keeping obligations.

CSA Classification

Controlled substances are categorized into five schedules under the CSA. The schedules range from Schedule I to Schedule V, with Schedule I drugs having the highest potential for abuse and no accepted medical use, and Schedule V drugs having accepted medical uses, and the lowest potential for abuse.

- Schedule I substances are characterized by a high potential for abuse and a lack of accepted medical uses.
- On the other hand, Schedules II to V substances have recognized medical applications but varying levels of abuse potential. It is essential for pharmacy technicians to be well-versed in the particular requirements associated with each schedule.
  - For instance, Schedule II substances, including opioids like oxycodone, are subject to stringent regulations such as no refill allowances and the necessity for a new prescription for each dispensing.

Schedule	Classification Criteria	Examples
C-I	Substances with high potential for abuse, no currently recognized medical use in the U.S., considered unsafe even when used under medical supervision	MDMA (Ecstasy), Heroin, LSD, Cannabis, Methaqualone, Peyote
C-II	Substances with high potential for abuse, which can lead to serious psychological or physical dependence. They have currently recognized medical uses, but with severe restrictions	Hydromorphone, Meperidine, Fentanyl, Opium, Codeine, Cocaine, Methadone, Amphetamine, Methamphetamine, Oxycodone, Methylphenidate, Morphine
C-III	Substances with lower abuse potential than substances in C-I or C-II. Abuse of these substances can lead to low or moderate physical dependence or elevated psychological dependence	Hydrocodone/Acetaminophen (Vicodin), Tylenol with Codeine, Benzphetamine, Phendimetrazine, Buprenorphine, Anabolic Steroids (Depo-Testosterone), Ketamine
C-IV	These substances are characterized by a lower abuse potential than class C-III substances	Alprazolam, Carisoprodol, Clonazepam, Clorazepate, Diazepam, Lorazepam, Midazolam, Temazepam, Triazolam
C-V	They have an even lower potential for abuse than the substances listed in C-IV. They are mainly preparations containing moderate amounts of certain narcotics	Robitussin AC, Ezogabine, Phenergan with Codeine

Controlled Substances Prescription Refills and Transfer

Federal regulations impose strict limitations on refilling prescriptions for controlled substances. Pharmacy technicians must be knowledgeable about these regulations to ensure compliance.

- Generally, Schedule II controlled substances cannot be refilled, while Schedule III to V controlled substances may have limited refills depending on state laws and prescriber discretion.
- The pharmacy technicians should understand and follow these regulations to prevent unauthorized refills or transfers.

Controlled Substances Records and Inventory

Accurate record-keeping and inventory management are critical for controlled substances. Pharmacy technicians are responsible for maintaining detailed records of controlled substance transactions, including dispensing, receiving, returning, and disposal.

- Examples of records include the Drug Enforcement Administration (DEA) Form 222 for ordering Schedule II substances and the DEA Form 106 for reporting theft or loss of controlled substances.
- Regular physical inventories are also necessary to reconcile the quantity of controlled substances on hand with recorded balances and identify any discrepancies.

Poison Prevention Packaging Act

The Poison Prevention Packaging Act, also known as the PPPA, requires child-resistant packaging for certain over-the-counter and prescription drugs to minimize the risk of accidental poisoning, particularly among children. Pharmacy technicians must understand the specific packaging and labeling requirements under the PPPA to ensure compliance and enhance medication safety.

Examples of child-resistant packaging include blister packs and safety caps that require simultaneous pushing and turning to open.

Restricted Drug Programs

Restricted drug programs are put in place to regulate the distribution and use of certain medications that have a higher risk of abuse, diversion, or adverse effects.

1. **Pseudoephedrine Regulations**: Over-the-counter cold and allergy medications frequently contain pseudoephedrine, which is a decongestant. Due to its potential use in the illicit production of methamphetamine, there are specific regulations governing its sale and distribution. These regulations aim to *prevent its misuse and diversion*.
   - Examples of acts and regulations related to pseudoephedrine include the Combat Methamphetamine Epidemic Act (CMEA) in the United States, which imposes restrictions on the sale and quantity limits of pseudoephedrine-containing products.
   - Pharmacies and retailers are required to maintain records and track sales of these products to comply with the regulations.

2. **Risk Evaluation and Mitigation Strategies (REMS):** REMS is a program implemented by the U.S. Food and Drug Administration (FDA) to *ensure the safe and appropriate use of certain medications that have known risks or serious adverse effects*. REMS programs are developed by drug manufacturers and approved by the FDA as a condition for drug approval.
   - These programs often involve additional requirements for healthcare providers, patients, and pharmacies to minimize the risks associated with the medication.
     - Examples of medications with REMS programs include opioids, certain antipsychotics, and medications used to treat acne.
   - Pharmacy technicians play a crucial role in REMS implementation by verifying and documenting compliance with the specific requirements of the program when dispensing these medications.

3. **Risk Minimization Action Plans (RiskMAPs)**: RiskMAPs are another type of restricted drug program that *focuses on specific safety concerns associated with a medication*. RiskMAPs are designed to manage known or potential risks by implementing additional measures beyond standard labeling and prescribing information.
   - Patients may be required to undergo counseling to ensure they understand the risks and safe use of the medication. Healthcare providers and pharmacies may be required to report certain adverse events or patient outcomes to the FDA.
   - Examples of medications that have implemented RiskMAPs include certain drugs used in the treatment of multiple sclerosis and isotretinoin, a medication used for severe acne.

FDA Recall Requirements: Recalls, Corrections, and Removals (Devices)

The U.S. Food and Drug Administration (FDA) has established guidelines and requirements for recalls, corrections, and removals of medical devices to protect public health and safety. When a medical device is found to be defective, poses a risk to patients, or violates FDA regulations, the manufacturer or distributor may initiate a recall. Here are key details regarding FDA recall requirements for medical devices:

1. **FDA Classification of Recalls**: Recalls are classified into three categories based on the level of risk associated with the device:
   - Class I: These recalls involve products that pose a significant risk of serious harm or death to the patient.
   - Class II: These recalls are related to products that carry the potential to cause temporary or reversible health problems or in rare instances, a remote possibility of serious harm
   - Class III: These recalls involve products that are unlikely to cause harm or have minimal risk to the patient, but are anyway in violation of law or FDA regulation
2. **Initiation of Recalls**: Recalls can be initiated by the manufacturer, distributor, or the FDA itself. Manufacturers are encouraged to voluntarily initiate recalls promptly when they become aware of a device defect or potential risk. The FDA may also request or order a recall, if required, to protect public health.
3. **Recall Strategy**: When initiating a recall, the manufacturer is required to develop a recall strategy that outlines the actions to be taken. This includes identifying the affected devices, notifying affected parties, and implementing appropriate corrective actions.
4. **Public Notification**: Manufacturers are responsible for notifying healthcare professionals, distributors, and other relevant parties about the recall. The FDA also publishes recall information on its website to ensure the public is aware of the issue and can take appropriate action.
5. **Correction or Removal:** Recalls may include either the implementation of corrective measures or the complete removal of the device from the market. Correction involves fixing the device or addressing the issue to prevent harm. Removal refers to physically removing the device from circulation, such as retrieving it from healthcare facilities or distributors.
6. **Effectiveness Checks**: Manufacturers must conduct effectiveness checks to ensure that the recall actions are successful and the defective devices are adequately removed or corrected. The FDA oversees these checks and may conduct audits for verification of compliance.
7. **Medical Device Reporting (MDR):** Manufacturers, importers, and device user facilities must report any incidents of serious injuries, deaths, or other adverse events linked to the device to the FDA via the Medical Device Reporting system. This reporting process enables the FDA to effectively monitor and evaluate the safety and performance of medical devices

Bonus Flashcards

Dear future Pharmacy Technician, we are grateful for the trust you are giving us by preparing for the PTCB Test with our Study Guide. That is why we are happy to share this exclusive and extremely valuable content with you!

Here the 2 main advantages of using our Flashcards:

- Help to store information quickly, facilitating long-term memorization through the "active recall" process, which involves recalling in your mind the same information over and over again. Which is exactly what happens when you train with Flashcards.

- Give you a clear idea of the questions you will be asked in the actual test. This way, your mind will already be used to the test you will face, giving you the right peace of mind to do it without the slightest anxiety. Which often makes the difference between passing or failing.

Are you ready to add this powerful tool to your exam-taking toolbox?

Scan the QR code and get your bonus Flashcards right away:

Dear Future Pharmacy Technician,

first of all, thank you again for purchasing our product.

Secondly, congratulations! If you are using our Guide, you are among those few who are willing to do whatever it takes to excel on the exam and are not satisfied with just trying.
We create our Study Guides in the same spirit. We want to offer our students only the best to help them get only the best through precise, accurate, and easy-to-use information.

That is why **your success is our success**, and if you think our Guide helped you achieve your goals, we would love it if you could take 60 seconds of your time to leave us a review on Amazon.

Thank you again for trusting us by choosing our Guide, and good luck with your new life as a Pharmacy Technician.

Sincerely,

H.S. Test Preparation Team

Scan the QR code to Leave a Review (it only takes you 60 seconds):

SECTION: 3 Patient Safety and Quality Assurance

Section 3 addresses the vital aspects of Patient Safety and Quality Assurance in pharmacy practice. It navigates through the intricacies of risk management, highlighting how pharmacy professionals identify and mitigate potential risks to ensure patient safety and adhere to regulatory standards. This section underscores the importance of implementing cutting-edge technology, fostering a culture of incident reporting, and embracing continuous improvement for the highest standards of pharmaceutical care.

Medication Safety and Quality Assurance

Risk Management

Risk management plays a crucial role in ensuring safe and effective pharmacy practices. It involves identifying, assessing, and minimizing potential risks associated with medication use, patient safety, regulatory compliance, and financial implications.

Risk Identification: The first step is identifying potential risks and hazards within the pharmacy setting.

- This includes conducting comprehensive assessments of various factors, such as medication dispensing processes, storage and inventory management, medication errors, adverse drug reactions, environmental factors, and technological systems.
- By analyzing these elements, pharmacists and pharmacy technicians can identify areas of vulnerability and prioritize risk mitigation efforts.

Risk Assessment: Once risks are identified, a thorough assessment is conducted to evaluate their potential impact and likelihood of occurrence.

- This involves considering the severity of potential consequences, the probability of risks materializing, and the existing control measures in place.
- Risk assessment tools, such as *failure mode and effects analysis* (FMEA) or *root cause analysis* (RCA), can be utilized to systematically analyze and prioritize risks based on their significance.

Risk Minimization and Prevention: After assessing risks, strategies are implemented to minimize their occurrence or impact. This includes developing and implementing policies and procedures that promote safe medication handling, storage, and administration.

- Pharmacy professionals ensure proper training and education for staff members regarding medication safety protocols, error prevention techniques, and adherence to regulatory guidelines.
- Implementing technology, such as computerized physician order entry (CPOE) systems and barcode scanning, can further reduce the risk of medication errors.
- Additionally, ongoing monitoring and audits help identify areas for improvement and ensure compliance with safety standards.

Incident Reporting and Analysis: An essential aspect of risk management is establishing a robust incident reporting system to capture and analyze adverse events, near misses, and medication errors.

- Pharmacy professionals encourage staff members to report incidents without fear of reprisal to foster a culture of transparency and continuous improvement. These reported incidents are thoroughly analyzed to identify contributing factors, root causes, and trends.
- Based on the analysis, appropriate corrective actions are implemented to prevent similar incidents from occurring in the future.

Regulatory Compliance: Pharmacy practices must adhere to various regulatory requirements and standards to minimize risks.

- Compliance with laws and regulations, such as those set by the Food and Drug Administration (FDA), Drug Enforcement Administration (DEA), and state pharmacy boards, is crucial to ensure patient safety and mitigate legal and financial risks.
- Regular audits, inspections, and adherence to proper documentation procedures help maintain compliance and reduce the likelihood of penalties or legal consequences.

Continuous Quality Improvement: Risk management in pharmacy practices is an ongoing process that involves continuous monitoring, evaluation, and improvement.

- By analyzing data, reviewing incident reports, and staying updated on industry best practices, pharmacy professionals can identify emerging risks and implement proactive measures.
- Collaboration with healthcare professionals, participation in quality improvement initiatives, and engaging in professional development activities contribute to the enhancement of risk management strategies within the pharmacy setting.

High Alert Medications

High alert medications (HAMs) are a distinct group of medications that possess an elevated risk of causing harm to patients, even when administered correctly as per medical guidelines. These medications exhibit specific characteristics that set them apart from others, including a narrow therapeutic index, which leaves minimal room for error during administration.

Some examples of high alert medications include:

- Chemotherapy drugs
- Insulin
- Opioids
- Anticoagulants (e.g., warfarin)
- Sedatives and hypnotics
- Potassium chloride injections
- Neuromuscular blockers

Incorrect administration of high alert medications has severe risks including severe bleeding, organ damage, respiratory depression, seizures, and even death.

The *Institute for Safe Medical Practices* (ISMP) has identified numerous categories of HAMs, each with its unique set of characteristics.

Point to remember: The Institute for Safe Medication Practices (ISMP) is a U.S.-based organization dedicated to preventing medication errors and advocating for safe medication practices. Their primary goal is to provide healthcare practitioners with a comprehensive understanding of medication errors from a systems perspective.

High Alert Medications List

This chart presents a comprehensive list of high-alert medications, encompassing various drug classes that carry a significant risk of causing severe harm if used incorrectly:

Medication Class	Examples
Adrenergic Agonists, IV	EPINEPHrine, Phenylephrine, Norepinephrine
Adrenergic Antagonists, IV	Propranolol, Metoprolol, Labetalol
Anesthetic Agents, General	Propofol, Ketamine
Antiarrhythmics, IV	Lidocaine, Amiodarone
Antithrombotic Agents - Anticoagulants - Direct Oral Anticoagulants and Factor Xa Inhibitors - Direct Thrombin Inhibitors - Glycoprotein IIb/IIIa Inhibitors - Thrombolytics	Warfarin, Low Molecular Weight Heparin, Unfractionated Heparin; Dabigatran, Rivaroxaban, Apixaban, Edoxaban, Betrixaban, Fondaparinux; Argatroban, Bivalirudin, Dabigatran; Eptifibatide
Cardioplegic Solutions	
Chemotherapeutic Agents	
Dextrose, Hypertonic, 20% or Greater	
Dialysis Solutions	
Epidural and Intrathecal Medications	
Inotropic Medications, IV	Digoxin, Milrinone
Insulin	
Liposomal Forms of Drugs	Amphotericin B
Moderate Sedation Agents, IV	Dexmedetomidine, Midazolam, LORazepam
Moderate and Minimal Sedation Agents, Oral	Chloral Hydrate, Midazolam, Ketamine
Opioids - IV - Oral - Transdermal	
Neuromuscular Blocking Agents	Succinylcholine, Rocuronium, Vecuronium
Parenteral Nutrition Preparations	
Sodium Chloride for Injection, Hypertonic	
Sterile Water for Injection	
Sulfonylurea Hypoglycemics, Oral	chlorproPAMIDE, Glimepiride, glyBURIDE, glipiZIDE, TOLBUTamide

Points to Remember:

- *Anticoagulants* are crucial in preventing blood clotting. However, their administration requires meticulous attention due to the risk of uncontrolled bleeding in case of injury or other medical interventions.
- *Insulin*, a hormone used to manage diabetes, demands careful dosage adjustment to prevent life-threatening hypoglycemia or hyperglycemia.
- *Narcotics/opioids*, powerful pain-relieving medications, carry a significant risk of respiratory depression and potential overdose.
- *Sedatives*, used to induce sedation and calmness, necessitate precise dosing to avoid adverse effects, such as respiratory suppression and potentially fatal outcomes.

Issues That Require Pharmacist Intervention

Certain roles performed by pharmacy technicians need monitoring and intervention by a pharmacist as these roles are beyond the scope of a pharmacy technician. Some of them are discussed below.

Drug Utilization Reviews (DURs): Pharmacy technicians play a vital role in assisting pharmacists with conducting Drug Utilization Reviews (DURs) at healthcare facilities. DURs involve systematic evaluations of medication prescribing and usage patterns. By analyzing electronic records, pharmacists and pharmacy technicians can assess the frequency of prescriptions, patient experiences, side effects, and the efficacy of various treatments. These reviews enable the gathering of valuable insights into medication utility and effectiveness.

Recommendations for OTC Therapy or Therapeutic Substitution: Pharmacists often provide recommendations to patients regarding over-the-counter (OTC) therapy or therapeutic substitution. Pharmacy technician supports pharmacists in this role.

- For example, a patient struggling to obtain insurance coverage for reflux medication may be informed about the availability of Prilosec as an OTC option.
- Additionally, pharmacy technicians under the observation of a pharmacist may discuss therapeutic substitution options with patients who receive frequent prescriptions for potentially addictive medications, such as Lorazepam, encouraging them to explore alternative therapies like working with a therapist to address underlying anxiety.

Preventing Medication Misuse: Pharmacy technicians have a significant role in preventing medication misuse, overuse, and addiction, particularly with opioids. They actively monitor patients' medication records to identify instances of obtaining the same medications from multiple pharmacies simultaneously. These concerns should be addressed with sensitivity, aiming to create a supportive environment that encourages patient collaboration and helps prevent medication misuse. Pharmacy technicians work closely with pharmacists to ensure appropriate interventions are made when potential misuse is identified.

Adverse Drug Event Reporting and Documentation

Reporting and documenting adverse drug events (ADEs) are essential for patient safety and quality assurance. Pharmacists and pharmacy technicians are encouraged to report any suspected ADEs to the appropriate regulatory agencies or medication error reporting programs. Depending on the severity of the

ADE, discontinuation of the medication may be necessary, and urgent medical attention may be required. Examples of ADEs include heart palpitations, shortness of breath, and extreme sleeplessness or anxiety. This should be documented in the patient's medical record, ensuring accurate and detailed information regarding the medication involved, the observed adverse reaction, and any actions taken. This documentation facilitates communication between healthcare providers and helps prevent similar incidents in the future.

Prescription Errors

Common Prescription Errors

Several factors can contribute to prescription errors. Some common types of prescription errors include:

- Illegible Handwriting: Poorly written prescriptions can lead to misinterpretation and medication errors.
- Incorrect Dosage or Frequency: Prescribers may inadvertently specify an incorrect dosage or frequency of administration, potentially resulting in under or overdosing.
- Drug Name Confusion: Similar-sounding drug names or look-alike packaging can lead to dispensing errors. Pharmacists must be vigilant and use verification systems to prevent these errors.
- Incomplete Information: Prescriptions may lack crucial information, such as patient allergies, relevant medical conditions, or necessary dosage adjustments.
- Wrong Drug Selection: Prescribers may select the wrong drug due to similarities in drug names or lack of familiarity with specific medications.

Understanding Medication Labels

Medication labels provide important information about the drug, including its name, strength, dosage form, directions for use, warnings, and storage requirements. Here's a breakdown of the key elements typically found on medication labels:

1. **Drug Name**: The label displays the brand name and/or generic name of the medication. Both names should be included for easy identification.
2. **Strength**: The strength of the medication indicates the amount of active ingredient(s) in each dosage unit. It helps ensure the correct dosage is administered to the patient.
3. **Dosage Form**: This describes the physical form of the medication, such as tablets, capsules, liquid, patches, or injections.
4. **Route of Administration**: It specifies the method by which the medication should be administered, such as oral (by mouth), topical (applied to the skin), intravenous (IV), or intramuscular (IM) injection.
5. **Quantity**: The label mentions the total quantity of medication contained in the package or container, usually in terms of dosage units (e.g., tablets, milliliters).
6. **Directions for Use**: This section provides instructions for proper administration of the medication. It includes the recommended dosage, frequency of administration, and any specific instructions related to timing or food intake.
7. **Patient-Specific Instructions**: If applicable, the label may include additional instructions tailored to the individual patient, such as "Shake well before use" or "Take with food."
8. **Warnings/Precautions**: Medication labels highlight important safety information and precautions associated with the drug. This may include allergy warnings, potential side effects, contraindications, and special precautions for certain populations (e.g., pregnant women, and elderly patients).
9. **Storage Requirements**: The label specifies the appropriate storage conditions for the medication, such as room temperature, refrigeration, protection from light, or avoidance of moisture.
10. **Expiration Date**: Every medication label must display the expiration date, indicating the date beyond which the drug should not be used. Pharmacists should ensure that patients are aware of this date and discard medications past their expiration.

11. **Pharmacy Information**: The label usually includes the name and contact details of the dispensing pharmacy, allowing patients to reach out with any questions or concerns.

Active Ingredients and Purpose

A pivotal aspect in comprehending medication labels lies in discerning the constituents of the product. While over-the-counter medications may contain a myriad of ingredients, the manufacturers simplify the process by prominently disclosing the active ingredient(s) at the forefront. These active ingredients constitute the specific compounds responsible for alleviating symptoms.

For example, a multi-symptom cold relief medication will have the following active ingredients:

1. Guaifenesin - Expectorant
2. Phenylephrine HCl - Decongestant
3. Diphenhydramine - Antihistamine

Within this formulation, the first active ingredient, Guaifenesin, belongs to the class of expectorants. Expectorants aid in thinning mucus, rendering it more facile to expectorate. The second active ingredient, Phenylephrine hydrochloride, falls under the category of decongestants.

Look Alike and Sound Alike Drugs

Despite sharing commonalities in names, certain drugs known as Look and sound alike drugs (LASA drugs) often have distinct mechanisms of action within the body, and mistaking one for another can lead to severe consequences.

- A characteristic feature of LASA drugs is their propensity to share resemblances in both brand and generic names.
  - Some instances involve brand names that bear striking similarities, such as Celebrex (a nonsteroidal anti-inflammatory drug) and Cerebyx (an anticonvulsant).
  - Alternatively, generic names can also contribute to confusion, as seen with hydroxyzine (an antihistamine) and hydralazine (an antihypertensive).
  - At times, even a brand name like Klonopin (an anticonvulsant) can be mistaken for a generic drug like clonidine (another antihypertensive).
- Furthermore, LASA drugs encompass formulations that share identical names but possess different characteristics, exemplified by Adderall and Adderall XR.

Insulin: A Unique LASA Category Insulin warrants a category of its own within the realm of LASA drugs. Brand names such as Humalog, Humulin, Novolog, and Novolin represent different insulin formulations, all intended to treat the same disease.

However, each formulation exhibits specific onset, peak, and duration characteristics. Some formulations even possess more specific names, such as Novolin N and Novolin R. Administering the incorrect formulation of insulin can have devastating, and in some cases, fatal consequences for the patient.

Oral Contraceptives: Common oral contraceptive pills, commonly referred to as birth control, include LoEstrin, LoEstrin FE, and Lo Loestrin. Ortho Cyclen, Ortho Tri Cyclen, and Ortho Tri Cyclen Lo represent another frequently miscommunicated group. Although these drugs share a common mechanism and purpose, they are not interchangeable and must not be mistaken for one another.

The Joint Commission, responsible for accrediting a majority of hospitals in the US and worldwide, mandates that each healthcare facility follow the list of LASA drugs for storage, dispensation, or administration purposes.

The Gold Standard In addition to the aforementioned policies, labeling practices, and storage protocols, the strategy of Read Back and Verify (RBAV or RB&V), also known as *Read Back and Confirm* (RBAC, RB&C), serves as the gold standard in medicine for mitigating errors associated with all medications, particularly LASA drugs.

- Whenever a verbal medication order is conveyed, the recipient should meticulously record it, read it back aloud, and verify or confirm that the transcribed order matches the original instruction provided by the prescriber.

Preventing Medication Errors

To mitigate the risks associated with HAMs, updated education ensures that the staff including the Pharmacist and Pharmacy Techiman have a comprehensive understanding of their medications, including potential risks and side effects.

Verifying medication packaging and administration equipment by two individuals enhances error detection. Additionally, reducing vial sizes, concentration ratios, and medication dosages in intravenous (IV) bags helps minimize the consequences of accidental overdose.

Adhering to the *Five Rights of Medication Administration* is a standard practice to prevent medication errors in all contexts, particularly when dealing with high alert medications. These principles include:

1. Right Patient: Checking the patient's identity by employing appropriate identification methods, such as their name, date of birth, or specific identifiers, before giving the medication.
2. Right Medicine: Ensuring the correct medication is administered to the patient, taking into account generic and brand names, as well as specific formulations.
3. Right Time: Right Time: Refers to administering the drug at the time set out in the prescription, while paying attention to elements like how often it should be taken and any specific timing guidelines.
4. Right Dosage: Calculating and administering the accurate dosage of the medication, following dosage guidelines and individual patient factors, such as weight or age.
5. Right Route: Ensures the medication is given using the appropriate administration method, which could be oral, intravenous, subcutaneous, or intramuscular, as specified in the prescription.

Enhancing Medication Safety

Deletion of Trailing Zeros and Leading Decimals

Ensuring accurate dosage and strength of medications is paramount. However, the presence of trailing zeros or decimals can introduce complexities and potential errors.

- For instance, consider a prescription for hydrocortisone lotion 1%. If the prescription is written as hydrocortisone lotion 1.0%, it may be misinterpreted as hydrocortisone 10%, leading to a tenfold increase in strength.
- Similarly, if the prescription is written as hydrocortisone lotion .5%, it may be mistakenly read as hydrocortisone 5%, resulting in incorrect dosing. Decimals should only be used when no viable alternatives are available.

Separation of Inventory

Thoughtful organization of medication inventory plays a significant role in preventing errors. Medications with similar packaging or names should be stored in separate locations to reduce the likelihood of confusion.

- For instance, placing glipizide and glyburide bins side by side increases the chances of grabbing the wrong medication, especially during moments of fatigue or haste.
- Additional organization tips, such as limiting inventory to prevent overcrowding, positioning medications at eye level with labels facing outward, and maintaining adequate lighting, contribute to enhanced medication safety.

Utilization of Tall Man Lettering

Certain medications share similar names and packaging, making them prone to confusion. To address this concern, the ISMP and FDA have developed a list of comparable drugs and introduced tall man lettering as a visual differentiating technique. Tall man lettering involves the use of bold, uppercase letters to emphasize the distinguishing portions of look-alike drug names.

- For example, using tall man lettering, acetaZOLAMIDE can be differentiated from acetoHEXAMIDE, thereby reducing the risk of medication mix-ups. This practice helps healthcare professionals recognize and select the correct medication, thus improving patient safety.

Commonly Used Drug Abbreviations, Medical Terminologies and SIG Codes

Note: *SIG codes* are standardized abbreviations used in prescription writing to provide instructions for the patient regarding medication usage.

Abbreviation	Meaning
a.c	Before meals
ad lib	Freely, as desired
APAP	Acetaminophen (paracetamol)
b.i.d.	Twice daily
c	With
comp	Compound
DAW	Dispense as Written
D/C	Discontinue
disp	Dispense
DS	Double strength
DX	Diagnosis
gtt	Drop(s)
h	Hour
h.s.	At bedtime

INR	International Normalized Ratio
IV	Intravenous
KCl	Potassium chloride
L	Liter
mcg	Microgram
MDI	Metered-dose inhaler
mg	Milligram
mL	Milliliter
NDC	National Drug Code
ng	Nanogram
NPO	Nothing by mouth
NSAID	Nonsteroidal Anti-Inflammatory Drug
o.d.	Once daily
p.o.	By mouth
OTC	Over-the-counter
p.c.	After meals
p.o.	By mouth
p.r.n.	As needed
q	Every
q.d.	Once daily
q.h.	Every hour
q.i.d.	Four times daily
q.s.	Sufficient quantity
q2h	Every 2 hours
q4h	Every 4 hours
q6h	Every 6 hours
q8h	Every 8 hours
SC	Subcutaneous
sig	Directions for using a prescription
SR	Sustained release
STAT	Immediately
tab	Tablet
tid	Three times daily
top	Topical
ung.	Ointment
XR	Extended release

Avoidance of Error-Prone Abbreviations

Abbreviations play a significant role in medical documentation, including medication instructions. However, their misuse or misinterpretation can lead to medication errors. To mitigate this risk, the FDA and ISMP have compiled a list of error-prone abbreviations commonly misinterpreted in healthcare settings.

- For instance, the abbreviation 'U' is often mistaken for a zero, potentially resulting in incorrect dosing. Instead, it is recommended to write out the word 'unit' to clarify the intended meaning.
- Similarly, abbreviations like 'QD' (daily) and 'QHS' (bedtime) can be mistaken for 'QID' (four times a day) and 'QHR' (every hour), respectively. To avoid confusion, it is best to write out the complete instructions using unambiguous terms.

Error-Prone Abbreviations List

Here's a list of Error-Prone Abbreviations shared by ISMP through the ISMP National Medication Errors Reporting Program (ISMP MERP):

Abbreviation	Intended Meaning	Misinterpretation	Best Practice
μg	Microgram	Mistaken as "mg"	Use "mcg"
AD, AS, AU	Right ear, left ear, each ear	Mistaken as OD, OS, OU (right eye, left eye, each eye)	Use "right ear," "left ear," or "each ear"
OD, OS, OU	Right eye, left eye, each eye	Mistaken as AD, AS, AU (right ear, left ear, each ear)	Use "right eye," "left eye," or "each eye"
BT	Bedtime	Mistaken as "BID" (twice daily)	Use "bedtime"
cc	Cubic centimeters	Mistaken as "u" (units)	Use "mL"
D/C	Discharge or discontinue	Premature discontinuation of medications if D/C (intended to mean "discharge") has been misinterpreted as "discontinued" when followed by a list of discharge medications	Use "discharge" and "discontinue"
IJ	Injection	Mistaken as "IV" or "intrajugular"	Use "injection"
IN	Intranasal	Mistaken as "IM" or "IV"	Use "intranasal" or "NAS"

HS	Half-strength,	Mistaken as bedtime, half-strength	Use "half-strength"
hs	At bedtime, hours of sleep	Mistaken as half-strength	Use "bedtime"
IU	International unit	Mistaken as IV (intravenous) or 10 (ten)	Use "unit(s)"
o.d., OD	Once daily	Mistaken as "right eye" (OD, oculus dexter), leading to oral liquid medications administered in the eye	Use "daily"
OJ	Orange juice	Mistaken as OD or OS (right or left eye), drugs meant to be diluted in orange juice may be given in the eye	Use "orange juice."
Per os	By mouth, orally	The "os" can be mistaken as "left eye" (OS, oculus sinister)	Use "PO," "by mouth," or "orally."
Q.D., QD, q.d., or qd	Every day	Mistaken as q.i.d., especially if the period after the "q" or the tail of the "q" is misunderstood as an "i"	Use "daily"
Qhs	Nightly at bedtime	Mistaken as "qhr" (every hour)	Use "nightly" or "at bedtime"
Qn	Nightly or at bedtime	Mistaken as "qh" (every hour)	Use "nightly" or "at bedtime"
Q.O.D., QOD, q.o.d., or qod	Every other day	Mistaken as "q.d." (daily) or "q.i.d. (four times daily) if the "o" is poorly written	Use "every other day"
q1d	Daily	Mistaken as q.i.d. (four times daily)	Use "daily"
q6PM, etc.	Every evening at 6 PM	Mistaken as every 6 hours	Use "daily at 6 PM" or "6 PM daily"
SC, SQ, sub q	Subcutaneous	SC mistaken as SL (sublingual); SQ mistaken as "5 every;" the "q" in "sub q" has been mistaken as "every"	Use "SUBQ" (all UPPERCASE letters, without spaces or periods between letters) or "subcutaneous"

ss or SS	Single strength, sliding scale (insulin), signs and symptoms, or ½ (apothecary)	Mistaken as "55"	Use single strength, sliding scale, signs and symptoms, or one-half or ½
SSRI, SSI	Sliding scale regular insulin, Sliding scale insulin	Mistaken as selective-serotonin reuptake inhibitor, Mistaken as Strong Solution of Iodine (Lugol's)	Use sliding scale (insulin)
TIW, tiw	3 times a week	Mistaken as "3 times a day" or "twice in a week"	Use "3 times weekly"
U, u	Unit(s)	Mistaken as the number 0 or 4, causing a 10-fold overdose or greater (e.g., 4U seen as "40" or 4u seen as "44"); mistaken as "cc" so dose given in volume instead of units (e.g., 4u seen as 4cc)	Use "unit(s)"
UD	As directed ("ut dictum")	Mistaken as unit dose (e.g., diltiazem 125 mg IV infusion "UD" misinterpreted as meaning to give the entire infusion as a unit [bolus] dose)	Use "as directed"

Source: Adapted from Institute for Safe Medication Practices (ISMP). ISMP List of Error-Prone Abbreviations, Symbols, and Dose Designations. ISMP; 2021.

Hygiene and Cleaning Standards

Maintaining hygiene and cleaning standards is crucial in healthcare settings to prevent the spread of infections. In this chapter, we will discuss hygiene practices related to equipment, personal protective equipment (PPE), handwashing, and more.

Equipment Hygiene

Proper cleaning and maintenance of equipment are essential to prevent cross-contamination and maintain a safe healthcare environment. Pharmacists and pharmacy technicians should be aware of the following key points related to equipment hygiene:

1. **Regular Cleaning**: Equipment should be cleaned regularly according to the manufacturer's guidelines and facility protocols. Regular cleaning helps remove dirt, debris, and potential pathogens from surfaces.
2. **Disinfection**: High-touch surfaces and reusable equipment should undergo appropriate disinfection using approved disinfectants. This process helps eliminate or reduce the number of microorganisms present, minimizing the risk of transmission.
3. **Sterilization**: Certain equipment, such as surgical instruments, must undergo sterilization to ensure complete elimination of microbial contamination. Sterilization processes, such as autoclaving, utilize high heat or chemicals to achieve this level of decontamination.

Personal Protective Equipment (PPE)

Proper use of PPE is crucial for protecting healthcare providers from exposure to infectious agents. Pharmacists and pharmacy technicians should be familiar with the following aspects of PPE:

1. **Selection and Use**: Appropriate PPE should be used based on the level of anticipated exposure to infectious agents. This may include gloves, masks, gowns, goggles, or face shields. The selection should align with established guidelines and protocols.
2. **Donning and Doffing**: Following the correct procedures for donning (putting on) and doffing (taking off) PPE to prevent self-contamination is important. This includes proper hand hygiene before and after donning and doffing, as well as the use of designated areas for PPE changes.
3. **Storage and Disposal**: Used PPE should be discarded in designated containers following appropriate waste management guidelines. Ensuring proper storage and disposal helps prevent the spread of pathogens and maintains a clean healthcare environment.

Handwashing

Effective hand hygiene is one of the most crucial practices in preventing the transmission of infections. Pharmacists and pharmacy technicians should understand the following key points regarding handwashing:

1. **Use of Soap and Water**: Washing hands with soap and water for at least 20 seconds is the preferred method for routine hand hygiene. Proper handwashing technique involves lathering all surfaces of the hands, including fingers, nails, and wrists, followed by thorough rinsing and drying.
2. **Alcohol-Based Hand Sanitizers**: In situations where soap and water are not accessible, it's recommended to use hand sanitizers that contain a minimum of 60% alcohol. These sanitizers are effective in reducing microbial contamination and should be applied to dry hands following proper technique.

3. Key times for handwashing:
- Before and after patient interactions: This includes activities such as counseling, administering vaccinations, or providing medication advice. It is important to cleanse hands before any direct contact with patients to prevent the transmission of pathogens.
- Before preparing or handling medications: Prior to handling medications, pharmacists should ensure their hands are clean to prevent cross-contamination.
- After removing gloves: If gloves are worn during procedures, it is essential to remove them properly and wash hands afterward.

SECTION 4: Order Entry and Processing

Section 4 offers a deep dive into the world of Order Entry and Processing, unraveling the complexities of pharmacology calculations and dosage determinations. It comprehensively covers essential measurements, conversions, and methodologies necessary for accurate medication administration, including oral and injectable dosages, BMI assessments, and alligations. This section also addresses the meticulous process of prescription interpretation, inventory management, and the nuances of pharmacy billing, underscoring the importance of accuracy and regulatory compliance in pharmacy practice. It serves as a detailed guide to mastering the critical skills required for efficient and safe pharmacy operations.

Pharmacology Calculations

The table below shows commonly used measurement quantities and conversions for pharmacological calculations:

Measurement	Conversion
1 ounce	28.3 grams
1 fluid ounce	29.57 mL (or 30 mL rounded-up)
1 teaspoon	5 mL
1 tablespoon	15 mL
Convert Celsius to Fahrenheit	Multiply by 1.8 and add 32
Convert Fahrenheit to Celsius	Deduct 32, multiply by 5, then divide by 9
BMI	kg/m^2
BSA	$\sqrt{(\text{height (cm)} \times \text{weight (kg)}/ 3600)}$
Kg to lbs.	1 kilogram = 2.2 pounds
1 US liquid quart	0.95 liters
1 grain	65 milligrams

Dosage Calculations and Proportions

Dosage calculations involve calculating the appropriate dosage for a patient based on their weight, age, or condition using proportions.

Proportions play a vital role in dosage calculations when determining the appropriate dosage for a patient based on various factors such as weight, age, or condition. Proportions provide a framework for comparing different quantities and finding the correct ratio between them. By using proportions, pharmacy technicians can accurately calculate the dosage of medication to be administered.

For example, when calculating oral medication dosage, a proportion can be set up to determine the number of tablets needed based on the prescribed dosage and the strength of each tablet. So, if a patient requires a medication dosage of 50 mg, and each tablet contains 25 mg, the pharmacy technician would need to provide two tablets. Some examples of the use of proportions to calculate oral and injectable dosage are explained below.

Calculating Oral Medication Dosage: This involves calculating the right dosage of medication based on the age, weight, and other characteristics of the patient. It may involve converting between different units of measurement (e.g., milligrams to grams) and ensuring accurate administration of the prescribed dosage.

- For example, suppose a patient is prescribed 0.1 mg/kg of medicine and weighs 60 kilos. The drug is offered as tablets, each of which contains 5 milligrams of the active ingredient. The required dosage for the patient would be 60 kg × 0.1 mg/kg = 6 mg.
    - To convert this to tablets, divide the required dosage by the strength of each tablet: 6 mg / 5 mg per tablet = 1.2 tablets.

Calculating Injectable Medication Dosage: Pharmacy technicians may need to calculate the appropriate dose of medication for injectable formulations. This often involves dilution calculations, where a concentrated solution is diluted with a specific volume of diluent to achieve the desired strength.

- For example, a physician orders an intravenous medication at a concentration of 50 mg/mL. The desired dosage for the patient is 25 mg. The pharmacy technician has a vial containing 10 mL of the concentrated solution. To determine the volume of the concentrated solution required, divide the desired dosage by the concentration: 25 mg / 50 mg/mL = 0.5 mL. Since the technician has a 10 mL vial, there is enough medication available.

Concentration Calculations: Concentration calculations are used to determine the strength or potency of a medication in a given solution. This is important for preparing medications with specific concentrations or diluting medications to achieve the desired strength.

- For example, if a medication vial contains 100 mg of the active ingredient in 10 mL of solution, the concentration would be 10 mg/mL.

Dilution Calculations: Dilution calculations are necessary when a medication needs to be diluted to a specific concentration before administration. Pharmacy technicians must accurately calculate the volume of the stock solution and the diluent required to achieve the desired concentration.

- For example, if a medication needs to be diluted to a concentration of 1:10, and the stock solution is 1 mL, the pharmacy technician would need to add 9 mL of diluent to achieve the desired concentration.

Formulation Calculations: Formulation calculations involve compounding medications by combining different ingredients and strengths.

- For example, if a prescription requires a cream with 2% hydrocortisone, and the technician has a 30 g base, they would need to add 0.6 g (2% of 30 g) of hydrocortisone to prepare the formulation.

Alligations

Alligation is a mathematical method that enables the calculation of the ideal proportion of two solutions with differing concentrations necessary to create a final solution of a desired concentration. This method proves especially advantageous when combining solutions of varying strengths to achieve a specific concentration.

To successfully solve an alligation problem, the following steps should be followed:

Step 1: Begin by drawing a line and marking the concentrations of the two solutions on this line.

Step 2: Position the desired concentration of the final solution in the center of the line.

Step 3: Determine the numerical distance between the desired concentration and each of the solution concentrations.

Step 4: Calculate the ratio of these distances.

Step 5: The ratio obtained in Step 4 denotes the relative quantities of each solution that ought to be blended together.

Body Mass Index (BMI) Calculations

Body Mass Index (BMI) is a simple yet important metric used in healthcare to evaluate an individual's body fat by considering their weight in proportion to their height. It serves as a quick screening method for identifying possible health problems related to weight. BMI offers a basic approximation of a person's weight category, be it underweight, normal, overweight, or obese, and this categorization can be indicative of their general health condition. While it is not a direct measure of body fat percentage and does not account for muscle mass, BMI is widely used because of its simplicity and has been shown to correlate with more complex health indicators. Understanding BMI and its implications is crucial for both healthcare professionals and patients, as it can inform decisions related to nutrition, exercise, and overall health management.

Knowing how to interpret BMI scores helps clinicians assess whether a person falls into the underweight, ideal weight, overweight, or obese category. BMI is calculated in kg/m^2.

- Under 18.5: Underweight
- 18.5 to 24.9: Ideal body weight
- 25 to 29.9: Overweight
- 30 and above: Obese

Example: What will be the BMI of a patient weighing 150 pounds with a height of 5.7 feet?

First, convert pounds to kilograms. Remember that 1 pound is approximately 0.45 kilograms.

150 pounds × 0.45 kg/pound = 67.5 kg

Next, convert the height from feet to meters. Since 1-foot equals 0.3048 meters:

5.7 feet × 0.3048 meters/foot = 1.73736 meters

Square the height:

1.73736 meters × 1.73736 meters = 3.01588 m^2

Finally, calculate the BMI:

BMI = 67.5 kg / 3.01588 m^2 = 22.4 kg/m^2.

This result indicates that the patient falls within the ideal weight range.

Storage and Disposal

Essential Equipment and Supplies Required for Drug Administration:

1. Package Size: Different medications come in various package sizes, such as bottles, vials, blister packs, or pre-filled syringes. Pharmacy technicians should ensure they have the appropriate package size based on the prescribed medication and dosage.
2. Unit Dose Packaging: Unit dose packaging provides individually sealed doses of medications, which are ready for administration. This packaging helps prevent medication errors and promotes convenience in healthcare settings.
3. Diabetic Supplies: For patients with diabetes, pharmacy technicians may need to provide diabetic supplies, including blood glucose monitors, lancets, test strips, insulin pens, insulin cartridges, and insulin vials. These supplies are essential for monitoring blood sugar levels and administering insulin.
4. Inhaler Spacers: Inhaler spacers or holding chambers are devices used with inhalers to improve the delivery of medication to the lungs. These spacers help patients coordinate their inhalation and ensure efficient drug delivery.
5. Oral Syringes: Oral syringes with clear markings are used to measure and administer liquid medications, particularly for patients who have difficulty swallowing or require precise dosing. These syringes come in different sizes to accommodate various medication volumes.
6. Injectable Syringes: Injectable syringes are required for the administration of medications via intramuscular (IM), subcutaneous (SC), or intravenous (IV) routes. They come in different sizes and have various markings to ensure accurate dosing and safe administration.
7. Needles: Pharmacy technicians should have a variety of needles available, including different lengths and gauges, depending on the specific medication and route of administration. Needle disposal must be done correctly after each use.
8. Safety Devices: Safety devices, such as retractable syringes and needlestick prevention devices, should be used to minimize the risk of accidental needlestick injuries and enhance workplace safety.
9. Alcohol Swabs: Alcohol swabs or wipes are used to clean the injection site before administering medications. They help reduce the risk of infection and ensure proper hygiene during drug administration.
10. Sharps Containers: Sharps containers are essential for the secure disposal of used needles, syringes, and other sharp instruments. They should be puncture-resistant and clearly labeled to prevent accidental injuries.

Regulating Temperature

Thermometers: Are utilized in various areas of the pharmacy, including storage shelves, refrigerators, freezers, and warming cabinets. Medications typically fall into different temperature categories based on their specific storage requirements.

Most medications are stored at room temperature, which ranges from 20 to 25 degrees Celsius. Controlled substances, excipients (inactive substances mixed with medications), and active pharmaceutical ingredients (API) are among the medications stored at room temperature.

Certain medications necessitate cooler storage, maintained at temperatures between 8 and 15 degrees Celsius, to prevent degradation. Cold storage, ranging from 2 to 8 degrees Celsius, is employed for highly sensitive medications, vitamins, and chemicals, as it inhibits bacterial growth and chemical reactions.

Freezer storage, ranging from -25 to -10 degrees Celsius, is employed for specific vaccines until they are ready for use.

Warmers: Also known as warming cabinets, are rarely utilized in pharmacy settings. They are designed to maintain injectable fluids and antibiotics at a consistent temperature between 35 and 50 degrees Celsius. This process ensures optimal substance preservation, minimizing the risk of degradation, and is performed immediately prior to administration.

- Tablets and capsules are stored in cool, dark, and dry places to shield them from light exposure.
- Emulsions, which contain multiple liquids, are placed in airtight containers, protected from light, high heat, and freezing temperatures.
- Suspensions are kept cool but not refrigerated, and shielded from light, heat, and sunlight in cool, dry locations.
- Ointments and pastes are stored in tightly closed containers in cool and dark areas.
- Syrups are stored in bottles with stoppers in cool, dark places protected from light. Oral drops require storage in cool, dry, and dark areas to prevent light exposure.
- Injections necessitate storage at temperatures below 30 degrees Celsius, shielded from light.

Disposal of Medical Materials

Proper management of disposal procedures for medical materials is essential for maintaining safety and compliance in a pharmacy setting. This knowledge is particularly crucial when faced with situations such as expired, returned, or recalled drugs.

Recalled Medications

Occasionally, medications are recalled due to various reasons, such as potential harm, packaging or labeling issues, or the presence of unintended substances. Pharmacies typically receive recall notifications from the drug manufacturer/wholesaler, the *Food & Drug Administration (FDA),* or the compounding pharmacy. Once informed of a recall, pharmacies must promptly notify their staff, prescribers, and affected patients in accordance with legal requirements.

To effectively manage a drug recall, proper documentation is crucial. The Joint Commission, a renowned healthcare facility accreditation organization, mandates specific information that must be recorded by pharmacies in the event of a drug recall. This includes:

- An official written policy outlining the pharmacy's procedures for handling drug and medical supply recalls.
- Date of notification regarding the recall.
- Date when the pharmacy initiated the necessary actions for the recalled drug.
- Number of affected drugs in stock.
- Number of patients impacted by the recall.
- Detailed description of the actions taken by the pharmacy regarding the recalled drug.

Disposal of Expired, Returned and Recalled Drugs

The appropriate disposal methods for expired, returned and recalled drugs depend on the specific type of material being discarded.

1. Red receptacle: Sharps, including needles and syringes, and any materials that may contain blood or bodily fluids (e.g., IV catheters, blood sample vials) should be disposed of in these containers. Red receptacles are constructed with thick plastic to prevent needle punctures.
2. Blue receptacle: Non-hazardous and non-controlled drugs such as aspirin or antibiotic ointments should be placed in blue receptacles.
3. Yellow receptacle: Materials containing minimal amounts of chemotherapy drugs should be deposited in yellow receptacles.
4. Black receptacle: Hazardous and controlled medications, including substances like epinephrine and chemotherapy drugs, should be placed in black receptacles.

Additionally, intravenous (IV) solutions that do not contain medications can be safely poured down the drain.

Drug Order Entry and Processing

Prescription Interpretation and Entry

During the medication order entry and fill process, it is essential to thoroughly review and interpret the prescription to ensure its completeness and accuracy. This crucial task can be undertaken by either the pharmacist or the pharmacy technician, but it is vital for a pharmacist to perform a final validation before dispensing the prescription to the patient. The following elements are carefully assessed:

1. Doctor's name, office address, phone number, and signature: These details help establish the legitimacy and accountability of the prescribing healthcare professional.
2. National Provider Identifier (NPI): This unique identifier ensures proper identification of the healthcare provider and facilitates accurate record-keeping.
3. Drug Enforcement Administration (DEA) number: This number is required for prescriptions involving controlled substances, helping to prevent illicit use and ensuring appropriate oversight.
4. Drug information: This includes the name of the medication, its strength, dosage form, route of administration, frequency, prescribed amount, number of refills, and an indication of whether a generic alternative is available.
5. Patient information: This includes the name and address of the patient, along with the date the prescription was ordered.

In a hospital setting, if the order entry process occurs within the hospital, additional information such as the doctor's name, DEA number, hospital identification number, patient identification number, patient's room number, and drug information must be included. The orders may be categorized as "stat" (requiring immediate attention), "as soon as possible" (ASAP), or "as needed" (PRN).

Once the prescription has been carefully reviewed and interpreted, it can be accurately entered into the computer system using prompts provided by the software. Metric units, such as grams and meters, are commonly used for data entry.

Prescription Filling and Drug Entry Process

The accurate filling of prescriptions is a crucial step in the pharmacy workflow. In outpatient settings, where automated dispensers may not be available, pharmacy technicians must follow a meticulous process to ensure precision and attention to detail. The following steps outline the prescription filling process:

1. Verify the completeness and accuracy of the prescription as entered into the computer system.
2. Match the medication label from the stock supply with the prescription order using the assigned National Drug Code (NDC) number issued by the FDA. Additionally, scan the Universal Product Code (UPC) barcode to confirm the correct drug.
3. Check the expiration dates of medications and store them appropriately in cool, dry areas unless specific storage requirements are indicated.
4. Accurately measure or count the medications, often in multiples of five, and double-check the count for precision.
5. Follow designated handling procedures for certain medications. For example, clean the counting tray with alcohol after handling penicillin or sulfa products, and use gloves and alcohol when dealing with oral chemotherapy drugs or hazardous medications.

6. Place the medications in suitable containers with child-resistant caps unless alternative specifications are provided. Different container types, such as bottles, vials, wide-mouth bottles, droppers, ointment jars or packages, boxes, tubes, and applicator bottles, are used based on specific requirements. These containers may serve purposes such as tamper-evidence, light resistance, single or multi-dose/unit dispensing, or prevention of contamination.

Following these steps ensures the accurate and safe dispensing of medications to patients.

The National Drug Code (NDC) is a unique identification number assigned to each medication by the Food and Drug Administration (FDA). It consists of three segments:

1. The labeler code
2. The product code
3. The package code

The labeler code identifies the manufacturer, repackager, or distributor of the medication. The product code identifies the specific drug formulation, strength, and dosage form. The package code indicates the package size and type.

Pharmacy technicians use **NDC** numbers to accurately match the medication label from the stock supply with the prescription order. By scanning the Universal Product Code (UPC) barcode associated with the NDC number, verify that the correct drug is being dispensed. The **UPC** barcode is a standardized barcode system used for product identification in various industries, including healthcare.

Inventory Management

Hospital pharmacies often employ a formulary, which is a curated list of approved medications. This practice eliminates the need to stock multiple medications within the same therapeutic class, thereby reducing costs.

- The inventory process in hospital pharmacies entails a comprehensive review of medication manufacturers and distributors.
- This evaluation ensures the pharmacy's focus on factors such as safety, value, negotiation of prices, partnerships with other organizations to decrease costs, and utilization of programs like the *340B drug program*. The 340B drug program, overseen by the federal government, provides reduced pricing for specific medications.

General Inventory Requirements

Irrespective of the pharmacy setting, certain inventory management practices remain universally important. These include:

1. Adhering to Drug Enforcement Administration (DEA) standards for controlled substances.
2. Analyzing data from invoices and medication usage to inform decision-making.
3. Regularly reviewing the formulary, medication costs, and available choices.
4. Properly stocking and storing medications in accordance with manufacturer instructions.
5. Implementing a scanning barcode system for accurate medication receipt and dispensing.
6. Employing a rotation system that prioritizes medications with closer expiration dates.
7. Monitoring storage temperatures to ensure medication integrity.
8. Establishing par levels to track medication usage effectively.
9. Addressing any discrepancies in inventory counts and scrutinizing access to medications.

Advantages of a computerized inventory system:

- Utilizing barcode technology. It enables precise tracking of medication receipt, dispensing, recalls, and waste.
- Detailed records encompassing medication names, strengths, dosages, container sizes, National Drug Codes (NDC), shipment dates, transaction history, and involved parties facilitate efficient management.
- Computerized systems can automatically generate reorders when predefined inventory levels are reached.

Medication shortages can significantly impact pharmacy inventory. In such cases, alternative medications may need to be utilized, necessitating adjustments in medication usage patterns. Temporary increases in inventory levels for substitute medications may be required until the shortage is resolved.

Proper disposal of medications is crucial and must comply with federal regulations. Disposal becomes necessary when medications are expired, recalled, or damaged.

- Disposing of opened medications that are contaminated or expired down drains can lead to environmental contamination. Likewise, discarding such medications in regular waste can pose risks if they end up in the wrong hands.
- Engaging the services of a waste management company ensures proper and safe disposal. Comprehensive documentation is essential for waste removal processes to provide accurate data regarding disposed medications.
- Unopened medications and certain expired medications can be returned to the manufacturer through a process known as reverse distribution. In some cases, pharmacies may receive a credit for such returns.

Ordering Process

1. Determining Stock Needs: Pharmacy technicians play a crucial role in assessing stock requirements by analyzing medication usage patterns, reviewing prescription volume, and considering anticipated demand. Collaborating with pharmacists and other healthcare professionals ensures accurate forecasting of medication needs. Factors such as seasonal variations, medication shortages, and patient demographics are considered to optimize inventory levels.
2. Vendor Selection: Pharmacy technicians assist in selecting reliable vendors and suppliers for medication procurement. They evaluate factors like pricing, product quality, delivery schedules, and customer support. Establishing strong vendor relationships streamlines the ordering process and ensures efficient supply chain management.
3. Placing Orders: Once stock needs are determined, pharmacy technicians assist in initiating the ordering process. They generate purchase orders, verifying product information, quantities, and pricing. Accurate communication of orders to vendors, including delivery timelines and special requirements, is ensured. Pharmacy technicians utilize electronic systems such as computerized order entry systems or electronic data interchange (EDI) for efficient and error-free order processing.
4. Receiving and Verifying Orders: Upon delivery, pharmacy technicians help in inspecting and verifying the accuracy and condition of received medications. They compare the delivered items to the purchase order, checking for discrepancies, damaged packaging, or expired products. Any issues or concerns are promptly communicated to the vendor for resolution.
5. Stock Replenishment and Documentation: After verifying the received order, pharmacy technicians update inventory records and stock shelves accordingly. They ensure proper storage of medications,

adhering to manufacturer guidelines for temperature control and environmental conditions. Accurate documentation of received stock, including lot numbers and expiration dates, is vital for inventory control and regulatory compliance.

Pharmacy Billing

Pharmacy billing is a crucial aspect of healthcare administration, and pharmacy technicians play a vital role in this process.

1. Insurance Coverage Verification: Pharmacy technicians are often responsible for verifying patients' insurance coverage before processing prescriptions. This involves confirming the patient's insurance information, such as the insurance provider, policy number, and coverage dates. Verifying insurance coverage helps ensure that prescriptions are appropriately billed to the correct insurance company.
2. Prescription Claim Processing: Once the insurance coverage is verified, pharmacy technicians may be asked to input relevant information, including medication details, dosage instructions, and patient information, into the pharmacy's billing system. The system then generates a claim that is sent to the insurance company for reimbursement.
3. Understanding Insurance Plans: Pharmacy technicians need to have a solid understanding of different insurance plans and their specific billing requirements. This includes knowledge of Medicare, Medicaid, private insurance companies, and other government-funded programs. Each insurance plan may have unique billing codes, formulary restrictions, and reimbursement policies that must be followed.
4. Billing and Reimbursement Codes: Pharmacy technicians use specific billing codes, such as National Drug Codes (NDCs), to accurately identify and bill for prescribed medications.
   - These codes ensure that the insurance company recognizes the medication being dispensed and properly reimburses the pharmacy for the cost. Pharmacy technicians must ensure the correct codes are used to prevent claim rejections or delays in reimbursement.
5. Coordinating Benefits: In cases where patients have multiple insurance plans, pharmacy technicians play a crucial role in coordinating benefits. They determine the primary and secondary insurance plans to ensure that claims are submitted in the correct order. Coordinating benefits helps prevent overpayment or duplicate payments for the same prescription.
6. Resolving Insurance Claim Issues: Occasionally, insurance claims may be rejected or encounter other issues. Pharmacy technicians assist pharmacists in resolving these issues by communicating with insurance companies, healthcare providers, and patients. They may need to gather additional information, clarify billing details, or appeal claim denials to ensure proper reimbursement.
7. Adhering to Regulatory Compliance: Pharmacy technicians must adhere to regulatory guidelines and privacy laws, such as the Health Insurance Portability and Accountability Act (HIPAA). They handle sensitive patient information with confidentiality and ensure that all billing practices comply with legal requirements and industry standards.

Medicare and Medicaid

As a pharmacy technician, it's crucial to have a clear understanding of Medicare and Medicaid, two important forms of insurance reimbursement provided by the Centers for Medicare and Medicaid (CMS).

Medicare

Medicare is a federal insurance program designed for specific patient groups, including:

- Individuals aged 65 and older

- Individuals under 65 but with disabilities

Medicare coverage is not income-dependent, meaning it is available to eligible individuals regardless of their income level. It consists of four parts:

- Part A: Covers hospital inpatient stays, care in hospice, and stays in skilled nursing facilities.
- Part B: Covers outpatient hospital visits, doctor visits, and durable medical equipment, such as blood glucose monitors, wheelchairs, and walking sticks.
- Part C: Known as the Medicare Advantage Plan, it allows private companies to offer Medicare coverage that includes Part A and Part B services.
- Part D: Provides prescription drug coverage.

Medicaid

Medicaid is a government-funded insurance program primarily intended for individuals with low incomes. It operates at the state level, and eligibility criteria and coverage may vary. Some individuals may qualify for both Medicare and Medicaid, which is referred to as dual eligibility.

The Affordable Care Act (ACA)

The Affordable Care Act (ACA) made health insurance more affordable and accessible for more people. It ensures that insurance companies must accept everyone, even those with pre-existing conditions. Here are some key points about the ACA:

Cost Sharing:

- The ACA created an insurance marketplace where people can find affordable health insurance options.
- Insurance policies in the marketplace are divided into four categories: Bronze, Silver, Gold, and Platinum.
  - Bronze: The insurance company covers 60 percent of medical costs.
  - Silver: The insurance company covers 70 percent of medical costs.
  - Gold: The insurance company covers 80 percent of medical costs.
  - Platinum: The insurance company covers 90 percent of medical costs.
- Each category has a different cost-sharing arrangement, with the insurance company covering a percentage of medical costs.
- Co-payments may be required for medical visits, and additional services during the visit may have their own costs.

Deductibles and Limits:

- Insurance policies allow individuals to choose their deductible amount, which is the amount they pay before insurance coverage starts.
- Higher deductibles generally mean lower monthly premiums.
- The ACA set limits on how much individuals have to pay for covered medical services.
- Once the limit is reached, the insurance company covers 100% of additional covered services for the rest of the year.

Covered Services:

- All insurance policies, whether from the marketplace or elsewhere, must cover specific medical services.

- The range of these services includes ambulance transport, emergency treatment, hospitalization, care for mothers and newborns, mental and behavioral health support, prescriptions, rehabilitation therapy, laboratory testing, preventive health measures, and healthcare for children.
- Preventive services, such as vaccinations and screenings, are fully covered, with no need for any co-payment.

Pharmacy Reimbursement

Pharmacy Networks: When it comes to pharmacy services, various network options are available for individuals to consider:

1. Pharmacy Provider Network: This involves a contract that brings together multiple providers within a network.
2. Community Pharmacy Network: In this network, specific pharmacies or any community pharmacy, whether independent or part of a chain, are selected.
3. In-House Network: This network is typically associated with HMOs and exclusively serves the members of the HMO.
4. Mail-Order Pharmacy: Managed care organizations operate mail-order pharmacies, allowing prescriptions to be filled and delivered through the mail.
5. Physician Dispensing Network: In some cases, physicians themselves may dispense medications to their patients.

Pharmacy Reimbursement from Third Party Organizations

Pharmacy reimbursement involves the cost of ingredients and a dispensing fee. The Average Wholesale Price (AWP) reflects the average charge by wholesalers, while the Actual Acquisition Cost (AAC) represents the amount pharmacies pay for medications. Maximum Allowable Cost (MAC) is a reimbursement formula used specifically for generic medications.

Considerations for Medication Costs and Plan Limitations:

Medication costs can vary depending on the reimbursement options available. It is important to be aware of a pharmacy's formulary, which is the list of approved medications covered by each third-party organization, in order to manage prescription costs effectively. Prior authorization may be required, where the physician must obtain approval from the third-party organization for each prescription. Rejected claims can occur due to missing or invalid information on the prescription claim. Additionally, plan limitations are put in place to regulate the amount of medication dispensed at one time and the costs associated with it.

Test 1: QUESTIONS

Our practice tests are designed to exactly mimic the real PTCB exam. Keep in mind, the actual exam has a time limit of 1 hour and 50 minutes. So time yourself to gain real-test experience and confidence, ensuring you are fully prepared for success.

1. **Inderal is the brand name of which of the following medications?**
   a) Propranolol
   b) Carvedilol
   c) Metoprolol
   d) Atenolol

2. **Which federal statute bestows the Food and Drug Administration (FDA) with the power to supervise the safety, effectiveness, and labeling of pharmaceuticals?**
   a) Health Insurance Portability and Accountability Act (HIPAA)
   b) Food, Drug, and Cosmetic Act (FD&C Act)
   c) Drug Enforcement Administration (DEA) Regulations
   d) The Drug Quality and Security Act (DQSA)

3. **Which of the following is NOT a step involved in risk management for pharmacy practices?**
   a) Risk identification
   b) Incident reporting and analysis
   c) Prescription dispensing techniques
   d) Risk minimization and prevention

4. **What role do proportions play in dosage calculations?**
   a) Proportions are used to determine the rate of adverse reactions
   b) Proportions provide a framework for comparing different quantities and finding the correct ratio between them
   c) Proportions are used to calculate the profit margin on medications
   d) Proportions are irrelevant in dosage calculations

5. **A prescription is written for Zoloft 50 mg QD. What medication and dosing schedule are being ordered?**
   a) Paroxetine 50 mg once daily
   b) Sertraline 50 mg once daily
   c) Citalopram 50 mg once daily
   d) Escitalopram 50 mg once daily

6. **How should the patient take a sublingual tablet?**
   a) Chew the tablet before swallowing
   b) Chew the tablet until tingling in the tongue is felt
   c) Swallow the whole tablet
   d) Keep the tablet under the tongue and do not drink, eat or smoke while the tablet is dissolving

7. **What is the main purpose of the Drug Quality and Security Act (DQSA)?**
   a) To regulate compounding practices for patient safety and quality
   b) To enhance the safety and security of the pharmaceutical supply chain
   c) To establish tracing, serialization, and verification systems to prevent counterfeit drugs
   d) To safeguard the privacy and security of protected health information

8. **Which tool can be utilized to systematically analyze and prioritize risks based on their significance?**
   a) Computerized physician order entry (CPOE) system
   b) Failure mode and effects analysis (FMEA)
   c) Barcode scanning technology
   d) Root cause analysis (RCA)

9. **How is the required dosage for oral medication calculated based on a patient's weight?**
   a) Multiply the patient's weight by the drug's concentration
   b) Multiply the patient's weight by the prescribed dosage per kg
   c) Divide the patient's weight by the drug's concentration
   d) Divide the patient's weight by the prescribed dosage per kg

10. **What dosing instruction is consistent with parenteral medication administration?**

a) Inhale
b) Swallow
c) Inject
d) Apply

11. **All of the following dosage forms are to be shaken well before use except:**

a) Suspensions
b) Emulsions
c) Oral solutions
d) Insulin vials

12. **A patient is taking Vicodin and Tylenol for pain management after surgery. Which active ingredient is present in both medications?**

a) Ibuprofen
b) Oxycodone
c) Hydrocodone
d) Acetaminophen

13. **Enema is administered via which route of medication administration?**

a) Intravenous
b) Rectal
c) Topical
d) Oral

14. **In compliance with DEA regulations, pharmacists are required to:**

a) Obtain and maintain a DEA registration
b) Implement appropriate security measures to protect patient data
c) Conduct periodic inventories of prescription drugs
d) Report medication errors and adverse drug events to the FDA

15. **Why is ongoing monitoring important in risk management for pharmacy practices?**

a) To assess the financial implications of medication errors
b) To identify emerging risks and implement proactive measures
c) To ensure adherence to FDA regulations
d) To minimize the impact of adverse drug reactions

16. **What does CPOE stand for in risk minimization and preventing strategies?**

a) Centralized Process of Evaluation
b) Clinical Protocol of Execution
c) Computerized Physician Order Entry
d) Comprehensive Patient Outcome Estimation

17. **What two primary measurements are needed to calculate Body Mass Index (BMI)?**

a) Height and blood pressure
b) Weight and height
c) Weight and age
d) Height and age

18. **What is often involved in calculating the dosage for injectable medications?**

a) Dilution calculations
b) Calculating profit margins
c) Estimating storage requirements
d) Calculating shipping costs

19. **What does the abbreviation PR stand for?**

a) Per rectum
b) Patient rights
c) Pre-meal
d) Per need

20. **You received a shipment of lotion that is separated into two layers within the bottle. You anticipate that the lotion has probably:**

a) Always been this way
b) Been exposed to extreme heat
c) Been opened from the bottle
d) Been leaked out from the bottle

21. **A physician writes an order for 500 mL of normal saline to be infused over 5 hours. The IV drop factor is 15 gtt/mL. How many drops per minute should be delivered?**

a) 20 gtt/min
b) 25 gtt/min
c) 30 gtt/min
d) 35 gtt/min

22. **Which of these is the correct sequence of risk management in a pharmacy setting?**

a) Risk Assessment, Risk Identification, Risk Minimization and Prevention, Incident Reporting and Analysis, Regulatory Compliance, Continuous Quality Improvement

b) Risk Identification, Risk Assessment, Risk Minimization and Prevention, Incident Reporting and Analysis, Regulatory Compliance, Continuous Quality Improvement

c) Incident Reporting and Analysis, Risk Assessment, Risk Identification, Risk Minimization and Prevention, Regulatory Compliance, Continuous Quality Improvement

d) Risk Minimization and Prevention, Regulatory Compliance, Risk Assessment, Risk Identification, Incident Reporting and Analysis, Continuous Quality Improvement

23. **What unit conversions may be involved in calculating oral medication dosages?**

a) Converting milligrams to grams
b) Converting dollars to cents
c) Converting gallons to liters
d) Converting feet to meters

24. **What does FMEA stand for?**

a) Failure Mode and Efficacy Assessment (FMEA)
b) Faulty Machinery Evaluation Approach (FMEA)
c) Failure Mode and Effects Analysis (FMEA)
d) Functional Model for Error Analysis (FMEA)

25. **What factor is crucial for calculating dosage in injectable medications?**

a) Temperature of the solution
b) Volume of the injection vial
c) Concentration of the solution
d) Color of the solution

26. **SC injection must be given with which of the following?**

a) A very fine needle
b) A very large needle
c) A needleless syringe
d) An IV line

27. **A patient takes two drugs together, and you know that one drug intensifies the action of the other. Which type of interaction will most likely be observed?**

a) Potentiation
b) Synergism
c) Antagonism
d) Additive effect

28. **Which of the following can be determined through the drug's half-life?**

a) How often a drug is given
b) When will the drug expire
c) When will the next refill be required
d) If there is a risk of an allergic reaction

29. **Which of the following suffixes of the drug is used for beta blockers?**

a) Azepam
b) Navir
c) Olol
d) Prazole

30. **What is the main purpose of reporting medication errors and adverse drug events mandated for pharmacy technicians by many state laws?**

a) To identify and analyze errors and discrepancies in drug dispensing
b) To regulate the scope of practice for pharmacy technicians
c) To ensure that pharmacy technicians collaborate with other healthcare providers
d) To enhance the safety and quality of pharmacy services and patient care

31. **Which of the following is NOT a characteristic of high alert medications (HAMs)?**

a) Narrow therapeutic index
b) Elevated risk of causing harm
c) Only administered intravenously
d) Belong to different drug classes

32. **What is the main role of The Institute for Safe Medication Practices (ISMP)?**

a) Providing comprehensive healthcare services
b) Enhancing medication safety in the healthcare industry
c) Offering medical training to healthcare practitioners
d) Developing new high alert medications

33. Which government program provides health coverage for individuals 65 and older?

a) Medicaid
b) Medicare
c) Affordable Care Act
d) Private Insurance

34. What is the primary aim of the Affordable Care Act (ACA)?

a) To provide free medication to all citizens
b) To expand health insurance coverage
c) To regulate drug prices
d) To improve healthcare infrastructure

35. You are planning to prepare 450 mL of 20% dextrose solution by mixing 5% and 50% dextrose solution. How much of each solution will be needed?

a) 150 mL of 50% and 300 mL of 5% dextrose solution
b) 300 mL of 50% and 300 mL of 5% dextrose solution
c) 300 mL of 50% and 150 mL of 5% dextrose solution
d) 150 mL of 50% and 150 mL of 5% dextrose solution

36. Which of the following determines the body's biological response to the drugs?

a) Pharmacokinetics
b) Pharmacodynamics
c) Therapeutic index
d) Half-life

37. What is the indication of benzodiazepines?

a) Anxiety
b) Asthma
c) Diabetes mellitus
d) Substance abuse

38. Which specific DEA form is utilized for reporting incidents of theft or significant loss of controlled substances?

a) DEA 106 form
b) DEA 222a Form
c) DEA 41 Form
d) DEA 222 Form

39. Which of the following is NOT an example of a high alert medication?

a) Insulin
b) Ketamine
c) Opioids
d) Metformin

40. Why do high alert medications pose an elevated risk of harm to patients?

a) They have a broad therapeutic index
b) They are always administered incorrectly
c) They possess a narrow therapeutic index
d) They are not regulated by healthcare guidelines

41. Which class of medication includes examples such as epinephrine, phenylephrine, and norepinephrine?

a) Neuromuscular blocking agents
b) Inotropic medications
c) Chemotherapeutic agents
d) Adrenergic agonists

42. What role do pharmacy technicians play in the pharmacy billing process?

a) They are responsible for medication dispensing only
b) They are responsible for verifying insurance coverage
c) They are responsible for setting drug prices
d) They are not involved in the billing process

43. How do you calculate the number of tablets needed for a patient if you know the required dosage and the strength of each tablet?

a) Multiply the required dosage by the strength of each tablet
b) Divide the required dosage by the strength of each tablet
c) Add the required dosage to the strength of each tablet
d) Subtract the strength of each tablet from the required dosage

44. Which of the following drugs requires specialized handling?

a) NSAIDs
b) Chemotherapy agents
c) Suppositories
d) Antibiotics

45. **Which of the following types of drug interferes with the action of the other drug, reducing its effect?**

a) Agonist
b) Antagonist
c) Synergist
d) Potent

46. **The combination of aminoglycosides and loop diuretics can lead to which of the following?**

a) Neurotoxicity
b) Anaphylaxis
c) Ototoxicity
d) Hepatotoxicity

47. **What federal agency oversees the regulations for controlled substances in the United States?**

a) FDA (Food and Drug Administration)
b) DEA (Drug Enforcement Administration)
c) CDC (Centers for Disease Control and Prevention)
d) SAMHSA (Substance Abuse and Mental Health Services Administration)

48. **Which organization provides a list of high alert medications?**

a) Centers for Disease Control and Prevention (CDC)
b) World Health Organization (WHO)
c) Food and Drug Administration (FDA)
d) Institute for Safe Medication Practices (ISMP)

49. **Which category of high alert medications includes medications like warfarin?**

a) Inotropic medications
b) Anticoagulants
c) Anesthetic agents
d) Epidural and intrathecal medications

50. **Which of the following is an example of a high alert medication?**

a) Multivitamins
b) Antihistamines
c) Antiarrhythmics
d) OTC pain relievers

51. **How do you calculate the volume of a concentrated solution required for an injectable medication if you know the desired dosage and the concentration?**

a) Multiply the desired dosage by the concentration
b) Divide the desired dosage by the concentration
c) Add the desired dosage to the concentration
d) Subtract the concentration from the desired dosage

52. **What is the concentration of a medication if a vial contains 100 mg of the active ingredient in 10 mL of solution?**

a) 1 mg/mL
b) 10 mg/mL
c) 100 mg/mL
d) 1000 mg/mL

53. **A client's asthma exacerbates soon after taking metoprolol. What type of interaction does this indicate?**

a) Drug food interaction
b) Drug-drug interaction
c) Drug disease interaction
d) Drug contraindication

54. **Which drug should be avoided with warfarin?**

a) Vitamin A
b) Vitamin B
c) Vitamin C
d) Vitamin K

55. **Which of the following routes undergo the first-pass effect?**

a) Oral
b) Vaginal
c) Topical
d) Parenteral

56. **What needs to be documented by the receiving pharmacy of a transferred controlled substance prescription?**

a) The date the prescription expires
b) The original prescription format (electronic, hand-written, fax, etc.)
c) The DEA number belonging to the transferring pharmacy
d) The patient's date of birth

57. Which of the following is NOT an example of a High alert medication?

a) Analgesic drug
b) Chemotherapy drug
c) Opioid drug
d) Sedative drug

58. Which medication class carries a significant risk of respiratory depression and potential overdose?

a) Anticoagulants
b) Insulin
c) Opioids
d) Chemotherapy agents

59. If a medication needs to be diluted to a concentration of 1:10, and the stock solution is 1 mL, how much diluent is needed to achieve the desired concentration?

a) 1 mL
b) 9 mL
c) 10 mL
d) 11 mL

60. Which mathematical principle is often applied in dosage calculations to ensure the correct dose is administered?

a) Quadratic equations
b) Proportions
c) Calculus
d) Pythagorean theorem

61. Liver toxicity can occur from which of the overdose of which of the following medications?

a) Diphenhydramine
b) Acetaminophen
c) Aspirin
d) Nitroglycerine

62. Which of the following is an example of nonsteroidal anti-inflammatory drug (NSAID)?

a) Acetaminophen
b) Naproxen
c) Lidocaine
d) Capsaicin

63. How long can an opened vial of insulin be usable?

a) 1 day
b) 1 week
c) 1 month
d) 1 year

64. Which of these controlled substance prescriptions cannot be refilled?

a) Schedule II
b) Schedule III
c) Schedule IV
d) Schedule V

65. What is the primary concern with administering insulin to manage diabetes?

a) Risk of uncontrolled bleeding
b) Potential for respiratory depression
c) Possibility of life-threatening hypoglycemia or hyperglycemia
d) Need for precise dosing to induce sedation

66. Why is meticulous attention required when administering anticoagulants?

a) Risk of respiratory suppression
b) Potential for life-threatening hypoglycemia
c) Possibility of uncontrolled bleeding
d) Need for careful dosage adjustment to manage diabetes

67. Why are narcotics/opioids considered high alert medications?

a) They are only administered intravenously
b) They require special storage conditions
c) They carry a significant risk of respiratory depression and potential overdose
d) They possess a broad therapeutic index

68. If a patient is prescribed 0.1 mg/kg of medication and weighs 60 kilos, what would be the required dosage for the patient?

a) 0.6 mg
b) 6 mg
c) 60 mg
d) 600 mg

69. A physician orders an intravenous medication at a concentration of 50 mg/mL. The pharmacy technician has a vial containing 10 mL of the concentrated solution. Is there enough medication available for a desired dosage of 25 mg for the patient?

a) Yes
b) No
c) Insufficient information
d) It depends on the diluent

70. Which of the following is a common type of chemical degradation of drugs?

a) Crystallization
b) Precipitation
c) Hydrolysis
d) Unexpected cloudiness

71. Suppose amoxicillin is available in 80 mg/2 mL vials. How many vials are needed to compound an IV bag containing 560 mg of amoxicillin?

a) 4 vials
b) 5 vials
c) 6 vials
d) 7 vials

72. If 1500 ml is to be infused over 3.5 hours, what is the infusion rate in milliliters per minute (mL/min)?

a) 214.57 mL/min
b) 109.16 mL/min
c) 428.57 mL/min
d) 7.14 mL/min

73. What is the purpose of Risk Evaluation and Mitigation Strategies (REMS) mandated by federal requirements?

a) To regulate the disposal of hazardous waste
b) To control the distribution of pseudoephedrine
c) To ensure safe medication processing for restricted drug programs
d) To monitor and manage risks associated with certain medications that have known risks or serious adverse effects

74. In which scenario might a pharmacy technician assist the pharmacist in recommending an over-the-counter (OTC) therapy?

a) When a patient requires a prescription-only medication
b) When a patient has insurance coverage for a specific medication
c) When a patient struggles to obtain insurance coverage for a reflux medication
d) When a patient needs medication for a chronic condition

75. What is one of the goals of pharmacy technicians in preventing medication misuse?

a) To increase opioid prescriptions
b) To monitor patients' medication records
c) To encourage patient collaboration in medication management
d) To identify instances of obtaining multiple medications from a single pharmacy

76. What is the importance of adverse drug event reporting?

a) Reporting adverse drug events is primarily done for legal purposes
b) Pharmacists and pharmacy technicians are discouraged from reporting suspected adverse drug events
c) Accurate and detailed documentation of adverse drug events helps improve patient care and prevent future incidents
d) Adverse drug events should only be reported if they lead to permanent disability or death

77. What is the first step in the prescription filling and drug entry process as described in standard procedures?

a) Counting the pills
b) Verifying patient information
c) Verifying the completeness and accuracy of the prescription as entered into the computer system
d) Billing the insurance

78. What is a common unit of measurement used in calculating oral medication dosages?

a) Inches
b) Miles
c) Milligrams
d) Gallons

79. If dopamine is available in a 200 mg/ml vial, how many milliliters are needed to compound an IV bag containing 600 mg?

a)   3 mL
b)   6 mL
c)   9 mL
d)   12 mL

80. You plan to administer a dose of medication over 10 hours. How many mLs are needed for the infusion to run 1 mL/minute?

a)   480 mL
b)   560 mL
c)   600 mL
d)   720 mL

81. The expiration date is required for which of the following drug packaging?

a)   Prescribed medicines only
b)   Over-the-counter drugs only
c)   All prescribed and over-the-counter drugs
d)   Liquid dosage forms of drugs only

82. Which of the following is TRUE about generic drugs?

a)   These are the most expensive forms of the drug
b)   They come in different dosage forms than the actual drug
c)   They are manufactured by different manufacturers other than the original developer
d)   They are manufactured by the original developer of the drug

83. What types of medications are subject to REMS?

a)   Over-the-counter medications
b)   Prescription medications with no abuse potential
c)   Prescription medications with a high potential for abuse and severe side effects
d)   All FDA-approved medications

84. Why is documentation of adverse drug events (ADEs) important in patient care?

a)   To promote the use of medication error reporting programs
b)   To track the number of ADEs occurring in a healthcare facility

c)   To facilitate communication between healthcare providers, and prevent similar incidents
d)   To avoid discontinuation of medications with potential side effects

85. What is the final step in solving an alligation problem in pharmacy?

a)   Calculate the total volume of the solution
b)   Determine the numerical distance between the desired concentration and each of the solution concentrations
c)   Calculate the ratio of the distances determined in the previous step
d)   Blend the solutions based on the calculated ratio

86. Which of the following establishes criteria for products to be classified as therapeutically equivalent?

a)   Drug manufacturer
b)   Prescriber
c)   Pharmacy
d)   FDA

87. Which of the following drugs has a narrow therapeutic index?

a)   Pantoprazole
b)   Lisinopril
c)   Digoxin
d)   Acetaminophen

88. Acetaminophen with codeine liquid is prescribed as "Give 2 teaspoons three times a daily dispense 90 mL." The patient is a 1-year-old boy. Which of the following would most concern the pharmacy technician?

a)   Age
b)   Gender
c)   Quantity of medication
d)   Amount of Tylenol

89. Which drug has specific regulations governing its sale and distribution?

a)   Antibiotics
b)   Antidepressants
c)   Antipsychotics
d)   Pseudoephedrine

90. Which of the following is an example of an adverse drug event (ADE)?

a)   Reduced blood pressure control after taking antihypertensive medication

b)   Increased appetite following the administration of an appetite suppressant

c)   Enhanced mood and decreased anxiety with the use of sedative medication

d)   Severe skin rash and itching after starting a new antibiotic

Test 1: ANSWERS

1. **Answer a)**: Inderal is the brand name for propranolol, which is a medication belonging to the class of beta-blockers. It is commonly used to treat high blood pressure, angina (chest pain), tremors, and other conditions related to heart and blood circulation. Carvedilol is a beta-blocker medication, but it is not sold under the brand name Inderal. Carvedilol is available under different brand names, such as Coreg and Coreg CR. Metoprolol is available under different brand names, including Lopressor and Toprol-XL. It is commonly used to treat high blood pressure, angina, and heart failure. Atenolol, marketed under various brand labels including Tenormin, is a beta-blocker commonly used in the management of hypertension, angina, and specific heart-related issues.

2. **Answer b)**: The Food, Drug, and Cosmetic Act is a pivotal federal law that empowers the FDA to regulate drugs and ensure their safety, efficacy, and proper labeling. This law sets forth requirements for drug approval, manufacturing practices, and post-marketing surveillance. Pharmacists must comply with FDA regulations to ensure that all drugs dispensed meet quality and safety standards, promoting patient safety and well-being. The other options, Health Insurance Portability and Accountability Act (HIPAA), Drug Enforcement Administration (DEA) Regulations, and The Drug Quality and Security Act (DQSA) are not specifically related to granting authority to oversee drug safety, efficacy, and labeling.

3. **Answer c)**: Prescription dispensing techniques are not directly related to the steps involved in risk management for pharmacy practices. While they are an essential part of pharmacy operations, they do not fall within the risk management process itself. Risk identification is the first step in the risk management process for pharmacy practices. It involves systematically identifying potential risks and hazards within the pharmacy setting. Incident reporting and analysis are essential aspects of risk management in pharmacy practices. It involves establishing a robust incident reporting system to capture and analyze adverse events, near misses, and medication errors. Risk minimization and prevention are critical components of risk

management in pharmacy practices. After assessing risks, strategies are implemented to minimize their occurrence or impact.

4. **Answer b)**: Proportions are fundamental in dosage calculations for determining the appropriate dosage for a patient based on various factors such as weight, age, or condition. They offer a way to compare different quantities and find the correct ratio between them. By using proportions, pharmacy technicians can accurately calculate the dosage of medication to be administered, ensuring patient safety and effective treatment.

5. **Answer b)**: Zoloft is the brand name for the medication sertraline. The dose specified is 50 mg, and QD stands for "once daily." Therefore, the prescription is for sertraline 50 mg to be taken once daily. Paroxetine is a different antidepressant medication commonly known by the brand name Paxil. Citalopram is another antidepressant medication, often prescribed under the brand name Celexa. Escitalopram is an antidepressant commonly sold under the brand name Lexapro.

6. **Answer d)**: To take a sublingual pill, place it under the tongue and wait for it to completely dissolve. The tablet shouldn't be chewed, swallowed, or crushed. The drug is designed to permeate through the mucous membranes located under the tongue, providing a direct path to the bloodstream, thereby avoiding the digestive process. This route of administration provides rapid absorption and onset of action.

7. **Answer b)**: The main purpose of the Drug Quality and Security Act (DQSA) is to improve the safety and security of the pharmaceutical supply chain. This is achieved through the implementation of two main provisions: the Drug Supply Chain Security Act (DSCSA) and the Compounding Quality Act (CQA). The DSCSA establishes systems to trace, serialize, and verify drugs, thereby preventing counterfeit products from entering the supply chain. The CQA, on the other hand, focuses on regulating compounding practices to ensure patient safety and quality, while also distinguishing between traditional compounding and manufacturing. While options to regulate compounding practices for patient

safety and quality and to establish tracing, serialization, and verification systems to prevent counterfeit drugs are partially correct, they do not encompass the main purpose of the DQSA. Additionally, the Drug Quality and Security Act (DQSA) does not ensure the privacy and security of protected health information.

8. **Answer b)**: Failure mode and effects analysis (FMEA) is a systematic approach used to identify potential failure modes (ways in which a process or product could fail) and their potential effects on a system. A Computerized Physician Order Entry (CPOE) system is a digital platform that allows healthcare providers to enter medical orders (e.g., prescriptions, lab tests, etc.) directly into a computer system rather than using paper-based methods. Barcode scanning technology is commonly used in healthcare settings to improve patient safety and reduce errors related to medication administration, patient identification, and inventory management. Root cause analysis (RCA) is a method used to identify the underlying cause or causes of a problem or an adverse event.

9. **Answer b)**: The required dosage for a patient is typically calculated by multiplying the patient's weight by the prescribed dosage per kilogram. For instance, if a patient weighs 60 kilos and is prescribed a dosage of 0.1 mg/kg, the required dosage would be calculated as $60 \, kg \times 0.1 \, mg/kg = 6 \, mg$. This ensures that the medication is tailored to the patient's body mass, providing an effective and safe treatment.

10. **Answer c)**: Parenteral medication administration refers to the delivery of medication through a route other than the digestive tract, such as injections. Therefore, the dosing instruction consistent with parenteral medication administration would be "inject." This typically involves the use of a syringe and needle to administer the medication directly into the body, bypassing the gastrointestinal system.

11. **Answer d)**: Insulin vials should not be shaken before use. Vigorous shaking of insulin can result' in air bubbles, potentially compromising the precision of the dosage. Instead, it's recommended to softly roll insulin bottles between the hands to mix the contents. Vigorous shaking should be avoided to prevent frothing or foaming.

12. **Answer d)**: Hydrocodone and acetaminophen are both ingredients in the pharmaceutical painkiller Vicodin. Acetaminophen alone makes up the whole composition of the over-the-counter pain reliever Tylenol. Both drugs are used to treat pain, but Vicodin is more effective for more severe pain because it also contains an opioid painkiller. Neither Tylenol nor Vicodin contain ibuprofen or oxycodone.

13. **Answer b)**: Enema is a medication administration method that involves delivering a liquid medication through rectal route. Some medications are required to be administered rectally due to their better absorption and depending upon their target tissues.

14. **Answer a)**: In compliance with DEA regulations, pharmacists handling controlled substances are required to obtain and maintain a valid Drug Enforcement Administration (DEA) registration. This registration allows pharmacists to handle, dispense, and administer controlled substances. Option Implement appropriate security measures to protect patient data is not specific to DEA regulations but rather pertains to the Health Insurance Portability and Accountability Act (HIPAA), which deals with safeguarding patient health information. Option Conduct periodic inventories of prescription drugs is a general requirement for pharmacies to ensure proper inventory management, but it does not solely relate to DEA regulations. Option Report medication errors and adverse drug events to the FDA is an important practice for patient safety, but it is not a specific requirement under DEA regulations.

15. **Answer b)**: Ongoing monitoring in risk management for pharmacy practices helps identify emerging risks and enable the implementation of proactive measures to prevent adverse events and enhance patient safety. By being vigilant and proactive, pharmacies can continuously improve their processes and minimize the occurrence of potential risks and errors. Ongoing monitoring in risk management for pharmacy practices is important for several reasons, but assessing the financial implications of medication errors is not the primary focus. While compliance with FDA regulations is an important aspect of risk management in pharmacy practices, ongoing monitoring serves a broader purpose in identifying and mitigating risks beyond regulatory compliance. Minimizing the impact of adverse drug reactions is a critical consideration in

pharmacy practice. However, ongoing monitoring plays a more comprehensive role in risk management.

16. **Answer c)**: Implementing technology, such as computerized physician order entry (CPOE) systems and barcode scanning, can be used in risk minimization and prevention to reduce the risk of medication errors. So, Computerized Physician Order Entry is correct.

17. **Answer b)**: To calculate Body Mass Index (BMI), two primary measurements are needed: weight and height. BMI is a useful screening tool to identify whether an individual is underweight, normal weight, overweight, or obese. The formula for BMI is weight in kilograms divided by the square of height in meters. This calculation is widely used in healthcare settings to assess a patient's nutritional status and risk for diseases related to body weight, such as diabetes or cardiovascular disease.

18. **Answer a)**: Calculating the dosage for injectable medications often involves dilution calculations. A concentrated solution is diluted with a specific volume of diluent to achieve the desired strength. Pharmacy technicians may need to accurately calculate the volume of the concentrated solution and the diluent required to ensure proper medication strength and patient safety.

19. **Answer a)**: The abbreviation PR can stand for multiple things depending on the context. However, in the medical field, the most common interpretation of PR is "Per rectum," which refers to the administration or examination of something through the rectum. For example, medications administered through the rectum may be labeled as PR medications. It is important to note that medical abbreviations can have different meanings depending on the context. So it is always crucial to consider the specific context when interpreting an abbreviation.

20. **Answer b)**: Heat can cause the ingredients in lotions to separate or undergo changes in consistency. High temperatures can destabilize emulsions, causing the separation of layers. If the lotion has been exposed to extreme heat during storage or transportation, it can lead to this separation.

21. **Answer b)**: To determine the number of drops per minute (gtt/min) that should be delivered, we can use the formula:

Drops per minute = (Volume to be infused × IV drop factor) / Time in minutes
Given:
Volume to be infused = 500 mL
IV drop factor = 15 gtt/mL
Time in minutes = 5 hours × 60 minutes/hour = 300 minutes
Substituting these values into the formula, we get:
Drops per minute = (500 mL × 15 gtt/mL) / 300 minutes
Calculating:
Drops per minute = 7500 / 300 = 25 gtt/min.
Therefore, the correct answer is B. 25 gtt/min.

22. **Answer b)**: Risk management starts with Risk Identification, the initial step of recognizing potential risks and hazards in the pharmacy setting. Following this, Risk Assessment occurs, which involves evaluating the potential impact and likelihood of occurrence of identified risks. After assessing risks, the focus shifts to Risk Minimization and Prevention, where strategies are put in place to reduce the occurrence or impact of these risks. Incident Reporting and Analysis then takes place, involving the capture and analysis of adverse events and medication errors. Regulatory Compliance is addressed, ensuring adherence to various regulations and standards. The sequence concludes with Continuous Quality Improvement, which involves ongoing monitoring and enhancement of risk management strategies.

23. **Answer a)**: When calculating oral medication dosages, pharmacy technicians may need to convert between different units of measurement. One common conversion is from milligrams to grams. This ensures that the medication dosage is accurate and aligns with the prescription, which ultimately contributes to effective treatment and patient safety.

24. **Answer c)**: Failure Mode and Effects Analysis (FMEA)," is the correct answer, as it accurately represents the acronym and the methodology behind FMEA. The other options are variations that do not accurately reflect the full meaning of FMEA.

25. **Answer c)**: The concentration of the solution is a crucial factor when calculating dosages for injectable medications. Pharmacy technicians must know the concentration to accurately determine the volume required for a given dose. For example, if the concentration is 50 mg/mL and

the desired dose is 25 mg, one would divide 25 mg by 50 mg/mL to get the required volume of 0.5 mL. Accurate concentration data ensures that the patient receives the correct dosage.

26. **Answer a)**: Subcutaneous injections are given just below the skin into the fatty tissue. The goal is to deliver medication into the subcutaneous layer, which is relatively close to the surface of the skin. Using a very fine needle helps minimize pain and discomfort for the patient.

27. **Answer a)**: Potentiation refers to an interaction where one drug enhances or increases the effect of another drug. In this case, one drug is augmenting the action of the other, leading to a more pronounced or prolonged effect than what would be expected from either drug alone.

28. **Answer a)**: The duration it takes for a drug's body concentration to reduce by half is referred to as its half-life. It provides information about the rate at which the drug is eliminated from the body. By understanding the drug's half-life, healthcare professionals can determine the dosing frequency of the medication. For example, if a drug has a long half-life, it means it stays in the body for a longer duration, and it may be administered less frequently. Conversely, a drug with a short half-life may require more frequent dosing to maintain therapeutic levels in the body.

29. **Answer c)**: "Olol" is the suffix commonly used for beta blockers. Beta-blockers are a class of medications that primarily block the effects of adrenaline (epinephrine) on beta receptors in the body. The suffix "-olol" is used to indicate a drug's classification as a beta blocker. Examples of beta blockers include propranolol, metoprolol, atenolol, and carvedilol, all of which have the "-olol" suffix.

30. **Answer d)**: The main purpose of reporting medication errors and adverse drug events mandated for pharmacy technicians by many state laws is to enhance the safety and quality of pharmacy services and patient care. By reporting errors, pharmacy technicians contribute to identifying potential risks and vulnerabilities in the medication management process, leading to the implementation of strategies and improvements to prevent future errors. Option a is partially correct, as reporting errors does involve identifying and analyzing errors and discrepancies in drug dispensing. However, the primary purpose

of reporting is to enhance patient safety and care quality rather than solely focusing on identifying errors. The scope of practice for pharmacy technicians is typically defined by state laws and regulations, outlining their roles, responsibilities, and professional activities related to medication preparation, dispensing, and other supportive tasks under the supervision of pharmacists. Reporting errors are not directly related to regulating their scope of practice. Collaboration among healthcare providers is essential for comprehensive patient care, but it is typically facilitated through other means, such as interprofessional communication protocols and teamwork within the pharmacy setting.

31. **Answer c)**: High alert medications can be administered through various routes, including oral, intravenous, intramuscular, subcutaneous, and others. The key defining features of HAMs are their narrow therapeutic index and elevated risk of causing harm, regardless of the route of administration. They can belong to various therapeutic classes and may have different indications and effects.

32. **Answer b)**: The main role of The Institute for Safe Medication Practices (ISMP) is to promote and improve medication safety in healthcare settings. The Institute for Safe Medication Practices (ISMP) is not primarily focused on providing comprehensive healthcare services. While The Institute for Safe Medication Practices (ISMP) may offer educational resources and training related to medication safety, its main role is not specifically focused on offering medical training to healthcare practitioners. It is also not involved in developing new high alert medications.

33. **Answer b)**: Medicare is a federal program that provides health coverage for individuals aged 65 and older, as well as for some younger people with specific disabilities. Unlike Medicaid, which is a joint federal and state program aimed at providing health coverage to low-income individuals and families, Medicare is primarily focused on the older population.

34. **Answer b)**: The primary aim of the Affordable Care Act (ACA), also known as Obamacare, is to expand health insurance coverage to more Americans. It also aims to improve the quality of healthcare and health insurance to regulate the

health insurance industry, and to reduce healthcare spending in the US.

35. **Answer a)**: To determine the amounts of each solution needed to prepare the desired 20% dextrose solution, we can use the concept of dilution. Let's calculate the quantities required:

Let x represent the volume of the 50% dextrose solution needed (in mL).

Then, the volume of the 5% dextrose solution needed would be (450 - x) mL (as the total volume is 450 mL).

Now, let's calculate the amount of dextrose in each solution:

For the 50% dextrose solution, the amount of dextrose is 50% of x mL, which is 0.5x mL.

For the 5% dextrose solution, the amount of dextrose is 5% of (450 - x) mL, which is 0.05(450 - x) mL.

The total amount of dextrose in the final 450 mL solution is 20% of 450 mL, which is 0.2 * 450 mL = 90 mL.

Since the dextrose amounts from both solutions combine to give the total, we can set up the following equation:

0.5x mL + 0.05(450 - x) mL = 90 mL

Solving this equation will give us the value of x:

0.5x + 0.05(450 - x) = 90
0.5x + 22.5 - 0.05x = 90
0.45x = 90 - 22.5
0.45x = 67.5
x = 67.5 / 0.45
x = 150

Therefore, the amount of the 50% dextrose solution needed is 150 mL, and the amount of the 5% dextrose solution needed is (450 - x) mL = 450 - 150 mL = 300 mL.

So, the correct answer is A. 150 mL of 50% and 300 mL of 5% dextrose solution.

36. **Answer b)**: The study of the relation between a drug's concentration at its site of action and the ensuing biological reaction in the body is known as pharmacodynamics. It involves understanding how drugs interact with specific receptors or target sites in the body to produce their effects. Pharmacodynamics encompasses the mechanisms of drug action, including receptor binding, signal transduction pathways, enzyme inhibition, and other biochemical and physiological processes that mediate the drug's effects. It aims to comprehend how the concentration of a drug

correlates with the strength and duration of its impact on the human body.

37. **Answer a)**: Benzodiazepines enhance the effects of gamma-aminobutyric acid (GABA) in the brain, leading to sedation, anxiety relief, and hypnotic effects. They are indicated for anxiety disorders, insomnia, and seizure disorders. Contraindications include a history of substance abuse and respiratory depression.

38. **Answer a)**: The DEA Form 106 is specifically designed to report thefts or significant losses of controlled substances. This form is part of the DEA's efforts to track and control the distribution of these substances to prevent their misuse. The DEA Form 222a is used for ordering Schedule I and II controlled substances, the DEA Form 41 is used for the destruction of controlled substances, and the DEA Form 222 is used for the transfer of Schedule I and II controlled substances.

39. **Answer d)**: Metformin is not an example of a high alert medication. It is an oral medication commonly prescribed to manage type 2 diabetes. Insulin, ketamine and opioids are examples of high alert medications.

40. **Answer c)**: High alert medications are drugs with a narrow therapeutic index, meaning that the difference between the therapeutic dose (the dose that provides the desired effect) and the toxic dose (the dose that can cause harm) is small. High alert medications do not have a broad therapeutic index. While high alert medications have an elevated risk of causing harm if used improperly, it does not mean they are always administered incorrectly. High alert medications are regulated by healthcare guidelines and safety protocols.

41. **Answer d)**: Adrenergic agonists are a class of medications that activate adrenergic receptors in the sympathetic nervous system. Examples of adrenergic agonists include drugs like epinephrine, phenylephrine, and norepinephrine. Examples of neuromuscular blocking agents include drugs like rocuronium, vecuronium, and succinylcholine. Examples of inotropic medications include drugs like digoxin and milrinone. Examples include drugs like cisplatin, doxorubicin, and paclitaxel.

42. **Answer b)**: Pharmacy technicians play a vital role in the pharmacy billing process, and one of their key responsibilities is verifying insurance coverage for patients. This is crucial for ensuring

that the billing process runs smoothly and that patients are appropriately charged for the medications and services they receive.

43. **Answer b)**: Calculating the number of tablets needed for a patient involves dividing the required dosage by the strength of each tablet. For example, if a patient requires a medication dosage of 50 mg and each tablet contains 25 mg, you would divide the required dosage (50 mg) by the strength of each tablet (25 mg) to find that the patient would need two tablets. This calculation ensures that the patient receives the appropriate amount of medication based on their prescription, taking into account the strength of the medication available in tablet form.

44. **Answer b)**: Some medications pose a risk to healthcare workers if proper precautions are not taken during handling. Hazardous drugs, such as chemotherapy agents (Key B), require specialized handling techniques to minimize exposure. All the other options are incorrect.

45. **Answer b)**: An antagonist (Key B) is a form of drug that interferes with the actions of another drug, reducing its effectiveness. Agonists (Key A) mimic the effects of naturally occurring substances that would normally bind to the receptor and activate it. A synergist (Key C) is a substance that enhances or potentiates the effect of another substance, but it does not necessarily bind to a receptor to inhibit activation. The term "potent" (Key D) refers to the strength or effectiveness of a drug but does not specifically describe a drug's mechanism of action in relation to receptor binding or activation.

46. **Answer c)**: The administration of aminoglycosides (e.g., Gentamicin, amikacin) in combination with loop diuretics (e.g., furosemide) heightens the risk of experiencing ototoxicity (Key C) and kidney damage. Key A, B and D are incorrect.

47. **Answer b)**: The DEA is the federal agency responsible for enforcing the Controlled Substances Act (CSA) and overseeing the regulations for controlled substances in the United States. The DEA's main role is to prevent the diversion, misuse, and abuse of controlled substances, such as opioids, stimulants, and sedatives. The FDA is a federal organization that is involved in supervising the regulation of food, drugs, medical devices, vaccines, and various other products within the United States. The CDC is a federal organization that manages issues related to public health and the prevention of disease. The EPA is a federal agency tasked with protecting human health and the environment. It is not involved in regulating controlled substances.

48. **Answer d)**: The ISMP provides a list of high alert medications, which are drugs that carry a higher risk of causing significant harm to patients when used in error. The CDC is a leading national public health organization in the United States. While the CDC focuses on disease prevention and control, it does not specifically provide a list of high alert medications. While the WHO sets global health standards and guidelines, it does not maintain a specific list of high alert medications. The FDA does not provide a specific list of high alert medications.

49. **Answer b)**: Anticoagulants are a category of high alert medications that are used to prevent or treat blood clot formation. Warfarin is an example of an anticoagulant. Examples of inotropic medications include digoxin and milrinone. Warfarin is not an anesthetic agent or an epidural or intrathecal medication.

50. **Answer c)**: Antiarrhythmics medications are classified as high alert medications because of their potential to cause significant harm if used in error. Multivitamins are supplements offering a varied mix of essential vitamins and minerals. They are generally considered low-risk medications and are available over-the-counter. Antihistamines are medications commonly used to treat allergy symptoms, such as sneezing, itching, and runny nose. They are also available over-the-counter and are generally considered low-risk medications. While OTC pain reliever medications are available without a prescription, they are not considered high alert medications.

51. **Answer b)**: In order to calculate the volume of a concentrated solution required for an injectable medication, you would divide the desired dosage by the concentration. For instance, if a physician orders an intravenous medication at a concentration of 50 mg/mL and the desired dosage for the patient is 25 mg, you would divide the desired dosage (25 mg) by the concentration (50 mg/mL) to find that 0.5 mL of the concentrated solution is required. This calculation is crucial for ensuring that the patient receives the correct

amount of medication, particularly when dealing with injectable formulations that may be highly concentrated.

52. **Answer b)**: The concentration of a medication is calculated by dividing the amount of the active ingredient by the volume of the solution. In this case, if a medication vial contains 100 mg of the active ingredient in 10 mL of solution, the concentration would be calculated as 100 mg: 10 mL = 10 mg/ml. This is crucial information for pharmacy technicians, especially when preparing medications that require a specific concentration. Knowing the concentration allows for accurate dilution or administration procedures to ensure patient safety.

53. **Answer c)**: This represents a drug-disease interaction (Key C), where the drug can have negative effects on a pre-existing medical condition. Drug-food interaction (Key A) refers to the interaction between medication and certain foods or beverages. However, in a drug-drug interaction (Key B), the interaction occurs between two or more medications that can affect their efficacy or result in adverse effects when taken together. A drug contraindication (Key D) refers to a situation where a drug should not be used due to the potential harm it can cause to a particular individual or a specific condition.

54. **Answer d)**: In order to avoid potential interactions and maintain the effectiveness of warfarin, it is generally recommended to avoid excessive consumption of vitamin K (Key D) while taking the medication. This is because vitamin K performs coagulation whereas warfarin is an anticoagulant drug, Key A, B, and C are incorrect.

55. **Answer a)**: Only the oral route (Key A) undergoes significant first-pass metabolism, making it distinct from the other options. Vaginal administration (Key B) involves the direct placement of a drug into the vagina, allowing it to be absorbed directly into the local tissues or systemic circulation without passing through the liver. Topical administration (Key C) involves applying a drug to the skin, where it is absorbed into the local tissues or systemic circulation. This route also bypasses the liver. Parenteral routes (Key D), such as intravenous or intramuscular injections, involve delivering drugs directly into the bloodstream, bypassing the gastrointestinal tract and the liver.

56. **Answer c)**: Documentation of the DEA number from the transferring pharmacy is required when transferring a prescription for a controlled substance. This is part of the requirements set by the DEA to track the movement of controlled substances and prevent their diversion. While the date the prescription expires, the original prescription format, and the patient's date of birth may be part of the prescription information; they are not specifically required to be documented in the case of a transfer according to DEA regulations.

57. **Answer a)**: Analgesic drugs are medications used to relieve pain. They encompass a wide range of medications, from over-the-counter pain relievers like acetaminophen and ibuprofen. These aren't considered as High alert medications. Some examples of high alert medications include Chemotherapy drugs, Insulin, Opioids, Anticoagulants, Sedatives and hypnotics, Potassium chloride injections and Neuromuscular blockers.

58. **Answer c)**: Opioids have a strong potential for respiratory depression, especially when used in high doses or in combination with other sedative medications. Overdosing on opioids can lead to life-threatening respiratory suppression and even death. While anticoagulants carry their own set of risks, such as bleeding, they do not typically cause respiratory depression or overdose. Insulin can lead to hypoglycemia (low blood sugar) if not administered correctly, but it does not pose a significant risk of respiratory depression or overdose. Common side effects of chemotherapeutic agents include nausea, vomiting, hair loss, and a weakened immune system. Respiratory depression and overdose are not typical risks associated with chemotherapy.

59. **Answer b)**: When a medication needs to be diluted to a specific concentration, the amount of diluent required is calculated based on the desired concentration ratio and the volume of the stock solution. In this case, if the desired concentration is 1:10 and the stock solution is 1 mL, you would need to add 9 mL of diluent to achieve this concentration. The calculation follows the formula Diluent Volume = (Desired Ratio−1) × Stock Solution Volume, or (10−1) × 1 = 9 mL. This is an important calculation for pharmacy technicians to ensure the correct concentration of

medications, particularly for injectable formulations.

60. **Answer c)**: The mathematical principle often applied in dosage calculations to ensure the correct dose is administered is the use of proportions. Proportions provide a way to compare quantities and find the correct ratio between them. This is especially useful in pharmacy, where dosage calculations are critical for patient safety. Proportions help in determining the appropriate dosage based on various factors such as weight, age, or condition of the patient. Pharmacy technicians use proportions to calculate the right amount of medication for individual patients, ensuring safety and effectiveness.

61. **Answer b)**: Acetaminophen (Key B), is a popular over-the-counter medicine used for its analgesic and antipyretic properties. While it is generally safe when taken at recommended doses, excessive or prolonged use of acetaminophen can lead to liver damage. The rest of the options do not lead to liver toxicity.

62. **Answer b)**: Naproxen (Key B) is an example of a nonsteroidal anti-inflammatory drug (NSAID). Acetaminophen (Key A) is not an NSAID, although it is commonly used to relieve pain and reduce fever. Lidocaine (Key C) is a local anesthetic that is used to numb a specific area of the body and relieve pain. It is not classified as an NSAID. Capsaicin (Key D), present in chili peppers, is utilized as an analgesic. Its mechanism of action involves reducing levels of substance P, a neurotransmitter responsible for conveying pain sensations.

63. **Answer c)**: An opened vial of insulin can be used for 1 month (Key C). All other options are incorrect.

64. **Answer a)**: Refills are not permitted for Schedule II controlled substance prescriptions. In accordance with federal regulations, Schedule II controlled substances are classified as medications with a high potential for abuse and are regarded as the most hazardous among all controlled substances. Schedule III, Schedule IV and Schedule V controlled substance prescriptions may have limited refills allowed based on state and federal regulations.

65. **Answer c)**: Insulin is a potent hormone that lowers blood sugar levels by facilitating the uptake of glucose into cells. However, if too much insulin is administered or if the dose is not appropriately adjusted based on the individual's blood sugar levels and carbohydrate intake, it can lead to dangerously low blood sugar levels (hypoglycemia). Uncontrolled bleeding and respiratory depression are not primary concerns with administering insulin to manage diabetes. Inducing sedation is not the purpose of administering insulin for diabetes management. Insulin is not used for sedation.

66. **Answer c)**: Anticoagulants work by inhibiting blood clotting factors, which can increase the time it takes for blood to clot. Meticulous attention is not required when administering anticoagulants due to the risk of respiratory suppression. Life-threatening hypoglycemia is not a concern when administering anticoagulants. Careful dosage adjustment to manage diabetes is not related to anticoagulant administration.

67. **Answer c)**: Opioids, such as morphine, fentanyl, oxycodone, and others, are powerful pain-relieving medications. The way they operate is by binding to specific receptors located in the brain and spinal cord, leading to pain relief but also causing side effects like respiratory depression. While some opioids may be given intravenously for specific medical situations, the primary reason narcotics/opioids are classified as high alert medications is their inherent risk of respiratory depression and potential overdose when used in any form of administration. While proper storage is essential for all medications, including opioids, the need for special storage conditions alone does not make narcotics/opioids high alert medications. Narcotics/opioids do not possess a broad therapeutic index.

68. **Answer b)**: To find the required dosage for a patient who is prescribed medication based on their weight, you would multiply the weight of the patient by the prescribed dosage per kilogram. In this example, the patient is prescribed 0.1 mg/kg and weighs 60 kilos. The required dosage would be calculated as $60\,kg \times 0.1\,mg/kg = 6\,mg$. This calculation is crucial for ensuring the patient receives an appropriate and safe dosage of the medication, tailored to their specific weight.

69. **Answer a)**: To determine whether there is enough medication available for a desired dosage, the pharmacy technician would first calculate the volume of the concentrated solution required. This

is done by dividing the desired dosage by the concentration of the medication. In this case, 25 mg: 50 mg/mL = 0.5 mL. Since the technician has a vial containing 10 mL of the concentrated solution, and only 0.5 mL is needed for the desired dosage of 25 mg, there is more than enough medication available to meet the patient's needs.

70. **Answer c)**: Chemical stability refers to a drug's ability to remain unchanged when exposed to various environmental conditions that could cause degradation. One common type of chemical degradation is hydrolysis (Key C), where the drug reacts with water, resulting in its breakdown. Physical stability refers to a drug's ability to maintain its physical properties over time, such as crystallization (Key A) and precipitation (Key B). Microbiological stability relates to the prevention of microbial contamination during the storage and transportation of drugs (Key D).

71. **Answer d)**: The question asks how many vials, each containing 80 mg of amoxicillin, are needed to compound an IV bag containing 560 mg of the drug.
To determine the number of vials needed, we should divide the total required dose (560 mg) by the quantity of the drug in each vial (80 mg/vial).
560 mg ÷ 80 mg/vial = 7 vials
So, 7 vials of amoxicillin are needed to compound an IV bag containing 560 mg of the drug.

72. **Answer d)**: Determining the infusion rate involves transforming the given data into the appropriate measurement units.
The infusion rate is typically expressed in mL per minute.
Given:
Total dose = 1500 mg
Infusion time = 3.5 hours
First, we need to convert the infusion time from hours to minutes since the infusion rate is expressed in mL per minute.
Hours * 60 minutes/hour = 210 minutes
Next, we can calculate the infusion rate using the formula:
Infusion rate (mL/min) = Total dose (mg) / Infusion time (min)
Infusion rate = 1500 mg / 210 min
Infusion rate ≈ 7.14 mL/min

73. **Answer d)**: The purpose of Risk Evaluation and Mitigation Strategies (REMS) mandated by federal requirements is to monitor and manage risks associated with certain medications that have known risks or serious adverse effects. REMS is a program initiated by the U.S. The Food and Drug Administration (FDA), is responsible for ensuring that the advantages of specific medications outweigh their risks. Regulating the disposal of hazardous waste is not the primary purpose of Risk Evaluation and Mitigation Strategies (REMS). Controlling the distribution of pseudoephedrine is not the primary purpose of Risk Evaluation and Mitigation Strategies (REMS). While ensuring safe medication processing is important, it is not the primary purpose of Risk Evaluation and Mitigation Strategies (REMS).

74. **Answer c)**: If a patient is facing challenges with obtaining insurance coverage for a reflux medication, the pharmacist and pharmacy technician may collaborate to find an appropriate OTC alternative for managing reflux symptoms. The pharmacist, not the pharmacy technician, would be responsible for handling prescription medications and recommending appropriate prescription therapies. If a patient has insurance coverage for a specific prescription medication, the pharmacist may work with the patient's insurance plan to process the prescription and dispense the medication. The need for medication for a chronic condition does not necessarily involve recommending an over-the-counter (OTC) therapy.

75. **Answer b)**: One of the primary goals of pharmacy technicians in preventing medication misuse is to monitor patients' medication records. Pharmacy technicians play an essential role in maintaining and updating patient profiles, including medication histories, allergies, and any known drug interactions. Increasing opioid prescriptions is not the primary goal of pharmacy technicians in preventing medication misuse. While encouraging patient collaboration in medication management is a crucial aspect of pharmacy practice, it is not the primary goal in preventing medication misuse. Identifying instances of obtaining multiple medications from a single pharmacy is part of medication safety and monitoring, but it is not the primary goal of preventing medication misuse.

76. **Answer c)**: Reporting and documenting adverse drug events (ADEs) is crucial for enhancing patient care and preventing future incidents.

Pharmacists and pharmacy technicians should report suspected ADEs to regulatory agencies or medication error reporting programs. Documenting ADEs in the patient's medical record is essential. This documentation includes information about the medication involved, the observed adverse reaction, and any actions taken. Such comprehensive documentation aids in better communication among healthcare providers, leading to improved patient care, and serves as a tool to prevent similar incidents in the future. It is not done primarily for legal purposes. Pharmacists and pharmacy technicians should not be discouraged from reporting them. Reporting and documenting all adverse drug events should be done to enhance patient care and safety.

77. **Answer c)**: The first step in the prescription filling and drug entry process, as described in standard procedures, is to verify the completeness and accuracy of the prescription as entered into the computer system. This is a critical step to ensure that the prescription details match what is entered in the system. It helps in minimizing errors and is crucial for patient safety. Any discrepancies must be resolved before proceeding to the next steps of filling the prescription.

78. **Answer c)**: In the realm of pharmacology, especially when it comes to calculating oral medication dosages, the common unit of measurement is milligrams (mg). Milligrams are used to specify the strength or amount of active ingredient in each tablet or dosage form. For example, if a patient requires a medication dosage of 50 mg, the "mg" signifies the amount of the active ingredient that should be administered. Using the correct unit of measurement is crucial for ensuring that the patient receives the right amount of medication, thereby ensuring both efficacy and safety.

79. **Answer a)**: To determine the number of milliliters (mL) needed to compound an IV bag containing 600 mg of dopamine, we need to divide the total dose by the concentration of the dopamine vial.
Given:
Dopamine concentration = 200 mg/mL
Required dose = 600 mg
We can calculate the number of milliliters needed using the formula:
Volume (mL) = Required dose (mg) / Concentration (mg/mL)
Volume (mL) = 600 mg / 200 mg/mL

Volume (mL) = 3 mL
Therefore, the correct answer is a) 3 mL is needed to compound an IV bag containing 600 mg of dopamine.

80. **Answer c)**: To calculate the total volume of medication needed for a 10-hour infusion at a rate of 1 mL/minute, we can use the formula:
Volume (mL) = Rate (mL/minute) × Time (minutes)
In this case, the rate is 1 mL/minute, and the time is 10 hours. We need to convert the time to minutes by multiplying it by 60: Time (minutes) = 10 hours × 60 minutes/hour = 600 minutes
Now we can calculate the volume: Volume (mL) = 1 mL/minute × 600 minutes = 600 mL
Therefore, the correct answer is option c. 600 mL.

81. **Answer c)**: The expiration date on a medication signifies the time limit up to which the producer can assure the medication's maximum effectiveness and safety, provided it is stored correctly. It is important to adhere to the expiration date and not use medications beyond that point, as their effectiveness and safety cannot be guaranteed. This requirement applies to both prescribed medicines and over-the-counter (OTC) drugs.

82. **Answer c)**: Generic drugs are prescription pharmaceuticals that mirror their brand-name counterparts in aspects such as their active ingredients, dosage structure, strength, method of delivery, and designated use. They are commonly produced by different pharmaceutical entities after the patent protection on the brand-name drug has ended (Key c).

83. **Answer c)**: Risk Evaluation and Mitigation Strategies (REMS) are typically required for prescription medications with a high potential for abuse or serious side effects. REMS is mandated by the U.S. Food and Drug Administration (FDA) for certain medications that pose significant risks to patient safety or have the potential for abuse, misuse, or adverse events. Risk Evaluation and Mitigation Strategies (REMS) are generally not applicable to over-the-counter (OTC) medications. Prescription medications that do not have abuse potential are typically exempt from Risk Evaluation and Mitigation Strategies (REMS). Risk Evaluation and Mitigation Strategies (REMS) do not apply to all FDA-approved medications. REMS is a targeted

program established for specific prescription medications with known safety concerns or potential risks.

84. **Answer c)**: Documenting ADEs is crucial in facilitating communication between healthcare providers involved in a patient's care. While documentation of adverse drug events (ADEs) is essential for patient safety, promoting the use of medication error reporting programs is not the primary reason for documenting ADEs. Documenting ADEs can help track the number and types of adverse events occurring within a healthcare facility is valuable but not the primary reason for documenting ADEs. While documentation of ADEs can influence medication management decisions, the primary focus is not solely on avoiding the discontinuation of medications with potential side effects.

85. **Answer d)**: The final step in solving an alligation problem involves blending the solutions based on the calculated ratio of the distances between the desired concentration and each of the solution concentrations. This ratio denotes the relative quantities of each solution that should be mixed together to achieve the desired concentration. Following this step ensures that the final solution meets the specific concentration requirements, making it a critical skill for pharmacy technicians involved in medication compounding.

86. **Answer d)**: The FDA establishes criteria for products to be classified as therapeutically equivalent (Key D). All the other options are incorrect.

87. **Answer c)**: Digoxin (Key C) is a cardiac glycoside used for heart failure and certain arrhythmias. The difference between a therapeutic dose and a hazardous dose is known to be fairly small due to its narrow therapeutic index. Pantoprazole (a proton pump inhibitor used for treating acid-related disorders), lisinopril (an angiotensin-converting enzyme inhibitor used for hypertension and heart failure), and acetaminophen (a common pain reliever and fever reducer) are not typically associated with having a narrow therapeutic index.

88. **Answer a)**: In this case, the patient is a 1-year-old boy. Pediatric patients, especially those under a certain age, may have specific dosing requirements and considerations due to their age-related differences in drug metabolism,

physiology, and potential for adverse effects (Key A). While gender, the quantity of medication, and the amount of Tylenol (acetaminophen) are factors to consider in certain situations, the age of the patient is the most relevant reason that would alert the pharmacist in this specific case.

89. **Answer d)**: Pseudoephedrine is a restricted drug and due to its potential use in the illicit production of methamphetamine, there are specific regulations governing its sale and distribution. It is commonly found in over-the-counter cold and allergy medications. Antibiotics are not restricted drugs in the same sense as pseudoephedrine. Prescription medications known as antidepressants are utilized for treating depression and various other mental health conditions. Prescription medications known as antipsychotics are employed for treating different mental disorders, including schizophrenia and bipolar disorder. These drugs are only provided based on a doctor's prescription but are not considered restricted drugs.

90. **Answer d)**: A severe skin rash and itching that occurred after starting a new antibiotic is an example of an adverse drug event because it is an unintended and harmful reaction caused by the medication (antibiotic). Skin rashes and itching can be a sign of an allergic reaction to the antibiotic, which can be serious and requires immediate attention from healthcare providers. Reduced blood pressure control after taking antihypertensive medication is a desired therapeutic effect, not an adverse reaction. Increased appetite following the administration of an appetite suppressant may not be the intended effect but does not pose significant harm to the patient. Enhanced mood and decreased anxiety with the use of sedative medication are expected therapeutic effects of sedatives and not adverse reactions.

Test 2: QUESTIONS

Our practice tests are designed to exactly mimic the real PTCB exam. Keep in mind, the actual exam has a time limit of 1 hour and 50 minutes. So time yourself to gain real-test experience and confidence, ensuring you are fully prepared for success.

1. **How many insulin vials will you dispense for a 120-day supply if the prescription states, "inject 12 units SC every morning and at bedtime and 6 units SC at lunch"?**
   a) 1
   b) 2
   c) 3
   d) 4

2. **Which of the following would require storage in a refrigerator?**
   a) Oral suspensions
   b) Injectables
   c) Suppositories
   d) Vaccines

3. **Which of the following should be avoided with phenelzine?**
   a) Tyramine
   b) Iodine
   c) Vitamin C
   d) Calcium

4. **What is the correct procedure for a pharmacy technician when handling a Class II controlled substance prescription that requires a refill?**
   a) Fill the prescription and inform the prescriber of a new prescription
   b) Fill the prescription and inform the patient that no further refills are allowed
   c) Do not fill the prescription, as it is not allowed to be refilled
   d) Fill the prescription and obtain approval from the state board of pharmacy for a refill

5. **What important safety information is typically found under "warnings/precautions" on a medication label?**
   a) Dosage instructions for children
   b) Special storage requirements
   c) Potential side effects and contraindications
   d) Patient-specific instructions

6. **What potential risk arises from confusing look alike and sound alike drugs?**
   a) Increased drug sales
   b) Confusion in drug marketing
   c) Medication errors leading to patient harm
   d) Improved drug packaging

7. **Which of these information is most likely to be found in the dosage form section of a medication label?**
   a) Injection
   b) Quantity in mL
   c) Generic name
   d) Intramuscular administration

8. **What is a formulary in the context of a hospital pharmacy?**
   a) A list of patients in the hospital
   b) A curated list of approved medications
   c) A record of all transactions
   d) A catalog of medical equipment

9. **Which of the following sedative-hypnotic is a benzodiazepine?**
   a) Phenobarbital
   b) Zolpidem
   c) Ritalin
   d) Lorazepam

10. **Which of the following medications is not the preferred choice to prescribe for a patient with parkinsonism?**
    a) Typical antipsychotics
    b) Atypical antipsychotics
    c) Tricyclic antidepressants
    d) Monoamine Oxidase Inhibitors

11. **A physician orders phenobarbital 80 mg for a patient. The drug is available in 20 mg/5 mL concentration. What is the dose amount in teaspoons per administration?**
    a) 1
    b) 2
    c) 3
    d) 4

12. Which controlled substance schedule encompasses medications with recognized medical use but significant potential for abuse and psychological dependence?

a) Schedule I
b) Schedule II
c) Schedule III
d) Schedule IV

13. Which of the following symptoms is an example of an adverse drug event (ADE) that should be reported and documented?

a) Temporary headache
b) Mild drowsiness
c) Improved appetite
d) Shortness of breath

14. Which of these strategies does not help to minimize the occurrence or impact of identified risks?

a) Conducting comprehensive assessments of medication dispensing processes
b) Regularly reviewing incident reports and industry best practices
c) Working based on patient requirements even when they contradict laws and regulations set by the FDA
d) Developing and implementing policies and procedures for safe medication handling

15. How does incident reporting contribute to risk management in pharmacy practices?

a) It fosters a culture of transparency and continuous improvement
b) It involves conducting regular audits and inspections
c) It reduces the likelihood of penalties or legal consequences
d) It analyzes data and identifies emerging risks within the pharmacy setting

16. What is the primary use of oral syringes in pharmacy?

a) To measure and administer injectable medications
b) To measure and administer liquid medications
c) To store medications
d) To blend different medications

17. What factors are considered in determining stock needs in a pharmacy?

a) Medication usage patterns and prescription volume
b) The pharmacy's interior design
c) The number of pharmacy employees
d) The weather forecast

18. Which of the following drugs requires monitoring of platelet levels?

a) Warfarin
b) Heparin
c) Rivaroxaban
d) Clopidogrel

19. Which of the following is a calcium channel blocker?

a) Atenolol
b) Lisinopril
c) Sildenafil
d) Amlodipine

20. The drugs that have the same active ingredient, dosage, strength and route of administration are called?

a) Superior
b) Inferior
c) Non-inferior
d) Equivalent

21. Which of the following drugs is NOT part of the U.S. Food and Drug Administration (FDA)'s Risk Evaluation and Mitigation Strategy (REMS) drug safety program?

a) Clozapine
b) Thalidomide
c) Isotretinoin
d) Methotrexate

22. Which of these does not set compliance regulatory requirements and standards to minimize risks at pharmacy practices?

a) FDA
b) DEA
c) State pharmacy boards
d) ISMP

23. Why is the "Expiration date" displayed on every medication label?

a) To indicate the total quantity of medication in the package
b) To provide the name and contact details of the dispensing pharmacy
c) To specify the appropriate storage conditions for the medication
d) To indicate the date beyond which the drug should not be used

24. What is the guiding principle for the proper disposal of medications in a pharmacy?

a) Customer convenience
b) Federal regulations
c) Cost-effectiveness
d) Pharmacy policy

25. What kind of reaction occurs if the absorption of iron from ferrous sulfate is reduced when taken with calcium medications?

a) Drug-drug interactions
b) Drug-food interactions
c) Drug-disease interactions
d) Synergistic effect

26. Which antihistamine is commonly known as Zyrtec?

a) Fexofenadine
b) Cetirizine
c) Loratadine
d) Budesonide

27. Which medication is a combination of a beta-2 agonist with an inhaled corticosteroid?

a) Advair
b) Cortef
c) Serevent
d) Flonase

28. Into which Schedule is a drug with the lowest potential for abuse classified?

a) Schedule I
b) Schedule III
c) Schedule IV
d) Schedule V

29. Which element on a medication label helps ensure the correct dosage is administered to the patient?

a) Drug name
b) Dosage form
c) Route of administration
d) Strength

30. What is the expiration date of a medication labeled as "Ibuprofen 200 mg tablets, Expiry Date: 2024-09"?

a) September 2022
b) September 2023
c) September 2024
d) September 2025

31. Which organization mandates specific documentation for managing drug recalls in a pharmacy?

a) FDA
b) WHO
c) The Joint Commission
d) CDC

32. Which federal insurance program is specifically designed for certain patient groups like the elderly?

a) Affordable Care Act
b) Medicaid
c) COBRA
d) Medicare

33. What is the term used to describe the process through which drugs move from the site of administration into the bloodstream?

a) Absorption
b) Distribution
c) Metabolism
d) Excretion

34. A medication is available in a concentration of 25 mg/5 mL. The prescribed dose for a patient is 50 mg. How many milliliters (mL) of the medication should be administered?

a) 5 mL
b) 10 mL
c) 15 mL
d) 20 mL

35. A drug has a volume of distribution (Vd) of 100 L and a clearance (Cl) of 20 L/h. What will be the half-life ($t_{1/2}$) of the drug?
a) 3.465 hours
b) 6.930 hours
c) 0.3465 hours
d) 34.65 hours

36. Which of the following drugs is classified under Schedule I, according to the DEA?
a) Methadone
b) Marijuana
c) Xanax
d) Robitussin A.C.

37. How should a medication labeled as "Diphenhydramine 50 mg/mL oral solution" be administered to the patient?
a) By intravenous injection
b) By inhalation using a nebulizer
c) By topical application
d) By mouth

38. Which of the following drugs is an antihypertensive that can be confused with an antihistamine due to their similar names?
a) Cerebyx
b) Novolog
c) Hydroxyzine
d) Hydralazine

39. In a pharmacy setting, what items should be disposed of in a red receptacle?
a) Paper waste and plastic wrappers
b) Food and drinks
c) Sharps, including needles and syringes, and any materials that may contain blood or bodily fluids
d) General trash

40. Which of the following is NOT typically considered a diabetic supply in a pharmacy setting?
a) Blood glucose monitors
b) Lancets
c) Insulin cartridges
d) Cough syrup

41. Which class of drugs increases the release and inhibits the reuptake of neurotransmitters, leading to increased alertness and focus?
a) Amphetamines
b) Methylphenidate
c) Selective Serotonin Reuptake Inhibitors (SSRIs)
d) Tricyclic Antidepressants (TCAs)

42. Which drug is a non-steroidal anti-inflammatory drug (NSAID) commonly used for pain relief and fever reduction?
a) Ibuprofen
b) Morphine
c) Diazepam
d) Fluoxetine

43. Which class of drugs does the drug "Metformin" belong to?
a) ACE Inhibitors
b) Beta-Blockers
c) Diuretics
d) Biguanides

44. What class of drugs blocks an enzyme responsible for cholesterol synthesis and enhances the liver's capability to remove cholesterol from the bloodstream?
a) Statins
b) Bile acid sequestrants
c) Fibrates
d) ACE inhibitors

45. What is a key characteristic of Schedule II drugs?
a) Schedule II drugs do not have medical use
b) Schedule II drugs pose a significant risk of abuse
c) Schedule II drugs cannot be obtained without a prescription
d) Schedule II drugs are not commonly abused

46. Which of the following insulin brands exhibits specific onset, peak, and duration characteristics and may have specific names like Novolin N and Novolin R?
a) Humalog
b) Novolog
c) Celebrex
d) LoEstrin

47. **Which group of oral contraceptive pills is frequently miscommunicated and must not be mistaken for one another?**

a) LoEstrin, LoEstrin FE, LoLoestrin
b) Celebrex, Cerebyx
c) Humalog, Humulin
d) Novolog, Novolin

48. **What is one of the privacy laws that pharmacy technicians must adhere to?**

a) GDPR
b) COPPA
c) HIPAA
d) CAN-SPAM Act

49. **What is one type of code used by pharmacy technicians for billing and reimbursement purposes?**

a) QR codes
b) Barcodes
c) National Drug Codes (NDCs)
d) ICD-10 codes

50. **Mannitol belongs to which class of drugs?**

a) Thiazide Diuretics
b) Loop Diuretics
c) Potassium-Sparing Diuretics
d) Osmotic Diuretics

51. **Which drug is classified as an antifungal?**

a) Acyclovir
b) Valacyclovir
c) Oseltamivir
d) Fluconazole

52. **What type of drug interaction affects the absorption, distribution, metabolism, or excretion of a drug?**

a) Pharmacodynamic interactions
b) Pharmacokinetic interactions
c) Antagonism
d) Drug-food interactions

53. **Which of the following drugs is classified under Schedule III?**

a) LSD
b) Methadone
c) Ketamine
d) Amphetamine

54. **Which of the following practices is essential to prevent self-contamination when dealing with Personal Protective Equipment (PPE)?**

a) Washing hands only after doffing
b) Using PPE only once
c) Following correct procedures for donning and doffing
d) Storing used PPE for future use

55. **Which of the following is the preferred method for routine hand hygiene?**

a) Using alcohol-based hand sanitizers
b) Washing hands with soap and water for at least 20 seconds
c) Wiping hands with a dry cloth
d) Rinsing hands with water only

56. **What is generally the first step in the medication ordering process within a pharmacy?**

a) Dispensing the medication
b) Receiving payment
c) Verifying the prescription
d) Stocking shelves

57. **What factors are considered in dosage calculations for patients in a pharmacy setting?**

a) Only the patient's age
b) Only the patient's weight
c) Patient's weight, age, or condition
d) Only the patient's medical history

58. **Which drug interaction increases the risk of bleeding and is further amplified by the concomitant use of SSRIs?**

a) Antiplatelet Drugs, NSAIDs, and Anticoagulant Drugs
b) Multivalent Ions and Various Drugs
c) Nitrates and PDE5 Inhibitors
d) Beta-Blockers and Calcium Channel Blockers

59. **Which vitamin is primarily responsible for blood clotting?**

a) Vitamin A
b) Vitamin D
c) Vitamin E
d) Vitamin K

60. Which vitamin deficiency can lead to compromised hair and nail health?

a) Vitamin B1
b) Vitamin B3
c) Vitamin B7
d) Vitamin B12

61. Which of these drugs has a lower potential for abuse than drugs in Schedule III?

a) Benzphetamine
b) Codeine
c) Marijuana
d) Triazolam

62. When soap and water are unavailable, what should be used for hand hygiene?

a) Water only
b) Any available liquid
c) Alcohol-based hand sanitizers with at least 60% alcohol content
d) Hand lotions

63. After usage, how should disposable Personal Protective Equipment (PPE) be handled?

a) Reused for the next patient
b) Stored for future use
c) Disposed of according to facility guidelines
d) Washed and reused

64. What does a BMI score typically indicate in a clinical setting?

a) Patient's ability to metabolize medication
b) Patient's weight status, such as underweight, ideal weight, overweight, or obese
c) Patient's blood pressure
d) Patient's hydration level

65. What purpose do retractable syringes serve in a pharmacy setting?

a) To measure liquid medications
b) To prevent accidental needlestick injuries
c) To store medications
d) To mix different solutions

66. A patient needs a dose of 500 mg of medication. The medication is in the form of tablets, with each tablet containing 250 mg. What is the recommended number of tablets for the patient?

a) 1 tablet
b) 2 tablets
c) 3 tablets
d) 4 tablets

67. Which condition is NOT an indication for the use of angiotensin II receptor antagonists/blockers?

a) High blood pressure
b) Heart failure
c) Asthma
d) Diabetic nephropathy

68. Which cephalosporin antibiotic is present in the drug Omnicef?

a) Cephalexin
b) Ceftriaxone
c) Cefdinir
d) Cefuroxime

69. Which of the following drugs is classified under Schedule II?

a) LSD
b) Marijuana
c) Methadone
d) Ketamine

70. For hand hygiene, in what scenario are alcohol-based hand sanitizers most recommended?

a) When hands are visibly soiled
b) After potential exposure to Clostridium difficile
c) For routine hand hygiene when soap and water are not available
d) After handling chemical substances

71. Why is it important to ensure the correct fitting of Personal Protective Equipment (PPE)?

a) To look professional
b) To allow for easy movement
c) To ensure maximum protection and minimize contamination risk
d) To be able to reuse the PPE

72. What is the primary function of inhaler spacers in a pharmacy setting?

a) To store inhalers
b) To improve the delivery of medication to the lungs
c) To clean inhalers
d) To administer oral medications

73. What type of materials should be deposited in yellow receptacles in a pharmacy setting?

a)   General trash
b)   Sharps and needles
c)   Materials containing minimal amounts of chemotherapy drugs
d)   Food and drinks

74. Which two drugs are present in Vicodin?

a)   Oxycodone and Acetaminophen
b)   Hydrocodone and Ibuprofen
c)   Hydrocodone and Acetaminophen
d)   Tramadol and Naproxen

75. Which medication is classified as a selective serotonin reuptake inhibitor?

a)   Sertraline
b)   Amitriptyline
c)   Trazodone
d)   Duloxetine

76. Which of the following medicines contains Ibuprofen as its active ingredient?

a)   Bayer
b)   Tylenol
c)   Aleve
d)   Advil

77. What is the primary reason Schedule II drugs can be provided with a doctor's prescription?

a)   They have no potential for abuse
b)   They are considered medically acceptable for certain cases
c)   They have a low probability of misuse and addiction
d)   They are less dangerous than Schedule I drugs

78. What is the recommended hand hygiene method when hands are visibly soiled?

a)   Using alcohol-based hand sanitizers
b)   Washing hands with soap and water for at least 20 seconds
c)   Wiping hands with a wet cloth
d)   Rinsing hands with water only

79. Which statement is true regarding the reuse of disposable Personal Protective Equipment (PPE)?

a)   It can be reused indefinitely as long as it's not damaged
b)   It should be washed and dried before reuse
c)   It should not be reused and must be disposed of after use
d)   It can be shared among healthcare workers

80. What is a primary advantage of using unit dose packaging in healthcare settings?

a)   It saves space in the pharmacy
b)   It eliminates the need for pharmacists
c)   It helps prevent medication errors
d)   It makes medications more affordable

81. What should pharmacy technicians do if they notice discrepancies or damaged packaging upon receiving medication deliveries?

a)   Ignore it and proceed with stocking
b)   Communicate the issues to the vendor for resolution
c)   Dispose of the damaged items immediately
d)   Adjust the price and sell them as-is

82. What is the generic name for the drug NovoLog?

a)   Insulin Aspart
b)   Metformin
c)   Glipizide
d)   Sitagliptin

83. Ciprofloxacin is an example of which type of drug?

a)   Macrolide
b)   Fluoroquinolone
c)   Penicillin
d)   Cephalosporin

84. What is the generic name of Viagra?

a)   Tadalafil
b)   Sildenafil
c)   Vardenafil
d)   Prednisolone

85. What is the potential risk associated with taking SSRIs, such as fluoxetine or sertraline, in combination with tramadol?

a)   Increased risk of liver damage
b)   Increased risk of gastrointestinal bleeding
c)   Increased risk of serotonin syndrome
d)   Increased risk of allergic reactions

86. Which of the following drugs is classified under Schedule IV?

a) Methamphetamine
b) Fentanyl
c) Clonazepam
d) Ecstasy

87. For effective hand hygiene, how long should you wash your hands with soap and water?

a) 5 seconds
b) 10 seconds
c) 20 seconds
d) 1 minute

88. Do Look and sound alike drugs (LASA drugs) always have the same mechanisms of action within the body?

a) Yes, always
b) No, they often have distinct mechanisms of action
c) They always have similar side effects
d) They are always used for the same medical conditions

89. Which electronic systems are commonly used by pharmacy technicians for efficient and error-free order processing?

a) Social media platforms
b) Computerized order entry systems or electronic data interchange (EDI)
c) Gaming consoles
d) Video conferencing tools

90. Which drug, when taken with Aminoglycosides, can heighten the risk of kidney damage?

a) Calcium Channel Blockers
b) Loop diuretic
c) Thiazides
d) ACE inhibitors

Test 2: ANSWERS

1. **Answer d)**: To calculate the number of insulin vials needed for a 120-day supply, we need to determine the total units of insulin required for the given prescription.
   12 units SC every morning + 6 units SC at lunch + 12 units SC at bedtime = 30 units per day.
   Therefore, the total units needed for a 120-day supply would be: 30 units/day × 120 days = 3600 units.
   The standard vial of insulin typically contains 1000 units.
   To calculate the number of vials needed, we divide the total units by the units per vial: 3600 units / 1000 units/vial = 3.6 vials.
   Since we cannot dispense a fraction of a vial, we need to round up to the next whole number. Therefore, the correct answer is option d. 4 vials.

2. **Answer d)**: Vaccines (Key D) generally require refrigeration for proper storage. Oral suspensions are liquid medications for oral use (Key A), injectables are medications intended for injection (Key B), and suppositories are solid medications inserted into the rectum or vagina (Key C). While some medications in these forms may require refrigeration, it is not a general requirement for all of them. For each medication, the storage recommendations from the producing company or healthcare provider should be meticulously complied with.

3. **Answer a)**: One of the most important dietary restrictions for individuals taking phenelzine or other MAOIs is the avoidance of foods and beverages high in tyramine (Key A). This is because the combination of phenelzine and tyramine can cause a sudden and dangerous rise in blood pressure, known as hypertensive crisis. The rest of the options are inappropriate.

4. **Answer c)**: When handling a Class II controlled substance prescription that requires a refill, pharmacy technicians must be aware that Class II controlled substances, according to federal requirements, cannot be refilled. Filling the prescription and then informing the prescriber of a new prescription is not the correct procedure for Class II controlled substances. While it is essential to inform the patient about the lack of refills for a Class II controlled substance, filling the prescription for a refill is not appropriate in the first place. Class II controlled substances cannot be refilled, even with approval from the state board of pharmacy. The appropriate procedure involves obtaining a new prescription from the prescriber for each dispensing.

5. **Answer c)**: The "warnings/precautions" section of the medication label contains important safety information, including potential side effects and contraindications of the medication. Dosage instructions for children may be included in the "directions for use" section of the medication label. Special storage requirements, such as refrigeration, protection from light, or avoiding moisture, are typically mentioned under the "storage requirements" section of the medication label. Patient-specific instructions, if applicable, are included in the "patient-specific instructions" section of the medication label.

6. **Answer c)**: Confusing look alike and sound alike drugs can lead to medication errors, potentially resulting in patient harm. It's vital to differentiate these drugs to ensure that patients receive the correct medication.

7. **Answer a)**: The "dosage form" section of a medication label typically provides information about the physical form in which the medication is available for administration. In this case, "Injection" refers to the medication being formulated for injection. The quantity in mL is not specific to the "dosage form" section but is more commonly found in the "quantity" section of the medication label. The generic name of the medication is usually mentioned in the "drug name" section of the medication label. Information about the route of administration, such as "intramuscular," is generally found in the "route of administration" section of the medication label.

8. **Answer b)**: In the context of a hospital pharmacy, a formulary refers to a curated list of approved medications. This practice streamlines the stocking process by eliminating the need to have multiple medications within the same therapeutic class. It also aids in reducing costs. Understanding the formulary is essential for pharmacy technicians as it helps in managing prescription

costs effectively and ensures that the medications being dispensed are approved for use within the hospital.

9. **Answer d)**: Lorazepam (Key D) is a benzodiazepine and falls under the category of sedative-hypnotic medications. Phenobarbital (Key A) is a barbiturate, not a benzodiazepine. While it is a sedative-hypnotic medication, it belongs to a different class of drugs. Zolpidem (Key B) is a non-benzodiazepine sedative-hypnotic medication, also known as a "Z-drug." It is used primarily for the short-term treatment of insomnia. Ritalin (Key C) is a stimulant drug used for the management of narcolepsy and ADHD.

10. **Answer a)**: Typical antipsychotics (Key A), also known as first-generation antipsychotics, can worsen the symptoms of parkinsonism. The rest of the options (Key B, C and D) are generally considered safer than typical antipsychotics in patients with Parkinsonism. For completeness, please note that typical antipsychotics may still be used in some cases with careful monitoring.

11. **Answer d)**: To determine how many teaspoonfuls should be given for each dose of phenobarbital, we need to calculate the volume of the medication required based on the concentration and prescribed dosage.
The concentration of phenobarbital is 20 mg/5 mL, which means that each 5 mL of the solution contains 20 mg of phenobarbital.
The prescribed dosage is 80 mg.
To find the volume of the medication required, we can set up a proportion: (20 mg / 5 mL) = (80 mg / x mL)
Cross-multiplying:
20 mg * x mL = 5 mL * 80 mg
20x = 400
x = 400 / 20
x = 20 mL
Since 1 teaspoonful is approximately equal to 5 mL, we can divide the required volume by 5 to determine the number of teaspoonfuls:
20 mL / 5 mL = 4 teaspoonfuls
Therefore, the correct answer is D.

12. **Answer b)**: Schedule II controlled substances include medications that have accepted medical uses but also have a high potential for abuse and may lead to severe physical or psychological dependence. Schedule I controlled substances are classified as having a high potential for abuse,

lacking accepted medical uses, and being considered unsafe for medical purposes. These substances are tightly regulated and not prescribed for medical purposes. Schedule III controlled substances are known for their moderate to high potential for abuse and psychological dependence. While they do have accepted medical uses, they are subject to regulations, including refill restrictions and requiring a new prescription for each dispensing. Schedule IV controlled substances possess a decreased likelihood of abuse and physical or psychological dependence in comparison to Schedule II substances. They are acknowledged to have accepted medical uses and are subject to less stringent regulations.

13. **Answer d)**: Shortness of breath is a significant symptom and is considered a severe adverse drug event that should be reported and documented immediately. It can be indicative of a severe allergic reaction or other serious adverse effects related to the medication. A temporary headache and mild drowsiness are common side effects that may occur with certain medications. Improved appetite is not a side effect.

14. **Answer c)**: It is essential for pharmacy professionals to prioritize patient safety and adhere to established laws and regulations governing medication use and patient care. Working based on patient requirements that contradict FDA regulations may put patients at risk and compromise the overall safety and quality of medication management. By conducting comprehensive assessments, pharmacy professionals can identify potential weaknesses and vulnerabilities in the medication dispensing process. Incident reports are essential tools in risk management as they capture and analyze adverse events, near misses, and medication errors. Regularly reviewing these reports helps identify patterns and trends, enabling pharmacy professionals to develop targeted interventions to prevent similar incidents from occurring in the future. By implementing developing and implementing policies, the pharmacy ensures consistency and adherence to safe practices, minimizing the occurrence of medication-related risks.

15. **Answer a)**: When incident reporting is encouraged and supported within a pharmacy setting, it creates an environment where staff members feel comfortable reporting adverse

events, near misses, and medication errors without fear of reprisal. This fosters a culture of transparency, where incidents are openly acknowledged and discussed, and accountability is encouraged. While conducting regular audits and inspections is essential for risk management, it is not the primary purpose of incident reporting. Incident reporting itself does not directly reduce the likelihood of penalties or legal consequences. While incident reporting contributes to data collection, the primary focus is on capturing and reporting incidents rather than data analysis.

16. **Answer b)**: Oral syringes are primarily used to measure and administer liquid medications. These syringes are particularly useful for patients who have difficulty swallowing or require precise dosing. They come in different sizes to accommodate various medication volumes. For pharmacy technicians, understanding how to use oral syringes correctly is essential for ensuring that patients receive the accurate dosage of their prescribed liquid medications.

17. **Answer a)**: Pharmacy technicians play a crucial role in determining stock needs by analyzing medication usage patterns and reviewing prescription volume. These assessments are important for accurate forecasting of medication needs and optimizing inventory levels. Factors such as seasonal variations, medication shortages, and patient demographics are also considered. By effectively determining stock needs, pharmacy technicians help to ensure that the pharmacy is well-equipped to meet patient demands and reduce the likelihood of medication shortages.

18. **Answer d)**: Clopidogrel (Key D) is an antiplatelet medication that inhibits the aggregation of platelets, thereby reducing the risk of blood clot formation. Warfarin (Key A) is an anticoagulant that works by inhibiting the synthesis of certain clotting factors in the liver. Monitoring of heparin therapy (Key B) is primarily done by measuring the activated partial thromboplastin time (aPTT) or anti-factor Xa levels to ensure that the therapeutic range is achieved. Rivaroxaban (Key C) is a direct oral anticoagulant (DOAC) that inhibits a specific clotting factor. It does not require routine monitoring of platelet levels but may require periodic monitoring of renal function and liver enzymes.

19. **Answer d)**: Amlodipine (Key D) is a commonly prescribed calcium channel blocker. Atenolol (Key A) is a beta-blocker that primarily affects beta receptors in the heart, reducing heart rate and blood pressure. Lisinopril (Key B) is an angiotensin-converting enzyme (ACE) inhibitor that helps manage hypertension by inhibiting the production of angiotensin II, which causes blood vessel constriction. Sildenafil is a medicine administered for the handling of conditions like erectile dysfunction and pulmonary arterial hypertension.

20. **Answer d)**: Drugs that have the same active ingredient, dosage, strength and route of administration are called equivalent drugs. They are considered to be clinically interchangeable, meaning that they can be used interchangeably without affecting the patient's outcome.

21. **Answer d)**: Methotrexate is excluded from the FDA's Risk Evaluation and Mitigation Strategy (REMS) drug safety program. The primary objective of REMS is to guarantee that the benefits of particular medications outweigh their risks, particularly when significant safety concerns are present. Clozapine is an antipsychotic and is a part of the REMS program. Thalidomide is a drug used in the treatment of cancer and is also a part of REMS. Isotretinoin used in the treatment of acne is a part of the FDA's REMS program.

22. **Answer d)**: The ISMP (Institute for Safe Medication Practices) is a non-profit organization that works towards preventing medication errors. While it provides valuable recommendations, its guidelines and alerts are not enforceable regulations or standards in the same way that directives from the FDA, DEA, or state pharmacy boards are. The Food and Drug Administration (FDA), Drug Enforcement Administration (DEA), and state pharmacy boards set compliance regulatory requirements and standards to minimize risks in pharmacy practices. They are essential for safeguarding patient welfare and reducing legal and financial liabilities.

23. **Answer d)**: The "Expiration date" displayed on every medication label indicates the specific date beyond which the drug should not be used, as its effectiveness and safety cannot be guaranteed after that date. The "Expiration date" has no relation to the total quantity of medication in the

package, pharmacy details and appropriate storage conditions.

24. **Answer b)**: The proper disposal of medications in a pharmacy is guided by federal regulations. When medications are expired, recalled, or damaged, they must be disposed of in a manner that is in accordance with these federal guidelines. Failure to adhere to these regulations could result in legal consequences for the pharmacy. Therefore, it's imperative for pharmacy technicians to understand and follow the correct disposal procedures to operate within the bounds of the law.

25. **Answer a)**: It is regarded as a drug-drug interaction when the reduction in iron absorption from ferrous sulfate is brought on by the concomitant use of calcium medicines. In this instance, the interaction between the calcium medicine and the iron supplement affects how well it is absorbed. When the effects of one medication are changed by the presence of another medication, it is known as a drug-drug interaction, which may result in decreased efficacy or increased side effects.

26. **Answer b)**: Cetirizine is an antihistamine medication commonly sold under the brand name Zyrtec. Fexofenadine is sold as Allegra, and Loratadine is sold as Claritin. Budesonide is a corticosteroid and is not an antihistamine.

27. **Answer a)**: Salmeterol + Fluticasone, sold under the brand name Advair, is a combination medication that includes a long-acting beta-2 agonist (salmeterol) and an inhaled corticosteroid (Fluticasone). Hydrocortisone is a corticosteroid but is not combined with a beta-2 agonist in Advair. Salmeterol alone (Serevent) and Fluticasone alone (Flonase) are not the correct options for the combination medication.

28. **Answer d)**: Drugs classified under Schedule V have the lowest potential for abuse compared to the other schedules. While they still have some potential for abuse, it is significantly lower than drugs in Schedules I, II, III, and IV. Schedule V drugs typically contain limited quantities of certain narcotics or controlled substances and are often used for medical purposes, such as antidiarrheal medications or cough suppressants that contain codeine in small amounts. As compared to the medications in higher schedules, they have recognized medical uses and are subject to less strict regulations and restrictions compared to drugs in higher schedules, they still necessitate a prescription for dispensing.

29. **Answer d)**: The element on a medication label that helps ensure the correct dosage is administered to the patient is the "Strength." The strength of the medication indicates the amount of active ingredient(s) present in each dosage unit, such as tablets, capsules, or milliliters of liquid. While the drug name is an important element on the medication label, it does not directly relate to ensuring the correct dosage. The dosage form and route of administration do not directly determine the correct dosage.

30. **Answer c)**: The expiration date of the medication labeled as "Ibuprofen 200 mg tablets, Expiry Date: 2024-09" is September 2024. The expiration date indicates the specific date beyond which the medication should not be used.

31. **Answer c)**: The Joint Commission mandates specific documentation that must be recorded in the event of a drug recall in a pharmacy. This includes details such as the medication's name, lot numbers, and actions taken to handle the recall. Adhering to these guidelines ensures compliance with regulations and aids in the effective management of such critical events. Proper documentation is crucial for transparency and for meeting the standards set forth by The Joint Commission.

32. **Answer d)**: Medicare is a federal insurance program that is specifically designed to provide healthcare coverage for certain patient groups, including the elderly. Unlike Medicaid, which is a joint federal and state program aimed at low-income individuals, Medicare focuses on age and specific conditions as eligibility criteria. Understanding the differences between Medicare and Medicaid is important for pharmacy technicians, as these programs often have different billing procedures and coverage limitations.

33. **Answer a)**: Absorption is the mechanism by which drugs move from their site of administration (for instance, the gastrointestinal tract or skin) into the bloodstream. During this process, the drug traverses different barriers, including cell membranes, to enter the bloodstream and ultimately reach its intended site of action. Distribution refers to the process by

which a drug is transported from the bloodstream to the various tissues and organs of the body. Metabolism, also known as biotransformation, is the process by which the body breaks down and transforms drugs into different metabolites. In the process of excretion, the drugs and their metabolites are removed or excreted from the body through various routes, such as urine, feces, sweat, and breath.

34. **Answer b)**: To calculate the volume of medication needed, we use the ratio method:
Step 1: Establish ratios: 25 mg/5 mL = 50 mg/x mL
Step 2: Multiply the means and extremes: 25 mg * x mL = 5 mL * 50 mg
Step 3: Solve for "x" algebraically: x = (5 mL * 50 mg) / 25 mg = 10 mL
Therefore, 10 mL of the medication should be administered.

35. **Answer a)**: Using the given values in the formula:
$t1/2 = 0.693 * (Vd / Cl)$
$t1/2 = 0.693 * (100 L / 20 L/h)$
$t1/2 = 0.693 * 5$
Now, calculate the value of t1/2:
$t1/2 = 3.465$ hours.

36. **Answer b)**: According to the DEA (Drug Enforcement Administration), marijuana is classified under Schedule I. According to DEA and FDA, Schedule I substances are deemed the most hazardous and currently lack any accepted medical use. Even though some states have legalized its use for medical and recreational purposes, at the federal level it remains a Schedule I substance. Methadone is classified under Schedule II. Xanax is classified under Schedule IV. Schedule IV drugs have lower chances of being abused compared to Schedule I, II, and III substances, and they have clear evidence of viable medical use. Robitussin A.C. is classified under Schedule V.

37. **Answer d)**: The medication labeled as "Diphenhydramine 50 mg/mL oral solution" should be administered to the patient by mouth as it is labeled as an "oral solution". This means the medication should be ingested or swallowed. The oral solution cannot be administered intravenously (IV) or cannot be inhaled using a nebulizer. It also cannot be applied topically.

38. **Answer d)**: Hydralazine is an antihypertensive medication that can be confused with hydroxyzine, an antihistamine, due to their similar names. It's important to distinguish between these medications to avoid adverse effects and ensure appropriate patient care.

39. **Answer c)**: In a pharmacy setting, red receptacles are designated for the disposal of sharps, including needles and syringes, as well as any materials that may contain blood or bodily fluids. These receptacles are constructed with thick plastic to prevent needle punctures. Proper disposal in these red receptacles is essential for minimizing the risk of accidental injury or exposure to hazardous materials.

40. **Answer d)**: In a pharmacy setting, diabetic supplies typically include items like blood glucose monitors, lancets, test strips, insulin pens, insulin cartridges, and insulin vials. These items are essential for monitoring blood sugar levels and administering insulin to patients with diabetes. Cough syrup is not specifically categorized as a diabetic supply, as it is not used for monitoring blood sugar levels or administering insulin.

41. **Answer a)**: Amphetamines work by augmenting the release of neurotransmitters and blocking their reuptake, leading to heightened alertness and concentration. They are often prescribed for treating disorders such as attention-deficit hyperactivity disorder (ADHD) and narcolepsy. Examples of amphetamines include amphetamine and dextroamphetamine. Methylphenidate is another CNS stimulant, similar to amphetamines. It functions by promoting the release of the neurotransmitters norepinephrine and dopamine. Methylphenidate is prescribed for ADHD and narcolepsy. SSRIs are not the correct answer in this case. While SSRIs do increase the level of serotonin by inhibiting its reuptake, they are primarily used for the treatment of depression, anxiety disorders, and obsessive-compulsive disorder. Although TCAs can affect neurotransmitter levels, they primarily block serotonin and norepinephrine reuptake. TCAs are prescribed for depression and chronic pain.

42. **Answer a)**: The correct answer is Ibuprofen. Ibuprofen is a widely used NSAID that helps reduce pain, inflammation, and fever. This medication is commonly utilized to alleviate mild to moderate pain. Morphine, an opioid analgesic, is used in the treatment of moderate or severe pain. It is not an NSAID and is not primarily indicated

for reducing inflammation or fever. Diazepam is a type of medication known as a benzodiazepine. It is used for its calming, anxiety-reducing, and muscle-relaxing effects. It is not an NSAID and is not indicated for pain relief or reducing fever. Fluoxetine, a selective serotonin reuptake inhibitor antidepressant, is not an NSAID and is not used for pain relief or for reducing fever.

43. **Answer d)**: Belonging to the class of drugs known as biguanides, metformin is frequently prescribed for the management of type 2 diabetes mellitus. Biguanides work in the body by lowering the amount of glucose produced in the liver and making the body more responsive to insulin by increasing sensitivity to insulin. ACE inhibitors are drugs used in the management of hypertension, heart failure, and specific kidney conditions. Beta-blockers are frequently prescribed for cardiovascular conditions like hypertension, angina, arrhythmias, and heart failure. Diuretics are drugs that increase urine production, aiding in lowering blood pressure and reducing fluid retention.

44. **Answer a)**: Statins function by inhibiting an enzyme crucial in cholesterol synthesis. They are drugs that help reduce cholesterol production in the liver while increasing the liver's ability to remove cholesterol from the bloodstream, making them a common choice for managing high cholesterol levels. Some examples of statins are atorvastatin, rosuvastatin and simvastatin. As for bile acid sequestrants, they belong to a class of drugs that work by binding to bile acids in the intestines, preventing their reabsorption Fibrates are a class of drugs that primarily work by reducing the production of triglycerides in the body and increasing the removal of LDL (low-density lipoprotein) molecules. ACE inhibitors are the drugs utilized for the management of hypertension, heart failure, and specific kidney conditions.

45. **Answer b)**: Schedule II drugs are characterized by the significant risk of abuse they pose due to their highly addictive nature. Despite sharing some medically acceptable uses, they differ from Schedule I drugs, which lack any recognized medical applications. Healthcare professionals can prescribe Schedule II drugs in certain cases, such as for addressing chronic pain or addiction. Nevertheless, it is crucial to emphasize that Schedule II drugs still carry a substantial potential for abuse and addiction. Obtaining these drugs without a prescription from a licensed healthcare professional is prohibited. The high potential for abuse and the risk of physical or psychological dependence underscores the importance of stringent controls and regulations surrounding Schedule II drugs.

46. **Answer b)**: Novolog is an insulin brand that exhibits specific onset, peak, and duration characteristics. It has specific formulations like Novolin N and Novolin R. Using the correct insulin formulation is crucial for effective diabetes management.

47. **Answer a)**: LoEstrin, LoEstrin FE, and LoLoestrin are oral contraceptive pills that share a common mechanism and purpose. However, they are not interchangeable and must not be mistaken for one another to ensure safe and effective birth control.

48. **Answer c)**: Pharmacy technicians are required to adhere to privacy laws like the Health Insurance Portability and Accountability Act (HIPAA). This law protects sensitive patient information and mandates that certain confidentiality measures be in place. Compliance with HIPAA is crucial not only for safeguarding patient information but also for avoiding legal ramifications that could impact the pharmacy and its employees.

49. **Answer c)**: National Drug Codes (NDCs) are used by pharmacy technicians for billing and reimbursement purposes. These codes are essential for identifying the medication being dispensed. While they may not be the only codes used, they are important for ensuring accurate billing and for facilitating reimbursement from insurance companies. Using the correct codes is vital for smooth pharmacy operations and avoiding claim rejections.

50. **Answer d)**: Mannitol belongs to the class of drugs known as osmotic diuretics. Osmotic diuretics are substances that promote urine production by generating an osmotic force within the renal tubules, thus hindering the reabsorption of water and electrolytes. Hydrochlorothiazide is an example of a diuretic known as a thiazide. It works in the kidneys' distal convoluted tubules, where it helps to inhibit the reabsorption of sodium. Furosemide, a loop diuretic, inhibits the reabsorption of sodium and chloride from the ascending loop of Henle. In contrast, Potassium-

sparing diuretics, such as spironolactone, prevent the reabsorption of sodium in the distal tubules of the kidney while retaining potassium.

51. **Answer d)**: Fluconazole is classified as an antifungal drug. It is a common medication utilized for treating fungal infections, including yeast infections, in various areas of the body. The other options, Acyclovir, Valacyclovir, and Oseltamivir, belong to the antiviral class and are prescribed for treating viral infections.

52. **Answer b)**: Pharmacokinetic interactions refer to alterations in the absorption, distribution, metabolism, or excretion of a drug. These interactions can impact the concentration and response of one or both drugs at the site of action in the body. Pharmacodynamic interactions involve alterations in the biological response of drugs without affecting their pharmacokinetics. Antagonism refers to the interference of one drug with the actions of another drug, reducing its effectiveness. Drug-food interactions happen when certain foods interfere with the absorption, metabolism, or effectiveness of medications.

53. **Answer c)**: Ketamine is a drug classified under Schedule III. Schedule III controlled substances have accepted medical uses but also possess a moderate to high potential for abuse, which may lead to physical or psychological dependence. LSD, on the other hand, is not classified under Schedule III. It is placed in the Schedule I category, denoting its absence of accepted medical applications and a heightened potential for abuse. Methadone is not categorized as Schedule III either; it is categorized as a Schedule II controlled substance owing to its considerable risk of abuse. Amphetamine is not under Schedule III; it is classified as a Schedule II controlled substance due to its stimulant properties and potential for abuse.

54. **Answer c)**: It's essential to follow the correct procedures for donning (putting on) and doffing (taking off) Personal Protective Equipment (PPE) to prevent self-contamination. Proper hand hygiene before and after these procedures, as well as the use of designated areas for PPE changes, are also crucial.

55. **Answer b)**: Washing hands with soap and water for at least 20 seconds is the preferred method for routine hand hygiene. Proper handwashing technique involves lathering all surfaces of the hands, including fingers, nails, and wrists, followed by thorough rinsing and drying.

56. **Answer c)**: The first step in the medication ordering process within a pharmacy is typically verifying the prescription. Before any medication can be dispensed, the prescription must be reviewed for accuracy and completeness. This involves checking the medication name, dosage, and directions for use, as well as confirming the identity of the prescribing physician. This crucial step ensures that patients receive the correct medication and dosage, thereby reducing the risk of medication errors.

57. **Answer c)**: Dosage calculations in a pharmacy setting involve a variety of factors, including the patient's weight, age, or condition. These factors are important for determining the appropriate dosage of medication to be administered. Proportions are used as a framework to compare different quantities and find the correct ratio between them. By considering these factors, pharmacy technicians can accurately calculate dosages, thereby reducing the risk of medication errors or adverse effects.

58. **Answer a)**: When taken individually, antiplatelet drugs, NSAIDs, and anticoagulant drugs increase the risk of bleeding. When combined, the risk of bleeding becomes even more pronounced. Moreover, the simultaneous use of selective serotonin reuptake inhibitors (SSRIs) intensifies the risk of bleeding. Multivalent ions, such as those found in milk, antacids, calcium, magnesium, and iron, can interact with certain medications and diminish their efficacy. However, this does not specifically increase the risk of bleeding or involve the concomitant use of SSRIs. The combination of nitrates and PDE5 inhibitors, such as sildenafil and tadalafil, can lead to severe hypotension due to their respective hypotensive effects. While this interaction poses a risk, it does not specifically increase the risk of bleeding or involve the concomitant use of SSRIs. The combination of beta-blockers (e.g., metoprolol) with calcium channel blockers (e.g., verapamil, diltiazem) can increase the risk of heart failure and bradycardia (reduced heart rate). However, it does not specifically increase the risk of bleeding or involve the concomitant use of SSRIs.

59. **Answer d)**: Vitamin K plays a critical role in the coagulation cascade as it is vital for the synthesis of blood clotting factors. Its primary function is to promote proper blood clotting and prevent excessive bleeding. Insufficient levels of vitamin K can lead to bleeding disorders and an elevated risk of uncontrolled bleeding. Vitamin A is not primarily responsible for blood clotting. It plays a vital role in vision, skeletal growth, and the regulation of mucous membranes. Vitamin D is not primarily responsible for blood clotting. It helps in the absorption of calcium and phosphorus ions and is involved in bone and teeth formation. Vitamin E primarily acts as an antioxidant, protecting cells from damage caused by free radicals, and is not directly involved in blood clotting.

60. **Answer c)**: Vitamin B7, commonly referred to as biotin, plays a crucial role in preserving the health of hair and nails. A deficiency of biotin can lead to brittle nails, thinning hair, and hair loss. Vitamin B1, also known as thiamine, is essential for converting food into energy and maintaining proper nerve function. Vitamin B3, commonly referred to as niacin, plays a crucial role in the body by aiding in energy production, facilitating DNA repair, and contributing to the synthesis of diverse compounds in the body. Insufficient niacin levels can result in a condition known as pellagra, which is marked by symptoms like skin rashes, digestive issues, and mental impairment. Vitamin B12, also known as cobalamin, is important for red blood cell production, nervous system function, and DNA synthesis. While it is vital to overall health, vitamin B12 deficiency is not directly associated with compromised hair and nail health.

61. **Answer d)**: Triazolam is classified as a Schedule IV controlled substance, indicating that it has a lower potential for abuse and a lower risk of dependence compared to drugs in Schedule III. Benzphetamine is classified as a Schedule III controlled substance. Codeine is classified as a Schedule II controlled substance. Schedule II drugs have a higher potential for abuse compared to drugs in Schedule III. Marijuana is classified as a Schedule I controlled substance which has a high potential of being abused.

62. **Answer c)**: In situations where soap and water are not accessible, it is recommended to utilize alcohol-based hand sanitizers containing a minimum of 60% alcohol. These sanitizers are effective in reducing microbial contamination and should be applied to dry hands following proper technique.

63. **Answer c)**: Disposable Personal Protective Equipment (PPE) should be disposed of according to facility guidelines after its usage. It's essential to ensure that used PPE doesn't pose a contamination risk to the environment or other individuals.

64. **Answer b)**: In a clinical setting, Body Mass Index (BMI) scores are used to assess a person's weight status. The categories include underweight, ideal weight, overweight, and obese. BMI is calculated using the formula BMI = weight in kg: height in m2. Knowing how to interpret these scores is important for clinicians and pharmacy technicians alike, as it can influence the selection and dosing of medications.

65. **Answer b)**: Retractable syringes are designed to prevent accidental needlestick injuries in a pharmacy setting. These syringes have a safety mechanism that allows the needle to retract into the barrel after use, minimizing the risk of accidental puncture. The use of safety devices like retractable syringes enhances workplace safety and is an important aspect of maintaining a safe environment for both pharmacy staff and patients.

66. **Answer b)**: To determine the required quantity of tablets, dimensional analysis can be employed as a calculation method. The formula is Dose ordered (D) × Quantity (Q) / supply on hand (H) = dose.
Given:
Dose ordered (D) = 500 mg
Quantity (Q) = unknown (let's call it X)
Supply on hand (H) = 250 mg (strength of each tablet)
Using the formula, we can set up the equation:
500 mg × X / 250 mg = 500 mg
Cross-multiplying, we have:
500 mg × X = 250 mg × 500 mg
Simplifying, we get:
X = 250 mg × 500 mg / 500 mg
Canceling out the units, we find:
X = 250 mg
Therefore, the patient needs 2 tablets (250 mg each).

67. **Answer c)**: Angiotensin II receptor antagonists/blockers are indicated for the treatment of high blood pressure, heart failure, and

diabetic nephropathy. However, they are not typically used in the management of asthma. So, options a, b and d are incorrect.

68. **Answer c)**: Cefdinir is the cephalosporin antibiotic present in the drug Omnicef. Cefdinir is prescribed to treat a range of bacterial infections such as infections in the respiratory tract. Cephalexin is present in Keflex. Ceftriaxone is present in Rocephin. Cefuroxime is present in Ceftin.

69. **Answer c)**: Methadone is classified under Schedule II, has a high potential for abuse and accepted medical use, and is subject to strict regulations and restrictions. LSD (Lysergic acid diethylamide) is classified under Schedule I, not Schedule II. Marijuana is not categorized as a Schedule II substance; instead, it remains listed as a Schedule I controlled substance by the federal government. Similarly, Ketamine is not classified as a Schedule II drug; it is classified as a Schedule III controlled substance by the DEA.

70. **Answer c)**: When soap and water aren't available, alcohol-based hand sanitizers are the preferred option for routine hand hygiene. They are effective in reducing microbial contamination but are not suitable for hands that are visibly soiled or after potential exposure to certain pathogens like Clostridium.

71. **Answer c)**: Ensuring the correct fitting of Personal Protective Equipment (PPE) is crucial to provide maximum protection to the wearer and minimize the risk of contamination. Ill-fitting PPE might not offer complete protection and could be a source of contamination.

72. **Answer b)**: Inhaler spacers, or holding chambers, are used with inhalers to improve the delivery of medication to the lungs. These devices help patients coordinate their inhalation, ensuring that the medication is efficiently delivered to the respiratory system. For pharmacy technicians, understanding the utility of inhaler spacers is important, as it aids in patient education and ensures effective drug administration.

73. **Answer c)**: In a pharmacy setting, yellow receptacles are designated for the disposal of materials containing minimal amounts of chemotherapy drugs. These specialized containers are part of waste segregation measures that ensure the safe and compliant disposal of hazardous waste. Understanding the purpose and usage of

different colored receptacles, such as the yellow one, is crucial for pharmacy technicians to maintain a safe and compliant work environment.

74. **Answer c)**: Hydrocodone and Acetaminophen are the two drugs present in Vicodin. Vicodin is an Opioid Analgesic and has these two drugs to provide relief from moderate to severe pain. Oxycodone, Ibuprofen, tramadol and naproxen are not present in Vicodin.

75. **Answer a)**: Sertraline, marketed as Zoloft, is classified as a selective serotonin reuptake inhibitor (SSRI). SSRIs function by elevating serotonin levels in the brain, aiding in mood regulation and alleviating symptoms of certain mental health conditions like depression and anxiety. Amitriptyline is a tricyclic antidepressant (TCA) used for depression, while Trazodone is a serotonin antagonist and reuptake inhibitor (SARI) often prescribed for insomnia and depression. Duloxetine is an example of a serotonin-norepinephrine reuptake inhibitor (SNRI) and is prescribed to treat major depressive disorder and chronic pain conditions.

76. **Answer d)**: Ibuprofen, a non-steroidal anti-inflammatory drug (NSAID), is the active ingredient in Advil. NSAIDs, or non-steroidal anti-inflammatory drugs, are broadly utilized pharmaceuticals that help in soothing pain, decreasing inflammation, and reducing high fever. Bayer contains aspirin as its active ingredient, while Tylenol contains acetaminophen. The active ingredient in Aleve is naproxen sodium.

77. **Answer b)**: The primary reason Schedule II drugs can be provided with a doctor's prescription is that they are considered medically acceptable for certain cases. Schedule II drugs are characterized by their high potential for abuse, making them dangerous substances. However, they are not without medical merit as they do have recognized medical applications. Schedule II drugs do have a high potential for abuse, which is why they are subject to stringent regulations and closely monitored. They are considered to be among the most addictive and potentially harmful substances. Schedule II drugs are not less dangerous than Schedule I drugs; they are both considered highly dangerous and subject to strict control and regulation.

78. **Answer b)**: When hands are visibly soiled, it is recommended to wash hands with soap and water

for at least 20 seconds. Alcohol-based hand sanitizers may not be as effective on visibly dirty hands. Proper handwashing removes dirt and reduces microbial contamination.

79. **Answer c)**: Disposable Personal Protective Equipment (PPE) is designed for one-time use and should not be reused. Reusing disposable PPE can compromise its effectiveness and increase the risk of contamination. After use, it should be disposed of according to facility guidelines.

80. **Answer c)**: Unit dose packaging provides individually sealed doses of medications that are ready for administration. This type of packaging is designed to help prevent medication errors by ensuring that each dose is individually labeled and sealed. It is particularly useful in healthcare settings like hospitals, where medication errors can have severe consequences. For pharmacy technicians, understanding the advantages of unit dose packaging can aid in patient education and contribute to safer medication practices.

81. **Answer b)**: Upon receiving medication deliveries, pharmacy technicians are responsible for inspecting and verifying the accuracy and condition of the items. If they notice any discrepancies, damaged packaging, or expired products, these issues should be promptly communicated to the vendor for resolution. This is a crucial step in the pharmacy workflow to ensure that only quality medications are stocked and dispensed to patients.

82. **Answer a)**: The generic name for NovoLog is Insulin Aspart. NovoLog is prescribed as a rapid-acting insulin to reduce the levels of blood sugar in patients who have diabetes. Administered through subcutaneous injection, it aids in regulating glucose metabolism. Metformin is an oral medication used to manage type 2 diabetes. Glipizide is an oral medication from the sulfonylurea class used to lower blood sugar levels. Sitagliptin is an oral medication to enhance insulin production and reduce blood sugar levels in individuals with type 2 diabetes.

83. **Answer b)**: Ciprofloxacin is an example of Fluoroquinolone. Fluoroquinolones are a category of antibiotics recognized for their wide-ranging effectiveness against a variety of bacterial infections. Macrolides, such as azithromycin and erythromycin, are a class of antibiotics. Penicillin is a beta-lactam antibiotic, while cephalosporins are a related group of antibiotics, both of which have a different mechanism of action compared to fluoroquinolones.

84. **Answer b)**: The generic name of Viagra is Sildenafil. Sildenafil, classified as a phosphodiesterase type 5 (PDE5) inhibitor, is a medication primarily employed to treat erectile dysfunction in men. By improving blood flow to the penis, it allows for the attainment of a strong and long-lasting erection. Tadalafil and vardenafil are also PDE5 inhibitors used to treat ED, marketed under the brand names Cialis and Levitra, respectively. Prednisolone, sold under the brand names Prelone and Flo-Pred, is not a phosphodiesterase type 5 (PDE5) inhibitor. Instead, it belongs to the class of corticosteroids.

85. **Answer c)**: Taking SSRIs like fluoxetine or sertraline in combination with tramadol can potentially increase the risk of a rare syndrome known as serotonin syndrome. Serotonin syndrome is a life-threatening condition, results from elevated levels of serotonin in the body. Taking SSRIs like fluoxetine or sertraline in combination with tramadol does not typically increase the risk of liver damage. There is a potential risk of gastrointestinal bleeding when combining SSRIs with certain medications like non-steroidal anti-inflammatory drugs (NSAIDs) or anticoagulants. Tramadol, although it can have analgesic properties, is not specifically associated with an increased risk of gastrointestinal bleeding when used in combination with SSRIs. While both SSRIs and tramadol can individually cause allergic reactions in some individuals, the combination of these two medications does not necessarily increase the risk of allergic reactions beyond what is typically associated with each medication.

86. **Answer c)**: The drug classified under Schedule IV is Clonazepam. Methamphetamine is not classified under Schedule IV. It is categorized as a Schedule II controlled substance due to its high potential for abuse and limited medical use. Fentanyl is also classified under Schedule II. Ecstasy, also known as MDMA, is not classified under Schedule IV either. It is categorized as a Schedule I controlled substance.

87. **Answer c)**: For effective hand hygiene, it is recommended to wash hands with soap and water for at least 20 seconds. This length of time

facilitates a comprehensive cleansing of all hand surfaces, including the back, interdigital spaces, subungual areas, and wrists. Effective handwashing is vital in preventing the spread of infections.

88. **Answer b)**: Despite sharing commonalities in names, Look and sound alike drugs (LASA drugs) often have distinct mechanisms of action within the body. This distinction is crucial to ensure appropriate medication use.

89. **Answer b)**: Pharmacy technicians often use electronic systems such as computerized order entry systems or electronic data interchange (EDI) for efficient and error-free order processing. These systems streamline the ordering process, ensuring accurate communication of orders to vendors, including delivery timelines and special requirements. Utilizing these electronic systems helps in reducing manual errors and enhances the overall efficiency of the pharmacy's operations.

90. **Answer b)**: Combining aminoglycosides (e.g., Gentamicin, amikacin) with loop diuretics (e.g., furosemide) increases the risk of ototoxicity damage to the inner ear (causing hearing loss or balance problems) and kidney damage. Calcium channel blockers, thiazides and ACE inhibitors are not known or associated with an increase in the risk of kidney damage when taken with aminoglycosides.

Test 3: QUESTIONS

Our practice tests are designed to exactly mimic the real PTCB exam. Keep in mind, the actual exam has a time limit of 1 hour and 50 minutes. So time yourself to gain real-test experience and confidence, ensuring you are fully prepared for success.

1. **Which drug class do medicines with the prefix -olol belong to?**

a) Beta-blockers
b) Diuretics
c) Nitrates
d) ACE inhibitors

2. **What are the characteristics of the sublingual route of drug administration?**

a) The drug is absorbed through the stomach lining and enters the systemic circulation slowly
b) It bypasses the first-pass effect and offers a quick onset of action, suitable for self-administration
c) It is suitable for all types of drugs and does not cause taste and compliance issues
d) The drug is absorbed through the skin, providing a gradual and continuous release

3. **Which route of administration targets specific conditions or infections in the ear?**

a) Topical route
b) Otic route
c) Ocular route
d) Inhalation route

4. **What distinguishes Schedule IV drugs from Schedule III drugs?**

a) Schedule IV drugs are more dangerous
b) Schedule IV drugs are only available over-the-counter
c) Schedule IV drugs have a lower potential for abuse
d) Schedule IV drugs have no medical use

5. **What is the purpose of the Poison Prevention Packaging Act (PPPA)?**

a) To require child-resistant packaging for all medications
b) To minimize the risk of accidental poisoning among adults
c) To ensure compliance with prescription drug regulations
d) To require child-resistant packaging for certain drugs to protect children from accidental poisoning

6. **What is the first step in the process of risk management in a pharmacy setting?**

a) Risk Minimization and Prevention: After assessing risks, strategies are implemented to minimize their occurrence or impact. This comprises the development and enforcement of policies and protocols that foster the safe management, storage, and administration of medications
b) Following the analysis, proper corrective measures are implemented to ensure that similar incidents do not happen in the future
c) This involves considering the severity of potential consequences, the probability of risks materializing, and the existing control measures in place
d) Risk Identification: The first step is identifying potential risks and hazards within the pharmacy setting

7. **Which of the following is an essential component of aseptic technique?**

a) Using expired medications
b) Avoiding hand hygiene
c) Preventing contamination of sterile items
d) Reusing single-use items

8. **What is crucial when storing medications in a pharmacy setting?**

a) Storing all drugs at room temperature
b) Storing drugs based on their colors
c) Following manufacturer's guidelines for storage conditions
d) Storing all drugs in a refrigerator

9. What information should pharmacy technicians confirm when verifying a patient's insurance coverage?

a) Patient's favorite color
b) Patient's pet's name
c) Insurance provider, policy number, and coverage dates
d) Patient's shopping preferences

10. Where in the pharmacy are thermometers commonly used to monitor medication storage conditions?

a) Only in freezers
b) Only on storage shelves
c) In storage shelves, refrigerators, freezers, and warming cabinets
d) Only in refrigerators

11. Which route of administration allows for self-administration and is particularly suitable for drugs with a long duration of action?

a) Intravenous route
b) Intramuscular route
c) Subcutaneous route
d) Intradermal route

12. Which type of medications have a higher potential for abuse and are subject to strict regulations?

a) Hazardous medications
b) Controlled substances
c) Compounded medications
d) Special packaging and labeling medications

13. Which of the following is a common side effect of furosemide?

a) Increased urination
b) Muscle cramps
c) Weight gain
d) Blurred vision

14. Which of the following is an example of child-resistant packaging under the Poison Prevention Packaging Act (PPPA)?

a) Bottles with easy-to-open caps
b) Single-use syringes
c) Blister packs
d) Medication vials with standard screw caps

15. In the context of pharmacy, what does 'compounding' refer to?

a) Counting tablets for a prescription
b) Recommending over-the-counter medications
c) Mixing or altering ingredients to create a medication tailored to an individual patient
d) Checking drug interactions

16. Why is it essential to avoid using medications past their expiration date?

a) Expired drugs become more potent
b) Pharmacies can charge more for expired medications
c) Expired drugs may lose potency and might not be safe or effective
d) There's no real reason; expiration dates are just guidelines

17. For what types of patients are oral syringes particularly useful?

a) Patients with difficulty swallowing
b) Patients who prefer tablets
c) Patients who require intravenous medication
d) Patients with no specific needs

18. What factors do pharmacy technicians consider when assessing stock requirements?

a) The color of the medication
b) Seasonal variations, medication shortages, and patient demographics
c) The popularity of the medication
d) The manufacturer's marketing strategies

19. Which medication class can potentially cause cardiac arrhythmias and prolonged Q.T. interval?

a) Nitroglycerin
b) Antihypertensives
c) Antiarrhythmics
d) Niacin

20. Which medication class is commonly associated with persistent cough as a side effect?

a) Angiotensin-converting enzyme (ACE) inhibitors
b) Opioids
c) Sedatives
d) Non-steroidal anti-inflammatory drugs (NSAIDs)

21. **What severe adverse effect can arise due to bone marrow suppression?**

a) Easy bruising or bleeding
b) Aplastic anemia
c) Agranulocytosis
d) Decreased platelet function

22. **What is the purpose of Risk Minimization Action Plans (RiskMAPs) for medications?**

a) To restrict access to medications for specific patient populations
b) To manage known or potential risks associated with a medication
c) To reduce the cost of medications for patients
d) To expedite the approval process for new medications

23. **Which of the following can be a potential consequence of medication errors?**

a) Increased pharmaceutical company profits
b) Improved patient-healthcare provider relationship
c) Adverse drug reactions or even patient harm
d) Faster recovery times for patients

24. **What is a drug interaction?**

a) The cost of a medication
b) A reaction between two drugs leading to decreased or increased drug effects
c) The process of compounding medications
d) A side effect experienced by a patient

25. **What types of medications typically require disposal?**

a) All medications after one year
b) Only over-the-counter medications
c) Medications that are expired, recalled, or damaged
d) Only antibiotics

26. **How are expired or damaged medications typically managed in a pharmacy setting?**

a) Given away as free samples
b) Properly disposed of according to federal regulations
c) Sold at discounted prices
d) Returned to the manufacturer for a refund

27. **What is the target International Normalized Ratio (INR) range for patients on warfarin therapy?**

a) 1.0-2.0
b) 2.0-3.0
c) 3.0-4.0
d) 4.0-5.0

28. **What role do pharmacy technicians play in the management of NTI medications?**

a) Counseling patients about potential side effects
b) Reporting adverse effects to healthcare providers
c) Double-checking prescriptions and ensuring accurate dispensing
d) Monitoring blood levels and dosage adjustments

29. **What are the key considerations for sterile compounding?**

a) Monitoring patient allergies during the compounding process
b) Cleaning and disinfection of the cleanroom
c) Adjusting dosages based on patient requirements
d) Using specialized equipment for compounding

30. **Which statement about Risk Minimization Action Plans (RiskMAPs) is true?**

a) RiskMAPs focus on improving the availability of medications to a wider population
b) RiskMAPs implement standard labeling and prescribing information for medications
c) RiskMAPs require patients to undergo counseling to understand the benefits of medications
d) RiskMAPs are designed to manage known or potential risks by implementing additional safety measures beyond standard labeling and prescribing information

31. **Why is medication adherence important for patients?**

a) To ensure that pharmacies make profits
b) To avoid interactions with food
c) To ensure the effectiveness of the medication and achieve the desired therapeutic outcomes
d) To reduce the number of medications a patient has to take

32. In a pharmacy setting, why is prescription verification essential?

a) To market new drugs to patients
b) To ensure the patient receives the correct medication and dose
c) To promote over-the-counter medications
d) To assess the financial status of a patient

33. What is one essential consideration when disposing of medical materials in a pharmacy?

a) All waste can be categorized as hazardous
b) Medical waste should be separated from common waste
c) All expired medications can be donated
d) Medical waste can be disposed of in regular trash bins

34. What type of equipment is commonly used for administering oral liquid medications?

a) Nebulizer
b) Oral syringe
c) IV drip
d) Autoinjector

35. What types of medications are typically prepared through sterile compounding?

a) Creams and ointments
b) Tablets and capsules
c) Intravenous injections and intramuscular injections
d) Over-the-counter medications

36. Which organization provides guidelines for non-sterile compounding?

a) United States Pharmacopeia (USP)
b) Food and Drug Administration (FDA)
c) Centers for Disease Control and Prevention (CDC)
d) World Health Organization (WHO)

37. What are the recommended steps in the compounding process for non-sterile medications?

a) Formula creation, preparation, ingredient measurement, mixing and blending, documentation and labeling
b) Sanitization, ingredient quality and compatibility, packaging and labeling, accurate measuring and compounding techniques

c) Clean environment, ingredient quality and compatibility, accurate measuring and compounding techniques, packaging and labeling
d) Equipment acquisition, mixing and blending, formula creation, documentation and labeling, ingredient measurement

38. What are the three categories of recalls for medical devices established by the U.S. Food and Drug Administration (FDA)?

a) Category A, Category B, Category C
b) Class I, Class II, Class III
c) High Risk, Moderate Risk, Low Risk
d) Major Recall, Minor Recall, Voluntary Recall

39. Which piece of information is NOT typically found on a drug label?

a) The manufacturer's marketing strategy
b) Active ingredients
c) Recommended dosage
d) Potential side effects

40. Why is it important to store certain medications at specific temperatures?

a) To alter the medication's color
b) To ensure the medication remains effective and stable
c) To increase the medication's shelf life beyond the expiration date
d) To change the medication's taste

41. What is the primary goal of effective inventory management in a pharmacy?

a) To ensure customer loyalty
b) To minimize cost while maintaining an adequate supply of medications
c) To maximize profits by overstocking medications
d) To advertise new medications

42. What role do pharmacological calculations play in ensuring effective treatment?

a) They help in marketing the medication
b) They ensure the patient receives the appropriate dosage
c) They extend the shelf life of the medication
d) They make the medication more affordable

43. Which type of formulation is commonly used as a base for topical creams?

a) Mixtures
b) Liquids
c) Emulsions
d) Suppositories

44. What role do excipients play in drug incompatibilities?

a) They enhance the stability and solubility of drugs
b) They can cause the chemical decomposition of drugs
c) They affect the solubility of drugs in the chosen vehicle or diluent
d) They interact with the materials used in containers, affecting drug stability

45. What is the generic name of the drug Plavix?

a) Ezetimibe
b) Heparin
c) Clopidogrel
d) Methimazole

46. Which classification of recall involves medical devices that pose a significant risk of serious harm or death to the patient?

a) Class I
b) Class II
c) Class III
d) Class IV

47. Why is proper disposal of unused or expired medications important?

a) To make space for new medications
b) To prevent potential harm and environmental contamination
c) To allow pharmacies to resell the medication
d) To change the appearance of the medication

48. Which of the following is a primary concern when considering medication safety?

a) Maximizing profit for pharmacies
b) Ensuring patient adherence to over-the-counter supplements
c) Reducing the risk of medication errors and patient harm
d) Promoting new and experimental drugs

49. Which of the following is NOT a common type of medication package for storage?

a) Bottles
b) Vials
c) Blister packs
d) Cardboard boxes

50. What is the most critical factor for storing temperature-sensitive medications?

a) Light
b) Moisture
c) Temperature
d) Height

51. Which medication belongs to the class of benzodiazepines?

a) Lorazepam
b) Zolpidem
c) Guaifenesin
d) Dextromethorphan

52. Through which route is route Gentamicin excreted from the body?

a) Urine
b) Bile
c) Feces
d) Exhaled air

53. Through which route is the drug Erythromycin excreted from the body?

a) Urine
b) Bile
c) Feces
d) Exhaled air

54. What does a recall strategy for medical devices include?

a) Identifying affected parties only
b) Implementing corrective actions only
c) Outlining actions to be taken, identifying affected devices, notifying affected parties, and implementing corrective actions
d) Sending a letter to the FDA informing them about the recall

55. Why is handwashing considered a crucial practice in a pharmacy setting?

a) To avoid smudging prescription labels
b) To maintain personal aesthetics
c) To prevent the spread of germs and reduce the risk of contamination
d) To improve grip on medication bottles

56. What is the primary purpose of using Personal Protective Equipment (PPE) in a pharmacy?

a) To showcase the latest fashion trends
b) To identify staff members
c) To protect the staff from potential hazards and contamination
d) To promote brand loyalty

57. Which material is NOT commonly used for medication packaging?

a) Glass
b) Plastic
c) Metal
d) Wood

58. What is generally NOT a concern when storing medications?

a) Temperature
b) Moisture
c) Light
d) Color of the storage area

59. Which of these drugs can lead to tooth discoloration in infants when taken by a lactating mother?

a) Ibuprofen
b) Acetaminophen
c) Tetracycline
d) Aspirin

60. Which of the following medications is available over-the-counter (OTC) without a prescription?

a) Amoxicillin
b) Prednisone
c) Loratadine
d) Simvastatin

61. Which of these is true about over-the-counter (OTC) medications in the United States?

a) There are approximately 50 classes of OTC medications available
b) OTC medications are only suitable for minor health concerns
c) OTC medications require a doctor's prescription for purchase
d) The U.S. market has over 80 classes of OTC medications

62. Who can initiate a recall for a defective medical device?

a) Healthcare professionals
b) Patients
c) Manufacturer or distributor
d) Insurance companies

63. What is the generic name of the drug Zyprexa?

a) Risperidone
b) Quetiapine
c) Olanzapine
d) Clozapine

64. Why is maintaining equipment hygiene essential in a pharmacy?

a) To increase the lifespan of the equipment
b) To prevent contamination and ensure safe medication preparation and dispensing
c) To make the equipment look more appealing
d) To reduce electricity consumption

65. Which factor is NOT commonly considered in dosage calculations?

a) Patient weight
b) Patient age
c) Type of medication
d) Time of day

66. What is the primary purpose of using proportions in dosage calculations for pharmacy technicians?

a) To calculate the shelf life of medications
b) To determine the appropriate dosage based on various factors like weight, age, or condition
c) To find the cost of medications
d) To identify possible drug interactions

67. A nurse needs to administer 2.5 liters of intravenous (IV) fluid to a patient. The IV fluid bags available in the stock are 500 mL each. What is the quantity of IV fluid bags required by the nurse?

a) 3 bags
b) 4 bags
c) 5 bags
d) 6 bags

68. A patient requires a continuous intravenous (IV) infusion of medication at a rate of 1.5 mg/min. The available medication concentration is 4 mg/mL. What should be the infusion rate that the nurse needs to set for the IV pump?
a) 15 mL/h
b) 22.5 mL/h
c) 30 mL/h
d) 45 mL/h

69. Which drug class does alprazolam belong to?
a) Antidepressants
b) Antihistamines
c) Benzodiazepines
d) Methylphenidate

70. What is the main purpose of the Medical Device Reporting (MDR) system?
a) To monitor and evaluate the safety and performance of medical devices
b) To request recalls from manufacturers
c) To conduct audits for verification of compliance
d) To retrieve defective devices from healthcare facilities

71. What is the primary goal of adhering to hygiene and cleaning standards in a pharmacy?
a) To create a pleasant aroma in the pharmacy
b) To ensure a visually appealing environment
c) To prevent the spread of infections and ensure the safe preparation of medications
d) To reduce the need for equipment maintenance

72. Which of the following is NOT typically considered as Personal Protective Equipment (PPE) in a pharmacy setting?
a) Face mask
b) Stethoscope
c) Gloves
d) Safety goggles

73. What is the purpose of the Drug Enforcement Administration (DEA) number on a prescription?
a) To indicate the expiry date of the medication
b) To prevent illicit use and ensure appropriate oversight of controlled substances
c) To specify the manufacturer of the medication
d) To indicate the retail price of the medication

74. How is the concentration of a medication typically expressed in pharmacology calculations?
a) Milliliters per gram
b) Milligrams per milliliter
c) Pounds per gallon
d) Inches per meter

75. To which drug class does Valsartan belong?
a) Beta-blockers
b) Calcium channel blockers
c) Angiotensin-converting enzyme (ACE) inhibitors
d) Angiotensin II receptor blockers (ARBs)

76. For which of these conditions can beta-blockers be prescribed?
a) Asthma
b) Severe Bradycardia
c) Heart block
d) Hypertension

77. To which class of drugs does Diltiazem belong?
a) Beta-blockers
b) Calcium channel blockers
c) Angiotensin-converting enzyme (ACE) inhibitors
d) Angiotensin II receptor blockers (ARBs)

78. What role do pharmacy technicians play in the prescription filling?
a) Providing patient-specific packages
b) Assisting with placing inventory orders
c) Compounding medications from scratch
d) Sanitizing and stocking equipment in the pharmacy

79. Which of the following best describes the main reason for rigorous handwashing in a pharmacy setting?
a) To achieve a pleasant scent
b) To pass time between tasks
c) To prevent contamination and ensure medication safety
d) To improve skin texture

80. Which element on a medication label provides instructions for proper medication administration, including dosage and frequency?

a) Patient-specific instructions
b) Directions for use
c) Pharmacy information
d) Storage requirements

81. What is a key characteristic of Look and sound alike drugs (LASA drugs)?

a) They have similar colors and shapes
b) They have resemblances in both brand and generic names
c) They are always over-the-counter medications
d) They have the same mechanisms of action within the body

82. When diluting a medication to a specific concentration, what do pharmacy technicians often need to calculate?

a) The volume of the stock solution and the diluent required
b) The color of the medication
c) The retail price of the medication
d) The taste of the medication

83. To which drug class do drugs with the suffix "prazole" belong?

a) Antacids
b) Prokinetic agents
c) Proton pump inhibitors
d) Laxatives

84. Which group of patients should be cautious when using mineralocorticoids?

a) Patients with asthma
b) Patients with rheumatoid arthritis
c) Patients with congestive heart failure
d) Patients with diabetes

85. Which of these medications should be avoided in individuals with a penicillin allergy?

a) Ampicillin
b) Ceftriaxone
c) Azithromycin
d) Ciprofloxacin

86. How does the Drug Quality and Security Act (DQSA) impact the role of pharmacy technicians in enhancing the safety and security of the pharmaceutical supply chain?

a) It grants pharmacy technicians the authority to inspect facilities and enforce compliance with quality standards
b) It requires pharmacy technicians to regulate compounding practices and distinguish between traditional compounding and manufacturing
c) It establishes tracing, serialization, and verification systems for pharmacy technicians to prevent counterfeit drugs
d) It introduces outsourcing facilities subject to FDA oversight, allowing pharmacy technicians to monitor and manage the pharmaceutical supply chain

87. Why should individuals taking statins be cautious when consuming grapefruit juice?

a) It can decrease the effectiveness of statins
b) It has the potential to elevate the risk of gastrointestinal side effects
c) When combined with statins, it may result in an allergic reaction
d) It can lead to an increased likelihood of experiencing muscle pain

88. After verifying a received order, what is one of the key responsibilities of pharmacy technicians regarding stock replenishment?

a) Discarding all the packaging material
b) Updating inventory records and stocking shelves
c) Selling the newly received items immediately
d) Changing the price tags of medications

89. For the treatment of vaginal yeast infection, which class of antifungal drugs should be utilized?

a) Fluconazole
b) Amphotericin B
c) Nystatin
d) Micafungin

90. What is the generic name for the drug Lasix?

a) Furosemide
b) Metoprolol
c) Hydrochlorothiazide
d) Amlodipine

Test 3: ANSWERS

1. **Answer a)**: Medicines with the suffix -olol, such as metoprolol and propranolol, belong to the drug class of beta-blockers. Diuretics are of different types and include furosemide and may have a suffix -ide or -amide. Nitrates don't have a common suffix. ACE inhibitors include Ramipril and have a suffix -pril.

2. **Answer b)**: The sublingual route bypasses the first-pass effect, meaning the drug is not metabolized in the liver before reaching the systemic circulation. This leads to a quick onset of action as the drug directly enters the bloodstream. The sublingual route involves placing medications under the tongue, not through the stomach lining. The sublingual route may not be suitable for all types of drugs, and some medications may not be effectively absorbed through this route. Additionally, taste and compliance issues may arise, especially if the drug has an unpleasant taste or texture. The sublingual route does not involve absorption through the skin. Instead, it relies on absorption through the buccal mucous membrane under the tongue.

3. **Answer b)**: The otic/ear route involves administering medication into or through the ear using formulations such as ear drops. This route provides a localized effect, targeting specific conditions or infections in the ear. The topical method entails the direct application of medications onto the skin or mucous membranes to achieve localized effects. It allows for targeted treatment at different sites, such as the oral cavity, rectum, anal canal, eyes, ears, nose, bronchi, and skin. The ocular/eye route involves administering medication into the eye using formulations such as eye drops or eye ointments. Inhalation involves the administration of volatile liquids and gases for systemic effects or the treatment of nasal disorders.

4. **Answer c)**: Schedule IV drugs are classified as such due to their reduced potential for abuse and lower risk of physical or psychological dependence when compared to drugs in Schedule III. These medications retain accepted medical uses, though their abuse potential is considered lower than that of Schedule III drugs. In terms of abuse potential and dependence, Schedule IV drugs are regarded as less dangerous than Schedule III drugs. To obtain Schedule IV drugs, a prescription from a licensed healthcare provider is required; they are not available over-the-counter. The classification of drugs into Schedule IV is based on their accepted medical uses, which distinguishes them from drugs in Schedule I, which lack any recognized medical applications and have the highest potential for abuse.

5. **Answer d)**: The primary objective of the Poison Prevention Packaging Act (PPPA) is to mandate child-resistant packaging for specific over-the-counter and prescription drugs, ensuring children are safeguarded against accidental poisoning. Child-resistant packaging is intentionally designed to make it challenging for young children to open containers and access potentially harmful medications. PPPA specifically targets certain medications that are deemed to be potentially hazardous to children. It does not require child-resistant packaging for all medications universally. While child-resistant packaging can provide some degree of protection for adults as well, the main objective of the act is to safeguard young children who may inadvertently ingest medications. The act primarily focuses on child-resistant packaging requirements rather than general prescription drug regulations.

6. **Answer d)**: The correct answer is d) Risk Identification: The first step is identifying potential risks and hazards within the pharmacy setting. The first stage of risk management is critical because it forms the basis for the subsequent actions. It involves identifying potential risks and hazards within the pharmacy setting.

7. **Answer c)**: Aseptic technique is a method used to prevent contamination of sterile items and environments. An essential component of this technique is to prevent contamination, ensuring that sterile conditions are maintained during procedures.

8. **Answer c)**: In a pharmacy setting, it's crucial to store medications according to the manufacturer's guidelines for storage conditions. Proper storage

ensures the medication's efficacy, stability, and safety.

9. **Answer c)**: Pharmacy technicians are often responsible for verifying a patient's insurance coverage before processing prescriptions. This involves confirming essential information like the insurance provider, policy number, and coverage dates. Accurate verification is crucial for ensuring that prescriptions are billed correctly and that patients receive the medications covered by their insurance plans.

10. **Answer c)**: Thermometers are commonly used in various areas of the pharmacy to monitor medication storage conditions. These areas include storage shelves, refrigerators, freezers, and warming cabinets. Medications often have specific temperature storage requirements, and thermometers help ensure that these conditions are consistently met. Proper temperature monitoring is essential for maintaining the efficacy and safety of medications.

11. **Answer c)**: The subcutaneous route involves injecting medication into the subcutaneous tissue through direct infusion or injection. It offers advantages such as self-administration in certain cases, convenience, and control over treatment. It is particularly suitable for drugs with a long duration of action, reducing the overall duration of drug effects. The subcutaneous route carries a lower risk of systemic infection compared to other routes of administration. The intravenous route delivers drugs directly into a vein through injections or infusions. It carries risks such as infections, allergic reactions, and phlebitis and requires skilled administration. The intramuscular route involves administering medication directly into specific muscles, such as the gluteus medius and deltoid. Certain drugs administered intramuscularly may cause pain or discomfort due to their irritating nature. The intradermal route is when medication is injected into the skin, just below the surface or epidermal layer. Administering medication intradermally requires a precise injection technique to ensure accurate placement in the dermis.

12. **Answer b)**: Controlled substances, such as opioids and certain sedatives, have a higher potential for abuse and are therefore subject to strict regulations. These medications are classified by government authorities based on their potential for addiction, misuse, and harm. Hazardous medications refer to medications that pose a risk to healthcare workers if proper precautions are not taken during handling. While they can be dangerous if mishandled, they are not specifically associated with a higher potential for abuse or are subject to the same strict regulations as controlled substances. Compounded medications are customized formulations prepared according to the needs of a specific patient. These medications are not inherently associated with a higher potential for abuse. Special packaging and labeling medications refer to medications that require specific packaging or labeling due to specific patient requirements or regulatory guidelines. While these medications may have unique packaging or labeling considerations, they are not specifically associated with a higher potential for abuse or subject to strict regulations like controlled substances.

13. **Answer a)**: Increased urination is a common side effect of furosemide. Furosemide is a loop diuretic that works by increasing the excretion of water and electrolytes through urine, which leads to increased urination. Muscle cramps, weight gain and blurred vision are not common side effects of furosemide.

14. **Answer c)**: The Poison Prevention Packaging Act (PPPA) requires child-resistant packaging for certain over-the-counter and prescription drugs to minimize the risk of accidental poisoning, particularly among children. Blister packs are an example of child-resistant packaging under the PPPA. Bottles with easy-to-open caps are not considered child-resistant packaging as they can be easily opened by children, which goes against the requirements of the PPPA. Single-use syringes are not directly related to child-resistant packaging. Medication vials with standard screw caps are also not considered child-resistant packaging under the PPPA.

15. **Answer c)**: Compounding in pharmacy refers to the process of mixing or altering components to produce a medication customized to meet the specific requirements of an individual patient. This can be for reasons such as a patient needing a specific dose or a different form of medication.

16. **Answer c)**: Using medications past their expiration date is discouraged because they may lose potency over time and might not be safe or

effective. The expiration date represents the time frame within which the medication is expected to remain stable and retain its stated potency.

17. **Answer a)**: Oral syringes are particularly useful for patients who have difficulty swallowing. They come with clear markings and are designed to measure and administer liquid medications. The syringes are available in different sizes to accommodate various medication volumes, making it easier for such patients to receive precise dosing.

18. **Answer b)**: Pharmacy technicians play a crucial role in determining stock needs and optimizing inventory levels. Factors such as seasonal variations, medication shortages, and patient demographics are considered when assessing stock requirements. By analyzing these factors, along with medication usage patterns and prescription volume, pharmacy technicians can accurately forecast medication needs and ensure that the pharmacy is adequately stocked.

19. **Answer c)**: Antiarrhythmics are medications specifically used to treat abnormal heart rhythms, including cardiac arrhythmias. Some antiarrhythmics have the potential to cause cardiac arrhythmias and prolonged Q.T. interval as adverse effects. Nitroglycerin is a medication prescribed for angina treatment, which is a condition characterized by chest pain or discomfort caused by inadequate blood flow to the heart. Cardiac arrhythmias and prolonged Q.T. interval are not commonly associated with nitroglycerin. Antihypertensives are drugs administered to individuals suffering from hypertension, aiding in the reduction of their elevated blood pressure. While some antihypertensives may cause changes in blood pressure, they are not typically associated with cardiac arrhythmias and prolonged Q.T. interval. Niacin, also known as vitamin B3, is used to manage cholesterol levels. While it can cause flushing as a common side effect, it is not typically associated with cardiac arrhythmias and prolonged Q.T. interval.

20. **Answer a)**: ACE inhibitors are commonly prescribed for conditions such as hypertension and heart failure. A common side effect of an ACE inhibitor is persistent dry cough. It is important to recognize this side effect as it can be bothersome to patients and may require a change in medication. Opioids, powerful pain-relieving medications, can cause various side effects, but persistent cough is not commonly associated with their use. Constipation, drowsiness, and nausea are among the common side effects associated with opioids. Sedatives are medications that promote relaxation, calmness, and sleepiness. While sedatives can cause various side effects, such as drowsiness, confusion, and impaired coordination, persistent cough is not typically associated with their use. NSAIDs, commonly used for pain relief and to reduce inflammation, are not commonly associated with a persistent cough as a side effect. However, NSAIDs can cause other gastrointestinal side effects such as stomach upset, indigestion, and gastric ulcers.

21. **Answer b)**: Bone marrow suppression, a severe adverse effect, can lead to a decreased production of blood cells, including red blood cells, white blood cells, and platelets. Aplastic anemia is marked by the bone marrow's inability to generate a sufficient number of blood cells, leading to symptoms such as fatigue, weakness, heightened vulnerability to infections, and easy bruising or bleeding. While easy bruising or bleeding is associated with medications affecting platelet function, it is not specifically linked to bone marrow suppression. Agranulocytosis is not a common side effect but is serious and is marked by a notable reduction in the number of granulocytes, a type of white blood cell. Decreased platelet function can contribute to easy bruising or bleeding, but it is not directly caused by bone marrow suppression.

22. **Answer b)**: The main purpose of RiskMAPs is to manage known or potential risks associated with a medication. RiskMAPs are formulated with the intention of ensuring that the advantages of a medication outweigh its risks and improving patient safety. Risk Minimization Action Plans (RiskMAPs) are not intended to restrict access to medications for specific patient populations. RiskMAPs are not related to reducing the cost of medications for patients. They are primarily concerned with safety and risk management. Risk Minimization Action Plans (RiskMAPs) are not involved in expediting the approval process for new medications.

23. **Answer c)**: Medication errors can lead to adverse drug reactions or even harm to the patient. Such errors can be due to various factors, such as

incorrect dosing, wrong medication, or administering drugs to the wrong patient. It's essential to follow procedures and double-check to prevent these errors.

24. **Answer b)**: A drug interaction occurs when the activity of one drug is modified by the simultaneous administration of another drug. This can lead to decreased or increased effects of one or both drugs, potentially causing harm or reducing efficacy.

25. **Answer c)**: Proper disposal of medications is essential for ensuring safety and compliance with federal regulations. The types of medications that typically require disposal include those that are expired, recalled, or damaged. By properly disposing of these medications, pharmacies can mitigate the risk of accidental ingestion or misuse, thereby promoting a safer community environment.

26. **Answer b)**: In a pharmacy setting, expired or damaged medications are typically managed by proper disposal according to federal regulations. This process ensures that these medications do not pose a risk to public health or the environment. Understanding the guidelines for proper disposal is crucial for pharmacy technicians, who are often responsible for managing waste in the pharmacy.

27. **Answer b)**: Warfarin is an anticoagulant medication that requires regular monitoring of the patient's INR to assess the effectiveness and safety of the therapy. The INR is a standardized measure of the blood's clotting ability, and the target range for patients on warfarin therapy is typically between 2.0 and 3.0.

28. **Answer c)**: Pharmacy technicians play a crucial role in preventing medication errors with NTI medications. They are responsible for double-checking prescriptions, verifying dosage calculations, and ensuring accurate dispensing of these medications to help prevent any errors that could have serious consequences. While pharmacy technicians may provide general information about medications, counseling patients about specific side effects is typically within the scope of pharmacists or other healthcare professionals. Pharmacy technicians can play a role in identifying and reporting adverse effects to healthcare providers. They may document patient-reported side effects or observations and communicate this information to the pharmacist or healthcare team for further evaluation and management. But this is not their major role for NTI drugs, so this is the second best choice. Monitoring blood levels and dosage adjustments typically falls within the purview of pharmacists or other healthcare professionals.

29. **Answer b)**: Cleaning and disinfection of the cleanroom is an essential key consideration in sterile compounding to maintain a clean and sterile environment. This process helps prevent the introduction of contaminants and ensures the sterility of compounded medications. While patient allergies are an important consideration in healthcare, monitoring patient allergies is not specifically a key consideration for sterile compounding. Adjusting dosages based on patient requirements is not directly related to the key considerations for sterile compounding. While using specialized equipment is important in sterile compounding to maintain a sterile environment, it is not a key consideration.

30. **Answer d)**: The main purpose of RiskMAPs is to manage known or potential risks associated with a medication. They do so by implementing additional safety measures beyond the standard labeling and prescribing information. These measures may include patient counseling, reporting adverse events, and other risk management strategies. Risk Minimization Action Plans (RiskMAPs) do not focus on improving medication availability. While RiskMAPs may involve additional safety information, they go beyond standard labeling and prescribing information. While RiskMAPs may require patient counseling, the primary purpose is to ensure that patients understand the risks and safe use of the medication, not just the benefits. They do so by implementing additional safety measures beyond the standard labeling and prescribing information.

31. **Answer c)**: Medication adherence is crucial for patients to ensure the effectiveness of the medication and achieve the desired therapeutic outcomes. When patients don't adhere to prescribed medication regimens, it can result in suboptimal treatment outcomes, increased disease complications, and higher healthcare costs.

32. **Answer b)**: Prescription verification in a pharmacy setting is vital to ensure that the patient receives the correct medication and dose as

prescribed by the healthcare provider. This step helps prevent medication errors, ensuring patient safety.

33. **Answer b)**: When disposing of medical materials in a pharmacy, it's essential to separate medical waste from common waste. This is important for ensuring that hazardous or potentially infectious materials are not mixed with general waste, posing a risk to public health and the environment. Pharmacy technicians need to be knowledgeable about the guidelines and procedures for waste separation and disposal as part of their role in maintaining a safe and compliant pharmacy environment.

34. **Answer b)**: Oral syringes are commonly used equipment for administering oral liquid medications. These devices are structured to deliver a precise amount of medication, ensuring accurate measurement. Being familiar with the types of equipment used for various routes of administration is essential for pharmacy technicians, as it enables them to provide effective patient counseling and ensures the safe administration of medications.

35. **Answer c)**: Sterile compounding is commonly used to prepare medications that are administered through these routes. These medications require the use of aseptic techniques to maintain sterility and reduce the chance of contamination. Creams and ointments can be prepared through compounding, but they do not necessarily require sterile compounding techniques. Tablets and capsules are typically manufactured commercially and do not require sterile compounding techniques. Over-the-counter medications are generally commercially manufactured and do not require sterile compounding techniques.

36. **Answer a)**: The USP is a non-profit organization that sets quality standards for medications and healthcare products in the United States. It provides guidelines and standards for compounding practices, including non-sterile compounding. The FDA, as a regulatory agency, upholds its responsibility of safeguarding public health by ensuring the safety, efficacy, and security of drugs and medical devices in the United States. While the FDA plays a role in regulating drug compounding, including non-sterile compounding, it primarily focuses on the approval and oversight of commercially manufactured drugs rather than providing specific guidelines for compounding practices. The CDC is a national public health agency in the United States that focuses on preventing and controlling infectious diseases. While the CDC provides guidance on infection prevention and control in healthcare settings, it does not specifically provide guidelines for non-sterile compounding. The World Health Organization (WHO) is a United Nations specialized agency that primarily deals with global public health matters. While the WHO provides guidance and standards for pharmaceutical practices and regulations, it does not specifically provide guidelines for non-sterile compounding.

37. **Answer c)**: Key considerations for non-sterile compounding include:
Clean Environment: Non-sterile Compounding should be performed in a clean and well-maintained area to minimize the risk of contamination. This includes the routine cleaning of work areas, equipment, and tools.
Sanitization: Compounding personnel must sanitize equipment, such as mortar and pestle, mixing utensils, and measuring devices, before use. Proper cleaning and sanitization procedures help prevent cross-contamination between different medications.
Ingredient Quality and Compatibility: It is essential to use high-quality ingredients and ensure their compatibility to maintain the stability and effectiveness of compounded medications. Compounding personnel should carefully select ingredients and verify the suitability of the ingredients and the medication for use.
Accurate Measuring and Compounding Techniques: Precise measurement and compounding techniques are crucial to ensure accurate dosing and consistent quality of compounded medications. Proper training and following standard operating procedures (SOPs) help in minimizing errors and maintain quality control.
Packaging and Labeling: Non-sterile compounded medications should be appropriately packaged and labeled with clear instructions for use, ingredients, and expiration dates. Proper packaging and labeling help ensure accurate identification, appropriate storage, and patient safety.

38. **Answer b)**: The correct classification for medical device recalls established by the U.S. Food and Drug Administration (FDA) is Class I, Class II, and Class III. Category A, Category B, and Category C are not the correct classification for medical device recalls. While Class I recalls may involve high risk and Class III recalls may involve low risk, these terms are not the official classification for medical device recalls by the FDA. Major Recall, Minor Recall, or Voluntary Recall is not the correct classification for medical device recalls.

39. **Answer a)**: Drug labels provide essential information for safe and effective medication use, including active ingredients, recommended dosages, and potential side effects. They do not typically include the manufacturer's marketing strategy.

40. **Answer b)**: Certain medications require storage at specific temperatures to ensure they remain effective and stable. Improper storage conditions can affect the medication's potency, stability, and overall safety.

41. **Answer b)**: The primary goal of effective inventory management in a pharmacy is to minimize cost while maintaining an adequate supply of medications. Proper inventory management ensures that the pharmacy has enough stock to meet patient needs without overstocking, which can lead to increased costs and waste. Pharmacy technicians play a crucial role in this process, as they often handle inventory tasks such as ordering, receiving, and rotating stock.

42. **Answer b)**: Pharmacological calculations play a critical role in ensuring that the patient receives the appropriate dosage of medication for effective treatment. By using standardized units and various factors such as the patient's weight or condition, healthcare professionals can accurately determine the right amount of medication to administer. This minimizes the risk of overdose or under-dose, thereby ensuring effective treatment and reducing the likelihood of adverse effects.

43. **Answer c)**: Emulsions consist of two immiscible liquids dispersed throughout each other. For example, an oil-in-water emulsion involves dispersing oil droplets throughout the water. Emulsions are frequently employed in topical creams, acting as a base for ointments and lotions to create a smooth and creamy texture that allows for effortless application on the skin. Mixtures encompass a range of formulations that consist of multiple active and inactive ingredients. They can involve the combination of solids and liquids, two liquids, or two solids. This is not used in topical creams. Liquids comprise a solute (active drug component) dispersed homogeneously in a solvent (liquid vehicle). Some medications come commercially in liquid form, while others may require compounding. This is not used in topical creams. Suppositories are solid formulations primarily used rectally and sometimes vaginally. They contain medication suspended in a base, such as cocoa butter.

44. **Answer d)**: Excipients are inactive ingredients used in formulations, but they can interact with the active drug and cause destabilization or degradation, affecting the overall stability of the compounded medication. Some excipients may interact with the materials used in containers or administration devices, such as plastic or glass. These interactions can lead to leaching of substances from the container or adsorption of the drug onto the container surface, which can affect the stability of the drug and introduce contaminants.

45. **Answer c)**: Plavix is a brand name for the medication that contains the active ingredient clopidogrel. Clopidogrel is an antiplatelet drug. Ezetimibe is a Cholesterol Absorption Inhibitor and is sold under the brand name Zetia. Heparin is an anticoagulant and is sold under the brand name Heparin Sodium. Methimazole is an antithyroid drug and sold under the brand name Tapazole.

46. **Answer a)**: Class I classification of recall involves medical devices that pose a significant risk of serious harm or death to the patient. These recalls are considered the most critical as they involve devices with the highest potential for harm. Class II classification of recall is related to medical devices that carry the potential to cause temporary or reversible health problems or, in rare instances, a remote possibility of serious harm. Class III classification of recall involves medical devices that are unlikely to cause harm or have minimal risk to the patient. Class III recalls are for devices with the lowest potential for harm. There is no Class IV classification for medical device recalls.

47. **Answer b)**: Proper disposal of unused or expired medications is essential to prevent potential harm, misuse, and environmental contamination. Incorrect disposal, like flushing down the toilet or sink, can lead to contamination of water supplies.

48. **Answer c)**: When considering medication safety, the primary concern is to reduce the risk of medication errors and potential harm to the patient. Proper procedures, double-checking, and patient counseling are essential to achieve this goal.

49. **Answer d)**: The correct answer is 'Cardboard boxes' because the statement in the question specifically mentions that common types of medication packages for storage include bottles, vials, and blister packs. Cardboard boxes are generally not used for storing medications due to issues with moisture control and stability.

50. **Answer c)**: The correct answer is 'Temperature'. For medications that are temperature-sensitive, maintaining the correct temperature is crucial for ensuring their efficacy and safety. Failure to store these medications at the right temperature can lead to degradation and loss of effectiveness.

51. **Answer a)**: Lorazepam is a medication that belongs to the class of benzodiazepines, which are a group of drugs primarily used for their sedative, hypnotic, anxiolytic, anticonvulsant, and muscle relaxant properties. Lorazepam is frequently used to manage anxiety, insomnia, and seizure disorders. Its action mechanism enhances the effectiveness of the neurotransmitter gamma-aminobutyric acid (GABA) in the brain, resulting in a soothing and tranquilizing impact on the central nervous system. Zolpidem is a medication used for short-term insomnia treatment, and is an example of a sedative-hypnotic. Meanwhile, Guaifenesin functions as an expectorant, helping to loosen and thin mucus in the airways, and dextromethorphan acts as an antitussive medication, effectively suppressing coughing.

52. **Answer a)**: Gentamicin is exclusively eliminated through renal excretion, which means it is primarily excreted in the urine. The kidneys are essential in the process of filtering Gentamicin from the blood and eliminating it via the urinary system. Gentamicin is not excreted through bile, feces, or exhaled air.

53. **Answer b)**: Erythromycin is primarily eliminated through bile. While a small portion of the drug may be detected in urine and feces, the main route of elimination for Erythromycin is through the bile, which is released into the intestines. It is not excreted through other routes, such as urine or exhaled air.

54. **Answer c)**: A recall strategy for medical devices must outline all the necessary actions to be taken, including identifying the specific devices affected by the recall, notifying all relevant parties (such as healthcare professionals and distributors) about the recall, and implementing appropriate corrective actions to address the issue and prevent harm to patients. A recall strategy for medical devices involves more than just identifying affected parties. A recall strategy involves more than just implementing corrective actions; while corrective actions are a crucial part of the strategy, they are not the only element. While notifying the FDA is an essential part of a recall process, it is not the only component of a recall strategy.

55. **Answer c)**: Handwashing is vital in a pharmacy setting to prevent the spread of germs and reduce the risk of contamination. Proper hand hygiene ensures that medications remain uncontaminated and safe for patients.

56. **Answer c)**: In a pharmacy setting, the primary purpose of using Personal Protective Equipment (PPE) is to protect the staff from potential hazards and contamination. This ensures the safety of both the staff and the medications being handled.

57. **Answer d)**: The correct answer is 'Wood'. Medications are commonly packaged in materials like glass, plastic, and metal. Wood is generally not used for medication packaging as it may not offer the required protection from external factors such as moisture and light.

58. **Answer d)**: The correct answer is 'Color of the storage area'. Critical factors for the proper storage of medications, as mentioned, include temperature, moisture, and light. The color of the storage area is not listed as a concern and is therefore the correct answer.

59. **Answer c)**: Tetracycline is known to cause tooth discoloration, especially in developing teeth in infants or young children exposed to the drug during pregnancy or while breastfeeding. Ibuprofen, acetaminophen and aspirin do not cause tooth discoloration in infants.

60. **Answer c)**: Loratadine is an antihistamine medication that is commonly available over-the-counter (OTC). Amoxicillin, prednisone and simvastatin are not available Over-the-counter.

61. **Answer: d)**: In the United States, the market offers more than 80 classes of OTC medications, catering to a multitude of health needs, not just 50 classes. While many OTC medications are indeed intended for minor health concerns, there are also OTC medications available for various health needs, including some more serious conditions. The main characteristic of OTC medications is that patients can get them at a pharmacy without a prescription from the healthcare provider.

62. **Answer c)**: The manufacturer or distributor of a medical device is responsible for initiating a recall when they become aware of a device defect or potential risk. Additionally, the FDA can also request or order a recall if deemed necessary to protect public health and safety. While healthcare professionals play a critical role in identifying potential issues with medical devices and reporting them, they do not have the authority to initiate a recall. Patients can report adverse events or issues related to medical devices, but they do not have the authority to initiate a recall. Insurance companies lack the authority to instigate a recall for a defective medical device.

63. **Answer c)**: Olanzapine is the generic name for the drug Zyprexa. Zyprexa is the brand name of a medication that includes the active ingredient Olanzapine. Olanzapine is classified as an atypical antipsychotic and is prescribed for the treatment of various mental health conditions, including schizophrenia, bipolar disorder, and certain types of depression. Risperidone, quetiapine and clozapine are not the generic name for the drug Zyprexa.

64. **Answer b)**: Maintaining equipment hygiene in a pharmacy is essential to prevent contamination. Clean equipment ensures that medications are prepared and dispensed safely, reducing the risk of harm to patients.

65. **Answer d)**: The correct answer is 'Time of day'. Common factors considered in dosage calculations include patient weight, patient age, and the type of medication. The time of day is not commonly considered in these calculations.

66. **Answer b)**: The primary purpose of using proportions in dosage calculations for pharmacy technicians is to determine the appropriate dosage for a patient based on various factors such as weight, age, or condition. Proportions provide a mathematical framework for comparing different quantities and finding the correct ratio between them. This is essential for ensuring that the patient receives the correct amount of medication, thereby maximizing the effectiveness of the treatment while minimizing the risk of adverse effects. By using proportions, pharmacy technicians can make accurate and safe medication calculations.

67. **Answer c)**: Using the formula method, we can calculate the number of IV fluid bags required:
Dose ordered (D) = 2.5 liters = 2500 mL
Supply on hand (H) = 500 mL per bag
Quantity (Q) = Unknown (number of bags to be administered)
D/H × Q = Dose
(2500 mL) / (500 mL per bag) × Q = 2500 mL
Q = (2500 mL) / (500 mL per bag) = 5 bags
So, the correct answer is 5 bags.

68. **Answer b)**: Using the formula method, we can calculate the infusion rate in milliliters per hour (mL/h): Dose ordered (D) = 1.5 mg/min Supply on hand (H) = 4 mg/mL (concentration of the medication) Quantity (Q) = Unknown (infusion rate in mL/h)
D/H × Q = Dose (1.5 mg/min) / (4 mg/mL) × Q = 1.5 mg/min
First, we need to convert the dose ordered to milliliters: 1.5 mg/min ÷ 4 mg/mL = 0.375 mL/min
Next, we convert the infusion rate from mL/min to mL/h: 0.375 mL/min × 60 min/h = 22.5 mL/h
So, the correct answer is 22.5 mL/h.

69. **Answer c)**: Alprazolam belongs to the drug class, benzodiazepine. Benzodiazepines typically have names ending with the suffix "pam" or "lam." These medications are known for their calming properties and are often prescribed to address conditions such as anxiety, panic disorders, insomnia, and seizures. By augmenting the function of the neurotransmitter GABA, they work to decrease excessive brain activity and induce relaxation. It is important to note that benzodiazepines do not fall under the drug classes of antidepressants, antihistamines, or methylphenidate. ARBs are a group of medications used to treat.

70. **Answer a)**: The main purpose of the Medical Device Reporting (MDR) system is to collect and analyze reports of adverse events, serious injuries, deaths, and other incidents related to medical devices. By gathering this information, the FDA can monitor the safety and performance of medical devices and take appropriate actions, including recalls if necessary, to protect public health. While the FDA has the authority to request or order a recall for a defective medical device, this is not the main purpose of the Medical Device Reporting (MDR) system. The MDR system does not primarily involve conducting audits for verification of compliance. The MDR system is not directly involved in physically retrieving defective devices from healthcare facilities.

71. **Answer c)**: The primary goal of adhering to hygiene and cleaning standards in a pharmacy is to prevent the spread of infections and ensure the safe preparation and dispensing of medications. Proper hygiene practices ensure patient safety and maintain the integrity of medications.

72. **Answer b)**: In a pharmacy setting, face masks, gloves, and safety goggles are commonly used as Personal Protective Equipment (PPE) to ensure safety and hygiene. A stethoscope, while used in medical settings, is not typically considered PPE in this context.

73. **Answer b)**: The Drug Enforcement Administration (DEA) number on a prescription serves the purpose of preventing illicit use and ensuring appropriate oversight for controlled substances. This unique identification number is mandatory for prescriptions involving controlled substances. It helps in establishing the legitimacy of the prescription and facilitates monitoring and regulation by appropriate authorities. The DEA number is a critical aspect of prescription validation, especially for medications that have the potential for abuse or misuse.

74. **Answer b)**: In pharmacology calculations, the concentration of a medication is typically expressed in milligrams per milliliter (mg/mL). Concentration calculations are used to determine the strength or potency of a medication in a given solution. For example, if a medication vial contains 100 mg of the active ingredient in 10 mL of solution, the concentration would be 10 mg/mL. Understanding concentration is crucial for pharmacy technicians, as it allows them to prepare medications with specific concentrations and ensures accurate and safe administration to patients.

75. **Answer d)**: Valsartan belongs to the drug class of Angiotensin II receptor blockers (ARBs). ARBs, which stands for Angiotensin Receptor Blockers, are a class of medications given for the management of hypertension (high blood pressure) and heart failure. Valsartan is not a Beta-blocker, Calcium Channel Blocker, or ACE inhibitor.

76. **Answer d)**: Beta-blockers are frequently recommended for the treatment of hypertension, which is commonly referred to as high blood pressure. These drugs work by impeding the effect of adrenaline on the heart and blood vessels, resulting in a reduction of both heart rate and blood pressure. This mechanism makes them effective in managing hypertension. It is essential to note that beta-blockers are not suitable for individuals with severe bradycardia (slow heart rate), heart block, or asthma, and are contraindicated in such cases.

77. **Answer b)**: Diltiazem is classified as a calcium channel blocker medication. These drugs function by obstructing calcium channels in the walls of blood vessels and heart muscle cells. As a result of this action, blood vessels relax, and the heart rate decreases. Diltiazem is not a beta-blocker, ACE inhibitor or ARB.

78. **Answer a)**: Pharmacy technicians play a crucial role in prescription filling by providing patient-specific packages. Once prescriptions are received from healthcare providers, pharmacy technicians accurately dispense the prescribed medications. They carefully measure or count the appropriate quantities of medications and then package them into individual packages for each patient. Assisting with placing inventory orders falls under the pharmacy technician's responsibility for inventory management, not prescription filling. Compounding medications from scratch is typically a responsibility reserved for pharmacists themselves. While maintaining a clean and organized workspace is important for prescription filling and other tasks, it is not directly related to the specific process of prescription filling itself.

79. **Answer c)**: Rigorous handwashing in a pharmacy setting primarily aims to prevent contamination and ensure medication safety. Proper hand

hygiene is a fundamental practice to ensure that medications are dispensed in a safe manner.

80. **Answer b)**: The "directions for use" section on a medication label provides detailed instructions for proper medication administration. It includes the recommended dosage, frequency of administration, and any specific instructions related to timing, food intake, or other considerations. Patient-specific instructions are personalized instructions provided to an individual patient based on their specific needs and health conditions. Pharmacy information refers to the details of the dispensing pharmacy, including its name and contact information. The "storage requirements" section specifies the appropriate conditions for storing the medication to maintain its stability and effectiveness.

81. **Answer b)**: A characteristic feature of Look and sound alike drugs (LASA drugs) is their propensity to share resemblances in both brand and generic names. This can lead to potential confusion and medication errors.

82. **Answer a)**: When diluting a medication to a specific concentration, pharmacy technicians often need to calculate the volume of the stock solution and the diluent required. Dilution calculations are essential for achieving the desired medication concentration. For instance, if a medication needs to be diluted to a concentration of 1:10, and the stock solution is 1 mL, the pharmacy technician would need to add 9 mL of diluent to achieve the desired concentration. Accurate dilution calculations are crucial for ensuring patient safety and the effectiveness of the treatment.

83. **Answer c)**: Drugs with the suffix "prazole" belong to the class of proton pump inhibitors (PPIs). PPIs (Proton Pump Inhibitors) are prescribed to decrease the production of stomach acid. Antacids, Prokinetics and laxatives do not have the suffix "prazole" in their names.

84. **Answer: c)**: Mineralocorticoids should be used with caution in patients with hypertension or congestive heart failure. These drugs can cause an increase in fluid and sodium retention, which may lead to elevated blood volume and worsen hypertension or congestive heart failure. While patients with asthma may require caution when using corticosteroids (glucocorticoids), mineralocorticoids are not directly related to asthma. Mineralocorticoids are not directly indicated or contraindicated in patients with rheumatoid arthritis. Mineralocorticoids are not typically contraindicated in patients with diabetes.

85. **Answer a)**: Ampicillin is a penicillin antibiotic, and individuals who are allergic to penicillin are at risk of having cross-reactivity and allergic reactions to ampicillin as well. Therefore, ampicillin should not be given to a person allergic to penicillin. Ceftriaxone is a cephalosporin antibiotic and is not directly related to penicillin. Azithromycin falls under the category of macrolide antibiotics and is not associated with penicillin. Similarly, ciprofloxacin is a fluoroquinolone antibiotic and has no relation to penicillin.

86. **Answer c)**: The Drug Quality and Security Act (DQSA) establishes tracing, serialization, and verification systems as part of the Drug Supply Chain Security Act (DSCSA) to prevent counterfeit drugs from entering the pharmaceutical supply chain. Pharmacy technicians play a crucial role in this process, as they are involved in receiving, storing, and dispensing medications. While pharmacy technicians are essential members of the pharmacy team, they do not have the authority to inspect facilities or enforce compliance with quality standards. Those responsibilities typically fall under the purview of regulatory agencies and qualified inspectors. While pharmacy technicians play a role in compounding medications, it is the responsibility of pharmacists and regulatory bodies to ensure compliance with compounding regulations. While pharmacy technicians may work in these facilities and be involved in supply chain management, they do not have a direct role in introducing such facilities or overseeing them under FDA regulations.

87. **Answer d)**: The main reason individuals taking statins should be cautious when consuming grapefruit juice is its interaction with enzymes involved in statin metabolism. Grapefruit juice contains furanocoumarins that inhibit these enzymes, leading to reduced breakdown of statins in the body. As a result, statin levels in the blood can increase, potentially leading to an increased risk of experiencing side effects like muscle pain and aches. Consuming grapefruit juice along with statins does not reduce the efficacy of the statins. Additionally, there is no direct evidence to suggest

that grapefruit juice increases the risk of gastrointestinal side effects when taken with statins. Furthermore, allergic reactions are not commonly associated with the combination of grapefruit juice and statins.

88. **Answer b)**: After verifying the received order, pharmacy technicians are responsible for updating inventory records and stocking the shelves accordingly. Proper storage of medications is also ensured, adhering to manufacturer guidelines for temperature control and environmental conditions. Accurate documentation, including lot numbers and expiration dates, is vital for maintaining inventory control and ensuring regulatory compliance.

89. **Answer a)**: Fluconazole, belonging to the azole class of antifungal drugs, is commonly prescribed for treating vaginal yeast infections, also known as vaginal candidiasis. Amphotericin B is a powerful antifungal medication primarily employed to treat severe systemic fungal infections. On the other hand, Nystatin is not the first-line treatment option for vaginal yeast infections. Micafungin is an antifungal medication from the echinocandin class, which is mainly used for certain invasive fungal infections. While effective against some systemic fungal infections, it is not commonly used for the treatment of uncomplicated vaginal yeast infections.

90. **Answer a)**: The generic name for the drug Lasix is Furosemide. Lasix is a brand name for the medication that contains the active ingredient Furosemide, which is a loop diuretic commonly used to treat conditions such as edema and hypertension. Metoprolol, hydrochlorothiazide and amlodipine are not the generic name for the drug Lasix.

Dear Future Pharmacy Technician,

first of all, thank you again for purchasing our product.

Secondly, congratulations! If you are using our Guide, you are among those few who are willing to do whatever it takes to excel on the exam and are not satisfied with just trying.
We create our Study Guides in the same spirit. We want to offer our students only the best to help them get only the best through precise, accurate, and easy-to-use information.

That is why **your success is our success**, and if you think our Guide helped you achieve your goals, we would love it if you could take 60 seconds of your time to leave us a review on Amazon.

Thank you again for trusting us by choosing our Guide, and good luck with your new life as a Pharmacy Technician.

Sincerely,

H.S. Test Preparation Team

Scan the QR code to Leave a Review (it only takes you 60 seconds):

References

Healthdirect Australia. (n.d.). Generic medicines vs. brand-name medicines. Retrieved from

National Center for Biotechnology Information. (n.d.). Bookshelf: Therapeutic Drug Monitoring - Principles and Protocols. Retrieved from

Merck Manual Professional Version. (n.d.). Drug Administration. Retrieved from

Merck Manual Professional Version. (n.d.). Pharmacokinetics Overview. Retrieved from

National Center for Biotechnology Information. (n.d.). Bookshelf: Principles of Pharmacology. Retrieved from

Brunton, L. L., Hilal-Dandan, R., & Knollmann, B. C. (Eds.). (no date). Goodman & Gilman's: The Pharmacological Basis of Therapeutics, 13e. Available at:

Merck Manual Professional Version. (n.d.). Penicillins. Retrieved from

Merck Manual Professional Version. (n.d.). Cephalosporins. Retrieved from

Merck Manual Professional Version. (n.d.). Fluoroquinolones. Retrieved from

Abhishek V et al. (2021). Clinical Evaluation of Antihypertensive Drugs. Journal of Cardiovascular Pharmacology and Therapeutics, 26(3), 195-207. doi: 10.1177/20587384211002621

Merck Manual Professional Version. (n.d.). Antifungal Drugs. Retrieved from

National Center for Biotechnology Information. (n.d.). Bookshelf: Principles of Antimicrobial Therapy. Retrieved from

Merck Manual Professional Version. (n.d.). Antifungal Drugs. Retrieved from

National Center for Biotechnology Information. (n.d.). Bookshelf: Principles of Antiviral Therapy. Retrieved from

American Heart Association. (n.d.). Understanding Blood Pressure Readings. Retrieved from

National Center for Biotechnology Information. (n.d.). Bookshelf: Principles of Diuretic Action. Retrieved from

National Center for Biotechnology Information. (n.d.). Bookshelf: Principles of Diabetes Mellitus. Retrieved from

Powers, A. C., & D'Alessio, D. (2017). Endocrine Pancreas and Pharmacotherapy of Diabetes Mellitus and Hypoglycemia. In: Brunton LL, Hilal-Dandan R, Knollmann BC (Eds.), Goodman & Gilman's: The Pharmacological Basis of Therapeutics. 14th ed. McGraw-Hill Education.

Textbook of Cardiology. (n.d.). Cardiac Pharmacology. Retrieved from

Centers for Disease Control and Prevention. (n.d.). Treating High Cholesterol. Retrieved from

Drugs.com. (n.d.). Drug Interactions Checker. Retrieved from

Merck Manual Professional Version. (n.d.). Medications for the Treatment of Gastric Acidity. Retrieved from

Merck Manual Professional Version. (n.d.). Drugs for Heart Failure. Retrieved from

National Center for Biotechnology Information. (n.d.). Bookshelf: Principles of Anticoagulant and Antiplatelet Therapy. Retrieved from

National Center for Biotechnology Information. (n.d.). Bookshelf: Pharmacokinetic Drug-Drug Interactions. Retrieved from

National Center for Biotechnology Information. (n.d.). Bookshelf: Pharmacodynamics. Retrieved from

National Center for Biotechnology Information. (n.d.). Bookshelf: Drug Metabolism. Retrieved from

Merck Manual Professional Version. (n.d.). Drug Interactions. Retrieved from

MSN Manuals. Factors Affecting Response to Drugs: Drug Interactions. Retrieved from

National Institutes of Health. What Is a Drug Interaction? Retrieved from

Drugs.com. Drug Interactions Checker. Retrieved from

AccessPharmacy. Drug Interactions. Retrieved from

StatPearls. Drug Interactions. Retrieved from

MSN Manuals. Adverse Drug Reactions. Retrieved from

Brunton, L. L., Hilal-Dandan, R., Knollmann, B. C., & Goodman, L. S. (Eds.). Goodman & Gilman's: The Pharmacological Basis of Therapeutics, 13e. Retrieved from

National Center for Biotechnology Information. Drug Interactions: Principles and Practice. Retrieved from

American College of Allergy, Asthma & Immunology. Drug Allergies. Retrieved from

U.S. Food and Drug Administration. Information Regarding Insulin Storage and Switching Between Products in an Emergency. Retrieved from

ScienceDirect. Drug Stability. Retrieved from

Journal of Pharmacy and Pharmacology. (2021). Drug Interactions: Principles, Evaluation, and Management. Retrieved from

U.S. Food and Drug Administration. Drug Compounding and Drug Shortages. Retrieved from

National Center for Biotechnology Information. Drug Interactions. Retrieved from

Drug Enforcement Administration. Drug Scheduling. Retrieved from

U.S. Food and Drug Administration. Federal Food, Drug, and Cosmetic Act. Retrieved from

U.S. Food and Drug Administration. Drug Supply Chain Security Act (DSCSA). Retrieved from

Pharmacy Technician Certification Board. Pharmacy Technician Code of Ethics. Retrieved from

National Center for Biotechnology Information. Drug Interactions: Principles and Practice. Retrieved from

Drug Enforcement Administration. Controlled Substances - Alphabetical Order. Retrieved from

National Center for Biotechnology Information. Adverse Drug Reactions. Retrieved from

U.S. Food and Drug Administration. Legal Requirements for the Sale and Purchase of Drug Products Containing Pseudoephedrine, Ephedrine, and Phenylpropanolamine. Retrieved from

U.S. Food and Drug Administration. Risk Minimization Action Plans (RiskMAPs) for Approved Products. Retrieved from

U.S. Food and Drug Administration. Medical Device Reporting. Retrieved from

U.S. Food and Drug Administration. Recalls, Corrections, and Removals (Devices). Retrieved from

United States Pharmacopeia. General Chapter <795> Pharmaceutical Compounding - Nonsterile Preparations. Retrieved July 28, 2023, from

Van der Schors, T., Amann, S., Makridaki, D., & Kohl, S. (2021). EAHP Position Paper on Pharmacy Preparations and Compounding. European Journal of Hospital Pharmacy, 28(4), 190–192.

Anderson, S. (2021). Pharmacy Compounding of High-Risk Level Products and Patient Safety. In S. Anderson & M. Currie (Eds.), Making Medicines: A Brief History of Pharmacy and Pharmaceuticals. Pharmaceutical Press. Retrieved from

American Society of Health-System Pharmacists. (n.d.). ASHP Technical Assistance Bulletin on Compounding Nonsterile Products in Pharmacies. Retrieved from

Elsevier Inc, Davis, K., & Guerra, A. (n.d.). Mosby's Pharmacy Technician E-Book. Elsevier Health Sciences. Retrieved from

National Center for Biotechnology Information. (2014). Adverse drug events: Prevention, detection, and management. Retrieved from

Institute for Safe Medication Practices. (2018). High-alert medications: Acute care. Retrieved from

National Center for Biotechnology Information. (2016). Medication errors: Cut your risk with these tips. Retrieved from

Academy of Managed Care Pharmacy. (n.d.). Drug utilization review. Retrieved from

National Center for Biotechnology Information. (2016). Medication reconciliation. In Medication safety. StatPearls Publishing. Retrieved from

National Center for Biotechnology Information. (2020). The pharmacist's role in addressing the opioid crisis. Retrieved from

U.S. Food and Drug Administration. (n.d.). Over-the-counter medicines: What's right for you? Retrieved from

National Institute on Drug Abuse. (n.d.). How can prescription drug misuse be prevented? Retrieved from

National Center for Biotechnology Information. (2016). Medication safety in the elderly. Retrieved from

National Center for Biotechnology Information. (2019). Principles of drug therapy. In Basic & clinical pharmacology. McGraw-Hill Education. Retrieved from

National Center for Biotechnology Information. (2010). Medication errors: Prevention. Retrieved from

WebMD. (n.d.). Slideshow: How to read drug labels. Retrieved from

World Health Organization. (2017). Patient safety solutions: Look-alike, sound-alike medication names. Retrieved from

Institute for Safe Medication Practices. (n.d.). List of confused drug names. Retrieved from

Pharmacy Times. (n.d.). Medication safety. Retrieved from

Pharmacy Times. (n.d.). Top 5 most common prescription drug errors. Retrieved from

University of Florida College of Medicine - Jacksonville. (n.d.). Safe prescribing practices. Retrieved from

U.S. Food and Drug Administration. (n.d.). FDA's name differentiation project. Retrieved from

Verywell Health. (n.d.). Understanding prescription abbreviations. Retrieved from

Drugs.com. (n.d.). Commonly used abbreviations in pharmacy prescriptions. Retrieved from

National Center for Biotechnology Information. (2018). Medication safety. In StatPearls. StatPearls Publishing. Retrieved from

LibreTexts. (n.d.). Dosage calculations. Retrieved from

Lindstrom. (n.d.). Maintaining hygiene in the pharmaceutical industry: A glimpse of effective practices to implement. Retrieved from

National Center for Biotechnology Information. (2020). Medication errors: A common concern in clinical practice. Retrieved from

National Center for Biotechnology Information. (2019). Medication errors: Improving practices and patient safety. In Advances in patient safety: From research to implementation (Volume 4: Programs, tools, and products). Agency for Healthcare Research and Quality. Retrieved from

Black Country Partnership NHS Foundation Trust. (n.d.). Medicines supply, storage, and disposal. Retrieved from

Open Textbook Library. (n.d.). Safe injection administration and preparing medication from ampules and vials. Retrieved from

National Center for Biotechnology Information. (2017). Safe medication use in the ICU. In Critical care nursing clinics of North America (Vol. 29, No. 2). Elsevier. Retrieved from

Sensoscientific. (n.d.). Why pharmacy temperature monitoring is important for medicine storage. Retrieved from

GoodRx. (n.d.). Drug recalls: What to do if your medication is recalled. Retrieved from

National Center for Biotechnology Information. (2018). Medical errors in the emergency department. In StatPearls. StatPearls Publishing. Retrieved from

Pharmacy Times. (n.d.). Prescription validation is a critical task. Retrieved from

Ingersoll, K. (2015). Inventory Management for the Pharmacy Technician. Elite Professional Education, LLC. Retrieved from

West, D. Purchasing and Inventory Management. In Pharmacy Management: Essentials for All Practice Settings, 3e. McGraw Hill Medical. Retrieved from

Thom, L. H., Reichert, M., Iochpe, C., & Palazzo, J. (2020). Why Rigid Process Management Technology Hampers Computerized Support of Healthcare Processes? X Workshop on Medical Informatics. Retrieved from

Basicmedical Key. Processing Medication Orders and Prescriptions. Retrieved from

American Society of Health-System Pharmacists. ASHP Guidelines on Remote Medication Order Processing. Retrieved from

Rx-Wiki. Pharmacy Billing and Reimbursement. Retrieved from

Buffington, D. E., & Vieson, K. J. Reimbursement for Pharmacist Services. In Medication Therapy Management: A Comprehensive Approach, 2e. McGraw Hill Medical. Retrieved from

National Council for Prescription Drug Programs. (2018). Billing Guidance for Pharmacists' Professional and Patient Care Services (Version 2.0). Retrieved from

Medicaid and CHIP Payment and Access Commission. (2018). Comparison of Medicaid Drug Coverage to Medicare Part D and Commercial Plans. Retrieved from

Centers for Medicare & Medicaid Services. Prescription Drugs. Retrieved from

Institute for Safe Medication Practices (ISMP). ISMP List of Error-Prone Abbreviations, Symbols, and Dose Designations. ISMP; 2021.

Credits

Cover:
this cover has been designed using assets from Shutterstock.com.
ID Foto stock: 2260500949
This item was purchased under a commercial license that allows use of the content for commercial and personal projects, on digital or printed media, without any time limits, from anywhere in the world, to make modifications and create derivative works.

Disclaimer

High Score Publishing is not affiliated with or endorsed by any official testing organization. All organizational and test names are trademarks of their respective owners.

Made in the USA
Middletown, DE
16 June 2024